DIAGHILEV

CREATOR OF THE BALLETS RUSSES

ART · MUSIC · DANCE

Edited and with text by

ANN KODICEK

With contributions by

ROSAMUND BARTLETT · LYNN GARAFOLA

GLEB POSPELOV · MILITSA POZHARSKAIA · ALEXANDER SCHOUVALOFF

IRINA VERSHININA

Barbican Art Gallery / Lund Humphries Publishers

eon Bakst:
rtrait of Diaghilev
th his Nanny (detail)
04–6
t.6

First published in Great Britain
by Barbican Art Gallery in association with
Lund Humphries Publishers Limited,
Park House, 1 Russell Gardens, London NW11 9NN
on the occasion of the exhibition
Diaghilev: Creator of the Ballets Russes
25 January – 14 April 1996
organised by Barbican Art Gallery, Barbican Centre,
London EC2Y 8DS

Barbican Art Gallery is owned, funded and
managed by the Corporation of London
Copyright © 1996 Corporation of London
and the authors

British Library Cataloguing in Publication Data:
A catalogue record of this book is available from
the British Library
ISBN 0 85331 688 0

Exhibition selector: Ann Kodicek
Exhibition organisers: Tomoko Sato
and Conrad Bodman, assisted by Alison Hart
Exhibition consultant: Alexander Schouvaloff
Russian co-ordinator: Jovan Nicholson
Exhibition designer: Paul Dart
Exhibition graphic designers: Oxygen

Catalogue editors:
Tomoko Sato, Barbican Art Gallery
Lucy Myers, Lund Humphries Publishers Ltd
Translator: Mary Hobson

Catalogue designer: Richard Hollis
Typographic assistant: Stuart Bailey

Catalogue typeset by
Nene Phototypesetters, Northampton
in Monotype Ehrhardt,
Franklin Gothic No. 2 and Baskerville Italic

Printed in Great Britain by
BAS Printers Limited,
Over Wallop, Stockbridge, Hampshire

Catalogue distributed in the USA by
Antique Collectors' Club
Market Street Industrial Park
Wappingers Falls
NY 12590
USA

CONTENTS

Foreword ✣ 6

Editor's Preface ✣ 7

Lenders to the Exhibition ✣ 9

Ann Kodicek *Sergei Diaghilev* ✣ 11

Rosamund Bartlett *Diaghilev as Musician and Concert Organiser* ✣ 49

Militsa Pozharskaia *Diaghilev and the Artists of the Saisons Russes* ✣ 53

Irina Vershinina *Diaghilev and the Music of the Saisons Russes* ✣ 67

Alexander Schouvaloff *Diaghilev's Ballets Russes: The First Phase* ✣ 87

Lynn Garafola *Diaghilev's Unruly Dance Family* ✣ 101

Gleb Pospelov *The Diaghilev Seasons and the Early Russian Avant-Garde* ✣ 107

Chronology: Sergei Diaghilev and His Times ✣ 115

CATALOGUE ✣ 123

Notes on Productions ✣ 157

Biographical Notes ✣ 167

Select Bibliography ✣ 172

Index of Artists ✣ 173

Photographic Acknowledgements ✣ 174

Acknowledgements ✣ 175

'I am, first, a great charlatan, though with dash, second a great charmer, third cheeky, fourth, a person with a lot of logic and few principles and, fifth, someone afflicted, it seems, with a complete absence of talent. I think I've found my true vocation: to be a patron of the arts. For that I have everything I need except the money. *Mais ça viendra …*' So Diaghilev wrote to his stepmother in 1895.

In these mercantilistic times, it is appropriate that we should be able to recognise one of the greatest creative geniuses of this century in these terms. Sergei Diaghilev would not have classified himself as an artist, although he aspired to be a composer in his adolescence. Benois called him 'a wild and undiscriminating enthusiast, but a man of flair from the start'. Yet once he had learnt how to secure patronage in St Petersburg and then in Europe, he became perhaps the most influential Russian cultural export that Europe has ever encountered.

Since his death in 1929, there have been many attempts to document his life and work, and this exhibition, *Diaghilev: The Creator of the Ballets Russes*, follows notable efforts, especially by Richard Buckle, to pay tribute to his artistic achievements. However, we hope that this project brings a fresh perspective by being the first Diaghilev exhibition in Europe to take place since the demise of Communism. The change in the post-*perestroika* cultural climate has brought greater recognition of Diaghilev in his homeland and, encouraged by a burgeoning of enthusiasm in Russia for information about the pre-Revolution cultural milieu and his own activities within that context, we have been allowed to include a substantial contingent of Russian loans not previously seen in the West. These, mixed with works from Western collections, enable us to create a new depth to the picture of Diaghilev's career, his upbringing and his early life in Russia.

Indeed, our study has focused upon his Russian roots in order to illuminate the huge impact that Russian art had upon European audiences following the launch of Diaghilev's enterprises in Paris in 1907. The *Saisons russes* sent ripples from country to country and his aura still casts a spell upon us today. We hope in due course to plan a sequel exhibition that will look at the last fifteen years of his career and his work with European artists.

Diaghilev: The Creator of the Ballets Russes could not have been properly realised without the support of the State Tretyakov Gallery and the State Russian Museum, alongside that of the State Museum of Theatre and Music, St Petersburg, the A. A. Bakhrushin State Central Theatre Museum, the Bolshoi Theatre Museum, the National Library of Russia, the State Museum Reserve, Peterhof and the Benois Family Museum. In particular, I would like to thank Valentin Rodionov, Lydia Iovleva, Tatyana Gubanova, Alla Gusarova, Roxana Rassudina, Yulia Zabrodina, Valery Gubin, Tatiana Klim, Vladimir Vasiliev and Valery Zarubin from Moscow; Vladimir Gusev, Evgenia Petrova, Irina Evstigeeva, Natalia Metelitsa and Dmitry Korolev from St Petersburg; Vladimir Znamenov, Nikita Vasiliev, Peter Macho and Irina Zolatinkina from Peterhof.

I would like to join with Ann Kodicek in thanking the following for their contributions: Alexander Schouvaloff, Rosamund Bartlett, Lynn Garafola, Gleb Pospelov, Militsa Pozharskaia, Irina Vershinina and Sarah Woodcock for their research work; Baroness Smith of Gilmorehill and Jovan Nicholson for their liaison work with Russian lenders; and all those owners who have generously lent material to the display.

Tomoko Sato, Conrad Bodman and Alison Hart have borne the brunt of the organisational work and the installation design has been theatrically devised by Paul Dart and his team.

John Hoole
Curator
Barbican Art Gallery

The inspiration for this exhibition was sown in 1991, when I first visited the Benois Family Museum, at Peterhof, near St Petersburg. There I met three enthusiastic young curators, who immediately invited me to tea, when the exhibition was conceived. Nikita Vasiliev, the Museum's then Director, and his colleagues, Igor Prudnikov and Nikolai Pavlov, have been energetic and selfless supporters ever since. On my return to Britain, I was much encouraged in my then tentative attempts to mount an exhibition by Richard Buckle and Charles Spencer, and in finding a suitable venue by Timothy Wilson and Larissa Salmina-Haskell of the Ashmolean Museum. The project was converted from a desirable possibility to a marketable proposition by the British Council, who sponsored a visit in December 1992 to research suitable loans in collections in St Petersburg and Moscow. My eternal thanks for this go to Henry Meyric Hughes and Ann Elliott, who worked at that time in the British Council's Visual Arts division, and to Jovan Nicholson, who has nursed the project at every stage in co-ordinating arrangements with Russian lenders, catalogue contributors and multifarious suppliers in the CIS. Without his help, the practicalities of this exhibition could not have been addressed. Without a host gallery, the exhibition would not have taken place. My sincere thanks go to John Hoole and the Corporation of London for underwriting the risks of this tricky undertaking and allowing the exhibition to be shown at Barbican Art Gallery.

During all stages of my research for this exhibition, a key figure has been Dmitry Korolev, Exhibition Curator of St Petersburg's National Library of Russia, who supplied me with up-to-date bibliographical information and arranged introductions to Russian writers and specialists, as well as overseeing loan arrangements from the rich collections in this library. Also in St Petersburg, I would like to thank my friend, Natalia Solomatina, who was unfailing and generous with help, advice and information for which I rarely had to ask.

Curators of museums everywhere have been of great help in advising on loan material. A great number of unique loans have come from St Petersburg's State Museum of Theatre and Music, where Irina Evstigeevna, Natalia Metelitsa and Elena Fedosova have been towers of strength since I first visited them in 1992. In Moscow, I received much assistance from friends and colleagues. In this connection, I must give special thanks to my friend Roxana Rassudina, who was already unwell when I embarked upon this project, but none the less was unstintingly supportive. Her dream was to see important sculpture from the State Tretyakov Gallery, in particular Mikhail Vrubel's *Volga*, on show for the first time. Sadly, she has not been able to see the results of her crusade. Important and numerous loans have been made available to us from that museum through the generosity of Lydia Ivanovna Evlova and the co-operation of her team of curators, led by Lydia Ivanovna Mashkova and admirably co-ordinated by Tatiana Gubanova.

Major paintings, seen in Britain for the first time, have been graciously supplied by Evgenia Nikolaevna Petrova of the State Russian Museum, whose curators could not have been more helpful. This is the first London exhibition to show loans from the A. A. Bakhrushin State Central Theatre Museum in Moscow and I am grateful to Tatiana Klim for making these available from that significant collection. The Bibliothèque Nationale is a major lender. The staff of all branches of this institution have been most accommodating and I particularly wish to thank Pierre Vidal and Mademoiselle Pouderoux for their kind forbearance with our complicated requests.

The greatest number of Western exhibits come from the Victoria and Albert Museum, and we are most grateful to this museum for overriding its usual rule of never lending more than twelve items. The National Art Library has lent books not previously exhibited from Mikhail Larionov's collection, and ballet costumes, never previously shown, come from the Theatre Museum, where curators and researchers have worked with unflagging enthusiasm. Among them, I must especially thank Sarah Woodcock for a vital supply of information regarding ballet exhibits, and the staff of the National Art Library and of the British Library for their friendly help with my personal research over the past fifteen years.

Having arranged the venue and earmarked the principal loans, a daunting degree of work remained to be done on finalising the selection and compiling a catalogue. On my own, I would have found this insuperable. Support came from private lenders and their representatives, who have been extremely generous not only with loans but with their time and knowledge. Of these, I would particularly like to thank Julian Barran, Asya Chorley, Valéric Dobužinskis, Philip Dyer, David Elliott, John Stuart and the Cecchetti Society. On suitable essay material for the catalogue I received irreplaceable advice from Igor Golomshtock and Gleb Pospelov. In undertaking the translation of Russian material in the catalogue, Mary Hobson faced a herculean endeavour, in which she supplemented finely tuned textual contributions with other arduous chores not strictly covered by her contract. Indeed, several of our collaborators have augmented their duties with gestures that can only be described as labours of love.

Our consultant, Alexander Schouvaloff, has been indispensable to me on every level. Not only did he supply crucial information about loan material but he proved tireless and adept in fielding from me an endless tirade of miscellaneous queries on an infinite range of subjects. He further acted, with consummate tact and patience, as midwife on the catalogue, for which my confinement was unbelievably protracted. Here, we were attended by our sympathetic and uncomplaining editors, Lucy Myers and John Gilbert. The fallout from all the above has been cheerfully faced by two members of my family, Dennis and Hugh Gilbert, who provided unfailing moral support, factual information and technical help at all hours on all matters and who asked for no reward.

My final acknowledgements go to those who have worked hardest of all on this project and without whom the exhibition could never have been realised. Our catalogue contributors, Rosamund Bartlett, Lynn Garafola, Gleb Pospelov, Militsa Pozharskaia, Alexander Schouvaloff and Irina Vershinina have produced professional work despite a variety of pressures. Above all, I must thank and congratulate Tomoko Sato, Conrad Bodman and Alison Hart of Barbican Art Gallery for their courage and good temper in tackling the gargantuan task of organising this exhibition and for their triumph in its accomplishment.

An enormous number of colleagues, friends and relatives, have helped and contributed in all kinds of ways. Many of them are listed below. Any names omitted are accidental and I am anxious, if that is the case, to thank them collectively:

Svetlana Andreeva, Patrick Baide, Kenneth Baird, Susan Bennet, Jean Bouvier, Graham Brandon, Theresa Brett, the Brodsky Museum, Igor Bytensky, Melanie Christoudia, Gennadi Chugunov, Daphne Cooper, Andrew Dempsey, Mary Jane Duckworth, Irina Duskina, Claire Edwards, Christine Edzard, Sergei Essaian, Victoria Field, Elena Filippova, Nina Golomshtock, Jane Grayson, Valery Gubin, Alla Gusarova, Vladimir Gusev, Marina Henderson, Pamela Howard, Martine Kahane, Elena Karpova, Daniel Katz, Valentina Kniazeva, Richard Knight, Galina Krechina, Lyudmila Kurenkova, Evgeny Kurochkin, Svetlana Lanceray, Irina Lapina, Alexander Laskin, Nadine Leenhi, Christina Lodder, Igor Makhaev, Geoffrey Mann, David Mardell, Leila Meinertas, Alison Meyric Hughes, Geneviève Musin, Erik Näslund, Kira Odar-Bogaevskaya, Anatole von der Pahlen, Eleonora Paston, Frances Pritchard, Catherine Régnault, Amanda Robertson, Galina Shoumiatskaya, Iraida Sirotinskaya, Natalia Skorospeshkina, Mary Stassionopoulos, John Steer, Deborah Stratford, Tatiana Sventorzheskaya, Michael Symes, Viviane Tarenne, Christine Thomas, Nigel Thorp, Germain Viatte, Ekaterina Voshinina, Laura Wilson, Sarah Wilson, Yulia Zabrodina, Valery Zarubin.

In conclusion, I must thank my mother, whom I have hardly seen in the last months. If she had not committed the indiscretion of informing me about Diaghilev in the 1950s, when I was eight years old, she would not now be reading this.

Ann Kodicek

Czech Republic	B. Stavrovski Collection, Prague, 103B
France	Bibliothèque Nationale de France, Paris , 131A, 145, 161C, 170, 171
	Valéric Dobužinskis, 150, 151, 152A-B, 153
	Musée d'Art Moderne et Contemporain de Strasbourg, 119A-B
	Musée des Arts Décoratifs, Paris, 104, 134, 136A
	Musée des Beaux-Arts, Rouen, 123
	Musée National d'Art Moderne, Centre Georges Pompidou, Paris, 131G, 133, 132B, 136B
Russian Federation	A. A. Bakhrushin State Central Theatre Museum, Moscow, 23, 95A, 96, 97, 99, 101, 107B, 131I, 157, 161A-B and D
	Benois Family Museum, St Petersburg, 5A-B, 40A-G, 50A-L
	Bolshoi Theatre Museum, Moscow, 142A-C
	National Library of Russia, St Petersburg, 12A-D, 41, 55
	State Museum of Theatre and Music, St Petersburg, 2, 54, 58, 89A-D, 106A, 106C-D, 108A-D, 113A, 114, 115, 118B-C, 120, 125A-C, 131B, 131D-F, 131H, 131J, 141A-C, 142D, 144, 146, 147, 154, 164
	State Museum Reserve, Peterhof, 11, 93, 95B, 162A-B
	State Russian Museum, St Petersburg, 3, 6, 129
	State Tretyakov Gallery, Moscow, 1, 4A-B, 7, 9A-B, 10, 13A-D, 14A-B, 15, 16A-C, 17A-C, 18, 21A-D, 22A-B, 24, 25, 26, 27, 28, 29, 30, 31, 32, 33, 34, 35, 36, 37, 38, 39, 42, 43, 44, 45, 46, 47, 48, 49, 51, 52, 56, 57, 61, 62, 63, 64, 65, 66, 67, 68, 70, 71, 72, 73, 74, 75, 76, 77, 79, 80, 81, 82, 83, 84, 85, 86, 87, 88, 92, 94A-E, 98, 100, 107A, 116, 126
United Kingdom	Visitors of the Ashmolean Museum, Oxford, 19, 20, 53, 69, 143A-D
	Mr and Mrs S. Bawarshi, courtesy of Browse & Darby, London, 160
	Board of Trustees of the British Library, London, 159
	Cecchetti Society, London, 127, 128
	Philip Dyer, Deal, 110, 149B, 158
	David Elliott, Oxford, 78, 165, 168, 169
	Mander and Mitchenson Theatre Collection, Beckenham, 149A, 149C-E
	Mercury Gallery, London, 124
	Sothebys, London, 60
	Theatre Museum, courtesy of the Board of Trustees of the Victoria and Albert Museum, London, 105, 106F, 107C, 108E, 109, 111, 113B-C, 121, 122, 130, 131C, 132A, 135A, 138, 139A-C, 140, 148, 163, 166
	Board of Trustees of the Victoria and Albert Museum, London, 8, 59, 106E, 112, 118A, 155A-B, 156, 172, 173
United States	Fine Arts Museums of San Francisco, Achenbach Foundation for Graphic Arts, 106B, 107E, 117, 119C, 135B
	Robert L. B. Tobin, courtesy of the McNay Art Museum, San Antonio, Texas, 90, 91, 137
Private collections	102, 103A, 107D, 119D, 132C, 135C, 162C, 167, 174

ANN KODICEK

Sergei Diaghilev

PROLOGUE

Whenever they saw him seated alone in the tenth row of the stalls, Sergei Diaghilev's schoolfriends would regard him with envy. The teenager was in flagrant breach of school rules for attending the theatre without his parents. Yet Sergei would not be punished, for his teachers were received at the soirées held at the Diaghilevs' townhouse at Perm, in the Russian Urals. In exchange for gentrified culture, the staff of the Perm gymnasium would turn a blind eye to the boy's peccadilloes and his laziness in preparing his lessons.[1]

Sergei's schoolfriends were in some awe of him, for his youthfully commanding presence, his relaxed attitude to his studies and his perfect mastery of German and French as well as Russian. Already a good pianist, Sergei was not shy of participating in school concerts, operatic and dramatic performances. The local papers record the success of such ventures.[2]

In 1890, at the age of eighteen, he was to matriculate ingloriously, just scraping into St Petersburg University. At the age of twenty-five, however, in the role of impresario, Sergei Diaghilev would embark on the first of a series of enterprises that Russia had never seen before. Before the age of forty, Diaghilev had his own Company, Ballets Russes, and had won the international reputation for which he is still famous.

In childhood letters to his father, away on professional military duties, Sergei reveals an avuncular regard for his younger brothers who, as he discovered later, were born of a different mother, his own mother having died at his birth.[3]

Records of Sergei's early promise are provided by his stepmother, Elena Valerianovna. In a letter to Sergei's paternal grandmother, she proudly announces that the boy is already reading fluently

at the age of six[4] and is most at home with adult reading-matter. Although almost all of his communications in later life were by telegram, the young Diaghilev was an assiduous correspondent, writing regularly to his stepmother, a woman whom he loved and respected always.[5]

As well as a house in Perm, the Diaghilevs possessed Bikbarda, an estate near by. It was close to the distillery where the family fortunes had been made. Its workers, like the domestic staff, were valued employees and retainers. When, in 1890, the eighteen-year-old Sergei removed to St Petersburg, he was accompanied by two family servants who were to remain with him for the rest of their active lives: his valet, Vassily (later Vaslav Nijinsky's dresser) and his nanny, Avdotya Alexandrovna, who had attended his birth and was thus his last link to his mother.

'Nanny Dunya' is immortalised in the background of a full-length portrait of Diaghilev by Léon Bakst [cat. 6]: a small insistent presence who kept up standards of hospitality by making and serving the tea and jam consumed at the vibrant meetings held at Diaghilev's apartment, the results of which were to make cultural history.[6]

Diaghilev's physical appearance has been vividly described by various associates. He was on the plump side and burly. When he first appeared in the capital, he had chubby, rosy cheeks. He had lively dark eyes, a moustache and, from the time he first worked at the Maryinsky Theatre, dark hair with a white forelock (memorably recorded in his portrait) which earned him the nickname 'Chinchilla'. The designer Erté recalls in his memoirs that Diaghilev had a deceptively lazy expression in his eyes and a lethargic handshake, which were instantly belied by the intense energy of his character.[7]

At St Petersburg University, where, with singular unoriginality,

Diaghilev as a student at St Petersburg University
early 1890s
Diaghilev Foundation, Perm

he registered to read Law, thus gaining automatic eligibility for civil service work, Diaghilev busily pursued his interests, if not his studies.[8] His talent for music impelled him to embark on an external course of composition at the Conservatoire with Rimsky-Korsakov. His powerful baritone voice underwent training for a period with Signor Antonio Cotogni. At this point, Diaghilev made much of a spurious blood tie with Tchaikovsky, whose death a few years later he was to mark with tearful affectation.[9]

In his copious spare time,[10] Sergei resolved to broaden his cultural horizons. His guide in metropolitan life was his cousin, Dmitry (Dima) Filosofov, whose mother, born Anna Pavlovna Diaghileva, was a prominent political activist. Dima's father, Vladimir Dimitrievich Filosofov, was a highly placed government official descended from an old Russian landowning family.

Diaghilev's aunt and Filosofov's mother,
Anna Pavlovna Filosofova
1880s
Diaghilev Foundation, Perm

Dima, a sophisticated young man-about-town, gravitated naturally to intellectual circles and soon introduced his cousin Sergei to the 'Society for Self Improvement', a group of young artists and literati, recent graduates of the May Gymnasium, a high school founded and run by the German Karl Ivanovich May. These young men would meet regularly to discuss culture as they had done since their schooldays. The original members included Alexandre Benois, Dmitry Filosofov, Konstantin Somov and Walter Nouvel. They were joined in 1890 by Evgeny Lanceray, Léon Bakst and, later, Sergei Diaghilev. At this point, two members with foreign links entered the Society: Charles Birlé from the French Embassy, and the half-English Alfred Nourok, whom Benois remembers as always having a volume of Baudelaire's *Fleurs du mal* or Huysmans's *A Rebours* protruding carelessly from his pocket. Both works were strictly forbidden in Russia. The two foreigners supplied the young Russians with foreign magazines not available in St Petersburg.

Despite the scholarly nature of their meetings (Benois once gave a talk on German art, Nouvel on Russian music, Filosofov on Alexander I) the group chose for themselves the enigmatically comic nickname, 'Nevsky Pickwickians'.[11]

It is alarming to note that those Pickwickians who were members of the University were breaking the law, or at least their oath of matriculation by these meetings. Diaghilev, on enrolling for his course, had sworn: 'I, the undersigned, undertake herewith that during my time as a student … of the Imperial St Petersburg University, I am bound not only not to belong to a secret society, but even, without permission … not to enter into societies allowed by the law …'

From 1890 onwards, Diaghilev was breaking his oath with every venture he undertook. All his enterprises were to arouse controversy in official circles.[12]

If Diaghilev had seemed a precocious young grandee to his schoolfellows in Perm, he looked to the conceited hothouse élitists of the Society like a provincial dolt. It was quickly noticed by the senior member of the group, and, to a large extent, Diaghilev's mentor, Alexander Benois, that the newcomer was a visual illiterate and he was derided for the lack of taste that led him to admire the music of Verdi and Massenet.[13] However, he knew well the scores of Mussorgsky, at a time when the composer was not generally known, and this impressed his associates.[14]

Diaghilev, at this stage, remained uncharacteristically reserved in the company of his peers, not participating in the discussions which were generated by learned papers presented by members of the group. Instead, he would give occasional music recitals, singing his own compositions, or playing piano duets with his student friend, Walter Nouvel (later to become business manager of the Ballets Russes). Benois says in his memoirs that he did not admire Diaghilev's compositions, nor his somewhat heavy-handed pianistic technique.[15]

Great was the astonishment of Benois and his colleagues when, five years later, Diaghilev and Dima returned from a European tour, the former now a man of assurance and style and an art collector.[16] Diaghilev had graduated in 1895, after the statutory six years of study. At that point, he had recognised, with the help of plain speaking by Rimsky-Korsakov, that he was not composer material,[17] nor did he incline to train as a professional singer. Subsequent events show, however, that Diaghilev never doubted that a great future was in store for him.

It has been said that Diaghilev did not leave Rimsky's music room without a confrontation, ending with Diaghilev's provocative challenge, 'The future will show … which of us history will judge the greater'.[18] Diaghilev's self-discovery was expressed in a letter to his stepmother in the mid-1890s. In it, he announced: 'As for me … it must be confessed … from observation, that I am, first, a great charlatan, though with dash, second a great charmer, third cheeky, fourth, a person with a lot of logic and few principles and, fifth, someone afflicted, it seems, with a complete absence of talent. I think I've found my true vocation: to be a patron of the arts. For that I have everything I need except the money. *Mais ça viendra …*'[19]

The future impresario, whose charisma and flair for organisation would occasionally turn into despotism, was on the brink of a unique career, in which he was to play the role, first and foremost, of Sergei Diaghilev. He created it, in large part, with the help of his Pickwickian friends, whom, from the end of the 1890s, he was mobilising in a series of arts projects. A dilettante in many ways (as Benois does not hesitate to remind us),[20] Diaghilev was always able to extract the essence of a subject and use it to his own ends. An unerring eye led him to make important art-historical discoveries; a sure judgement of new music was to lead to major musical innovations; a legal education caused him to devise impossibly complex contracts with artists, and to pursue tireless litigation with prominent outlaws from his ballet Company.[21]

Diaghilev's first project in St Petersburg was the exhibition, in March 1897, of Scottish and German watercolours which, without creating a stir, elicited widespread admiration.[22] His last was an exhibition in spring 1906 of contemporary Russian art, which was received coolly. However, it served as the dress rehearsal for the first of Diaghilev's Paris projects, a retrospective exhibition of Russian art at the Salon d'Automne. The inclusion in both shows of works by the young art student, Mikhail Larionov, is an important indication of Diaghilev's future career as a promoter of the latest phenomena of the modern movement in art, music and dance.

The high point of his St Petersburg career also marked the moment when he began preparations to leave Russia. It was 1905: the year of the 'First Russian Revolution', which had begun in early January with a cruel act of peasant repression. The *Historical Russian Portrait Exhibition*, held from March to September at St Petersburg's Tauride Palace, gave Diaghilev an opportunity to indulge his penchant for self-advertising. During a banquet held in his honour at Moscow's 'Metropol' restaurant, Sergei Pavlovich made a powerful speech, predicting the future direction of Russian society with an accuracy that is uncannily prophetic.

Léon Bakst:
**Portrait of Diaghilev
with his Nanny** 1904–6
Cat. 6

...There is no doubt that every tribute is a summing-up and every summing-up is an ending. Don't you feel that the long alley of portraits of big and small people that I brought to life in the beautiful halls of the Tauride Palace is only a grandiose summing-up of a brilliant, but, alas, dead period in our history ...

The end of a period is revealed here, in those gloomy dark palaces, frightening in their dead splendour, and inhabited today by charming mediocre people who could no longer stand the strain of bygone parades. Here are ending their lives not only people, but pages of history ...

We are witnesses of the greatest moment of summing-up in history in the name of a new and unknown culture, which will be created by us, and which will also sweep us away. That is why, without fear or misgiving, I raise my glass to the ruined walls of the beautiful palaces, as well as to the new commandments of an aesthetic.

The only wish that I, an incorrigible sensualist, can express is that the forthcoming struggle should not damage the amenities of life, and that the death should be as beautiful and as illuminating as the resurrection.[23]

In view of the accelerated rate of change and the rapid deconstruction of the Tsarist State, perhaps the speech was evidence of observation, not clairvoyance. What it did show was that Diaghilev, unlike many members of the Russian upper classes, was able to face up to change and consider alternatives.

The alternative did not yet include emigration. A report written for presentation to the Ministry of National Enlightenment in November of the same year shows Sergei Diaghilev still in St Petersburg and tilting against the windmills of Imperial hierarchy in the arts.[24] He observes that the institutions of art and music were administratively so hidebound that they blocked the possibility of innovation, leaving the arts in Russia, and therefore Russian civilisation in general, light years behind the rest of Europe. Although he does not mention the Imperial Theatres in his sweep of arts institutions, it is clear from the writings of members of Diaghilev's ballet troupe that such conditions obtained also at the Maryinsky Theatre. In 1904, with his scenario for *Daphnis and Chloë*, Michel Fokine had already plotted the reform of ballet choreography, which he saw to have become stultified.[25] Bronislava Nijinska, in her memoirs, states this situation to have been extreme enough for herself and her brother, Vaslav Nijinsky, to opt out unquestioningly of the Imperial Theatres, where their salaries, pension prospects and jobs as solo ballet dancers seemed assured but where the atmosphere was dead.[26] With relief and high idealism, they joined Diaghilev's travelling company, where the situation was volatile, but working conditions were creative. Thus, although Diaghilev got no change out of the Russian government for his painstaking report on its shortcomings, it was precisely this bureaucratic boneheadedness that forced the top Russian artists to opt for Diaghilev and freedom when in 1911 he formed the Ballets Russes.

Ultimately, ballet became the chief element of Diaghilev's *Saisons russes*, although operatic scenes were still an integral part, and it is with the brilliance of the Ballets Russes that Sergei Diaghilev has become associated. It is not generally known that Diaghilev, initially, was not a ballet enthusiast. In their memoirs, Alexandre Benois[27] and Serge Lifar[28] both insist that Diaghilev never transcended his antipathy to ballet and never really understood it. At the end of his life, Diaghilev seems once again to have lost interest in dance and taken to book-collecting instead.[29]

In 1889, the wealthy industrialist Savva Mamontov had had talks with the Director of Paris's Porte St Martin Theatre about transferring four productions by his Private Opera Company to Paris.[30] In the event, it was Diaghilev who would succeed in pulling off the venture, with *Boris Godunov*. Subsequently, Diaghilev's ballet productions also followed the course begun by Mamontov's Private Opera Company. The idea was to produce holistic works of art, where musical composition, choreography, sets and costumes were all of a piece and were devised, not by theatrical hacks and decorators, but by artists working harmoniously together on composition, designs and libretti. With *Le Pavillon d'Armide*, Alexandre Benois created in 1907 the first total ballet to be exported by Diaghilev.[31]

With an excellent team of young dancers from both St Petersburg and Moscow, Diaghilev was able to add a new element to the unique success of the Russian ballet: that of the preeminence of the male dancer. Adolph Bolm's notable performance in 1909 in the *Polovtsian Dances* from *Prince Igor* was surpassed in 1910 by those of Nijinsky in *Les Sylphides* and *Schéhérazade*.

With a short pause necessitated by the First World War, Diaghilev's Ballet Russes went from innovation to innovation until Diaghilev's death on the Venice Lido at the age of fifty-seven on 19 August 1929.

On the face of it, the variety of Sergei Pavlovich Diaghilev's enterprises is a random sequence of hobby-horses reflecting his dilettantism. Closer examination reveals a logical succession of events which always had the aims and personnel of the Society for Self Improvement (later, the World of Art group) as its basis and initial inspiration. Gradually, other artists were added, first composers, then dancers and choreographers. Succeeding chapters in this catalogue will show this development. They will also show how, up until 1914, most of the inspiration is Russian, or shows a Russian interpretation of Western culture. This road was cut off by the First World War, as was Diaghilev's association with many colleagues. The breakdown of some of these relations was also dictated by Diaghilev's loss of interest in collaborators and protégés: a process which was to upset a number of colleagues, who had always started as Diaghilev's close friends.

Dmitry Filosofov, centre, with the poet Zinaida Gippius and the writer Dmitry Merezhkovsky, 1900s
Central State Archive of Cinema and Photo Documents, St Petersburg

THE WORLD OF ART GROUP

Although not all the original members of Benois's Society for Self Improvement continued into the World of Art phase, the founder members, for the most part, remained. Except for Diaghilev himself, and the literati Dmitry Filosofov and Walter Nouvel (whose main interest was music), four of the original members were practising artists and writers. Two of them, Alexandre Benois and Léon Bakst, were prominent as designers during the early Ballets Russes period. Konstantin Somov left the group in the early stages to concentrate on easel painting. Evgeny Lanceray became absorbed in the birth of socialism and its popular propaganda. The magazine's writers, Dmitry Merezhkovsky, N. Minsky, V. Rozanov and Lev Shestov, all left the group's magazine during the early 1900s to found the journal *New Way* (*Novy put*).

World of Art artists
left to right: Benois, Somov, Lanceray, Dobuzhinsky
Details of silhouettes by Elizaveta Kruglikova
Cat. 14A, 14B

Their place on *World of Art* magazine was taken by the visual artists Anna Ostroumova-Lebedeva, Mstislav Dobuzhinsky, Alexandre Golovine, Ivan Bilibin and Nikolai Roerich, who, until 1904, produced graphic work for the magazine. During the following decade, the last three contributed towards Diaghilev's first opera and ballet productions in the West, Golovine already being associated with the Maryinsky Theatre.

The easel art of the World of Art group is characterised by an ironic nostalgia or 'historicism' shot through with Hoffmannesque romanticism. Stylistically, all World of Art protagonists combined a degree of patriotism with the decorative forms of Russian *style moderne*.

Overall influences of World of Art painters were the theatre, Japanese prints, Beardsley, Vallotton, Poussin, Puvis de Chavannes and, ultimately, Gustave Moreau. Their work is typified by imaginative nostalgia, executed with freedom, elegance and theatricality. Benois's *Italian Comedy* [cat. 66], for example, shows the artist using the perspective of a footlights view of a stage from the orchestra stalls, indicating the activity in the pit and the wings, whilst the *commedia dell'arte* theme is enacted by a cast of clowns. From here to the designs for *Petrushka* [see cat. 142A–D] was but a short stride.

Both in easel and graphic art, the emphasis was on technical innovation designed for maximum visual effect. The result was a form of anti-academic, pure painting so bold that Ilya Repin once described it as 'impudent'.[1] The scale of World of Art paintings is small, and the medium is as often gouache on card as oil on canvas, so facilitating formal experimentation.

Léon Bakst:
Portrait of Alexandre Benois 1898
Cat.3

The retrospective concerns of World of Art painters involve use of the history of Russian architecture, design and fashion as a distillation of decorative motifs. The apparent superficiality of this approach must in part have earned the group the label, 'decadents'. Behind the façade, however, was a *fin-de-siècle* intensity.

The group's interests and identity were in no small part motivated by parental tradition. Somov's father was senior curator of the Hermitage Museum; the forbears of Benois and Lanceray had been leading architects and musicians in St Petersburg.

In his memoirs, Benois reminds us that few of the World of Art's original members had come of pure Russian stock.[2] Benois himself was conscious throughout his childhood of the cultures of France, Italy and Germany. For a long time, the artist he most admired was Adolf von Menzel.

In their own art, World of Art painters favoured a range of historical periods. Alexandre Benois's interest in France was aroused during long periods spent there with his family, for the health of his young son. Benois was intrigued by Versailles and the theme of the court of Louis XIV [see cat. 61, 65].

Some of his paintings are inspired by the stories of Saint-Simon, a writer whose titles he borrows for the painting *Le Roi se promenait par tous les temps*, which was exhibited in St Petersburg at the World of Art exhibition of 1900. Saint-Simon's political writings seem to have influenced Benois's thinking upon the relative merits of religion and positivism in the culture of a society.[3]

Anna Ostroumova-Lebedeva:
White Nights early 1900s
CAT. 21A

Benois was also interested in eighteenth-century St Petersburg. He wrote numerous articles about its palaces and an entire book on Tsarskoe Selo in the reign of Empress Elizabeth [cat. 8]. A commission for a school history book to paint Tsar Paul inspecting his troops (1907, State Russian Museum, St Petersburg) [see cat. 50C] led to a series of paintings on the theme of this extraordinary Emperor's mania for playing soldiers. His powerful illustrations for Russian classics, notably Pushkin's 'The Bronze Horseman' [see cat. 7] dwell on St Petersburg, less as architecture than as environment. (In this case, of the inexorable advance of the threatening bronze idol against the poem's defenceless hero, Evgeny, washed up by the flooded Neva.)

The symbolism of the myth of St Petersburg is a strong element in the works of several World of Art artists and can also be traced in contemporary literature and film of the Symbolist school. It is strong in the St Petersburg works of Mstislav Dobuzhinsky, whose debt to the literature of Dostoevsky and Alexander Blok is underlined by his use of titles borrowed from their works, such as *Night, street, lantern, chemist* – a quotation from a poem by Blok. His theme of the hairdresser [see cat. 68] is later repeated in works by Mikhail Larionov and members of the 'primitive' futurist groups. The ethereal lighting of Dobuzhinsky's twilight city [see cat. 13A] exploits a common World of Art theme: the faint boundary between illusion and reality, effected through the phantasmagoric qualities of life's transient kaleidoscope.

Also interested in St Petersburg of the eighteenth century was Benois's nephew, Evgeny Lanceray, who was brought up in the Benois family home. Among other joint projects with his uncle, Lanceray illustrated Benois's book *Tsarskoe Selo in the Reign of Empress Elizabeth* [cat. 17A–C]. Based on Hoffmannesque caricature,

Alexandre Benois:
Catherine II's Walk *c.*1909
State Tretyakov Gallery, Moscow

Lanceray's illustration on the theme of the title, which was also the sketch for an easel painting, is both amusing and grotesque.

Lanceray's own interest in the city is focused on the period of its foundation by Peter the Great himself [see cat. 16A–C]. He painted a series of large canvases of historical scenes based on the lives of the eighteenth-century tsars [see cat. 15]. These can be compared with the Imperial hunting scenes of World of Art associate Valentin Serov who, despite his academic training under Repin, enjoyed experimenting with effects of light and perspective.

Evgeny Lanceray:
St Petersburg, Early Eighteenth Century 1906
State Tretyakov Gallery, Moscow

The urgent mood of Serov's *Peter the Great Out Hunting* (1902, State Russian Museum, St Petersburg) is conveyed by the informality of the composition's poses. Like Repin, he could invest a historical subject with drama, although Serov did not care for sentimentality.

Konstantin Somov was the third artist with an interest in the eighteenth century. On leaving the Academy, he had produced sensitive portraits, intimate interiors and country scenes, all related to his own life experience. From the 1890s, after further studies in Paris, he painted only imaginative scenes from the eighteenth and early nineteenth centuries. These took the form of '*fêtes galantes*' in unspecific arbours and belvederes. Early works, such as *Confidences* [cat.79] and *Evening* (1900–2), give the effect of a tableau of figures, arranged frontally in frieze-like compositions. Rural idylls, such as *The Rainbow, After Rain* (1896), with ladies in crinolines, are heightened by the addition of a rainbow. Later works, such as *Harlequin and Lady* (1912) lay heavy emphasis on the elements of masquerade, *billets doux* and

concealed voyeurs, intensified by dramatic lighting. Twilight revels are dramatically lit by bursts of fireworks, which pick out erotic episodes in dark corners.

The theme of illicit lovers surprised in bowers can be seen art historically to echo the subjects of paintings in the Hermitage which Somov must have known well. Several works by Somov, such as *The Ridiculed Kiss* (1908, State Russian Museum, St Petersburg), clearly recall Fragonard's *Stolen Kiss* and Watteau's *Embarrassing Proposal*, both in the Hermitage collection, while his porcelain figures have the fragile elegance of Boucher [see cat. 82, 83].

Whereas place in Somov's pictures is deliberately unspecific, time is, as it were, carefully frozen into his works. Occasionally, two historical periods are represented in the same work. *Times Past: Lady in Blue* (1897–1900, State Tretyakov Gallery, Moscow) combines eighteenth-century architecture with nineteenth-century costume, showing a mournful lady (actually the artist, Elizaveta Martynova) looming over the remains of an historic estate.[4]

Of all the group's work, Somov's is the most heavily ironic. In it, he exposes the vain banality of human endeavour. In a pair of fashion plates, *How they dressed in olden times / How they dress today* (1903), the caricature element calls in question the dignity of humanity, especially in modern times. Somov's figures are far more like marionettes than humans, and their helplessness in the face of destiny is apparent. A deep, disturbing melancholy overlays his works, whose protagonists, fully costumed, are clearly not playing themselves. The idea of cross-dressing presents itself as a possibility. Somov was homosexual.[5]

Somov's dedication to easel painting and his meticulous technique drew repeated acclaim from his colleagues, starting with a liberally illustrated monograph by Benois in *World of Art* magazine in 1899. Somov's art is featured again in the magazine in 1903, the year of his one-man exhibition.[6] The World of Art associate Stepan Yaremich compares Somov with Vermeer.[7] Conversely, from his seniors he earned opprobrium. Repin, his former tutor, described Somov's work as a reduction to 'childish stupidity in colours'.[8] His own father referred to it as 'lisping childish prattle'.[9] Until recently, Somov's easel art remained generally unappreciated in Russia, gaining more acclaim in its day in France and Germany.

A most unlikely colleague for this group was Vassily Kandinsky who in 1902 contributed a 'Letter from Munich' to the magazine.[10] It seems he must also have been influenced at one point by World of Art historicism. As late as 1909–10, he was producing works heavily laced with eighteenth-century flavour, such as *Ladies in Crinolines* (State Tretyakov Gallery, Moscow).

Alexandre Benois:
Italian Comedy: The Love Letter 1905
Cat. 66

Konstantin Somov:
Lady in Pink 1903
Cat.39

Mstislav Dobuzhinsky:
Trinity Cathedral, St Petersburg 1905
Cat.13D

Mstislav Dobuzhinsky:
The Hairdresser's Window 1906
Cat. 68

During the late 1890s a fellow student of Kandinsky's at Azbé's studio in Munich was Igor Grabar. It is probable that Kandinsky's World of Art phase came through Grabar who contributed regular 'letters from Munich' to the magazine and, after leaving Munich, clearly passed some of this work to Kandinsky.[11] On his return to Russia, Grabar became closely associated with the group.

It was Grabar who helped the younger artist Mstislav Dobuzhinsky (also a pupil of Azbé's) to enter the World of Art group. Although he showed a certain interest in historical themes, Dobuzhinsky's works focused mainly on the shabby and even seamy side of contemporary St Petersburg. His paintings are typically of unimposing backyards during Russian winters or of shop windows in twilight streets, such as *The Hairdresser's Window* [cat. 68]. His bold, expressive topographical prints [see cat. 50 F–H] are the most successful part of his production. They have a grainy, monochromatic quality reminiscent of the traditional German woodcut. They can be compared with Anna Ostroumova-Lebedeva's delicate uncluttered prints

celebrating the timeless qualities of St Petersburg [see cat. 50 J–L].

Emphasising the city's immense vistas, the scale of its towering buildings and the looming quality of its monuments, Ostroumova's woodcuts, which owe something to the school of Whistler, with whom she trained in Paris, counterpoise the delicate tracery of railings, the sparse parkland, and occasional human life, all in muted polychrome.

To the second wave of the World of Art we can ascribe a retrospective interest in medieval and pagan Russia. Ivan Bilibin's characterful miniature prints of old Russian churches are plentiful in *World of Art* magazine. His technique owes much to the traditional Russian *lubok* or woodcut; his information was built on long researches on site in northern Russia.

In 1908 Bilibin was chosen by Diaghilev to design the programme and some of the costumes for the Paris production of Modest Mussorgsky's opera *Boris Godunov* [see cat. 93].

Another artist whose interests in old Russia were scholarly and historical was Nikolai Roerich. His bright easel renditions of Russia's prehistoric past were shown in World of Art exhibitions. Roerich also designed for the 'primitive' ballets of Diaghilev's Company. A pupil of Arkhip Kuindzhi, Roerich's effects of light and colour are very powerful and he makes great play with a strong cosmic symbolism, opposing the manichaean forces of good and evil. This philosophy came into its own in his designs for the *Polovtsian Dances* [cat. 112] and, especially, in *The Rite of Spring* [cat. 161 A–D, 162 A–C], for which, with Stravinsky, he also wrote the libretto.

A different form of retrospection was practised by Léon Bakst. In easel painting, illustrations and theatre design, Bakst was drawn throughout his life to Ancient Greece. This passion was heightened by a visit to Greece with Valentin Serov in 1907,[12] an expedition which inspired the monumental canvas, *Terror Antiquus* (1908, State Russian Museum, St Petersburg) with its towering quality of aerial perspective.

Bakst's attraction to oriental subjects seems to have emerged only when he became involved with the Ballets Russes. His overwhelming success in theatre design came through an uniquely original art response to scholarly research. The international triumph achieved by Bakst during his later career underlines the importance of the Ballets Russes period as the culmination of artistic achievement for the World of Art group as a whole.

Given our awareness, with hindsight, of Bakst's stunning originality in ballet design, it is surprising to see how Benois described him in his book, *The Russian School of Painting*, as an unoriginal artist whose work would not stand the test of time.[13] However, this book was written in 1904, before Bakst had proved himself even as an easel

Isaak Levitan:
Haystacks 1899
Cat. 75

Isaak Levitan:
Copse by a Lake (Autumn) *c.*1898
Cat.19

painter. In his early career, Bakst's friends record him mainly as caricaturist. Better known today are his literary illustrations for stories such as *The Nose* (1904) by Nikolai Gogol, who recorded the topsy-turvy surreal world of late eighteenth-century landed gentry.

As a school of painting, World of Art could not claim to produce great art. This was clearly stated in 1906 by Benois himself in 'Artistic Heresies',[14] an important article in *Golden Fleece* (*Zolotoe runo*) magazine [see cat. 78]. Here, he bemoaned the fact that Russian artists had not adhered to a school, preferring a cult of individualism; and he regretted that, with the decline of religion, there was no longer a unified cause to inspire all artists. Such a view, at its worst, can be seen to unite the eschatological and erotic vision of artists such as Somov, Bakst and Benois. It also shows Benois at his most moralistic. It took Sergei Diaghilev to ignite this self-absorbed tendency and make World of Art a memorable movement of the twentieth century.

THE 'WORLD OF ART' MAGAZINE

'…*World of Art* is higher than anything earthly, among the stars, there it reigns, haughty, mysterious and alone, like the eagle on a snowy summit.' So wrote Léon Bakst to Alexandre Benois after composing the eagle insignia for the World of Art group's eponymous magazine, first published in 1898-9.[1]

The title 'World of Art [Mir Iskusstva]', if pretentious, captures the aims and identity of the organisation: a search for pure forms in art, effected through a deliberate eclecticism, which excluded only the insincere, the dogmatic or the aesthetically distasteful from a boundless acceptance of art of all periods and persuasions. A degree of intellectual snobbery among its members perhaps dictated the haughty eagle as an appropriate emblem.

The name of the movement was arrived at following long debate by Diaghilev and the group, headed by Benois, of young artists and writers who had first come together in St Petersburg as the Society for Self Improvement, on leaving high school in 1889.[2] The original name suggests a dilettante quality which undeniably played a part in the enthusiasms of the circle.

Ultimately, the element of positive energy outweighed the lack of obvious coherent interest. What had started as an amateur discussion group in Russia would attain its apogee with the universal acclaim of Western Europe.

The achievement of the Ballets Russes fulfilled the utopian aim of the group's aesthetic programme: a total synthesis of all the arts through the medium of beauty, a notion derived from Richard Wagner's theory of *Gesamtkunstwerk*.

The magazine was openly derivative. If its opinions were culled from Western and Russian thinkers, including Nietzsche, Dostoevsky and Chernyshevsky, its format owed and acknowledged a debt to contemporary Western art magazines, specifically *The Studio*, *Die Kunst* and *Pan*.[3] Its contents, however, were new in Russia and its production techniques, sophisticated even by Western standards, were to a large extent unknown. The magazine was copiously illustrated, both with reproductions and with decorative graphic work, which established the art of illustration in Russia for the first time as an effective form.

The launch of *World of Art* was a hard-won achievement, which was pulled off by Diaghilev where contemporaries (such as Alexandre Benois's brother, the watercolour painter Albert Benois) had failed.[4] The launch of the magazine was the first coup, effected, in the last analysis, by Diaghilev alone, with practical help from Dmitry Filosofov.

The magazine had an avowedly didactic agenda: to introduce the Russian public to art from the West that they would not have seen before; to reintroduce forgotten aspects of their indigenous culture; and to eradicate ingrained prejudices towards the interpretation of art.

World of Art was not the only contemporary Russian magazine devoted to the arts, but it was unusual in being run, not by an institution but by an independent group of young people who were themselves largely active practitioners of the visual arts.

Also unusual, in an age of egregious nationalism following the reactionary reign of Alexander III, was the extent to which by far the majority of the magazine's illustrations referred to the art of Western Europe. Generally defined in its day as an 'advanced' publication, *World of Art* contained no material that would now qualify as avant-garde. It scarcely featured Western art from Impressionism onwards until its later issues.[5]

The magazine's consistently avant-garde element concerned its presentation of art history. Not only were contemporary Western artists represented for the first time (favourite schools were Scandinavian, German and English); art was approached in a manner that stripped away considerations of subject matter and skill in the appraisal of the art object; looking beyond academism to the unique talents of particular artists.

Isolation and distance from the West were not the only factors that fuelled the group's enthusiasm for foreign art. The Censor, too, played a part; and it is to the credit of Diaghilev and his colleagues that censorship was manipulated to play a positive role. Each issue of *World of Art* proudly proclaims that it has been 'passed by the Censor'. Yet

World of Art, issue no.2, cover, 1902
Cat.12B

contemporary readers found officially prohibited material in almost every feature.

The magazine's programme, as defined by its benefactors, was originally to cover all the arts of Russia, including fine art, architecture and, particularly, the applied arts. The first issue conformed to these criteria. With the second issue, however, which contained twenty drawings by Aubrey Beardsley, *World of Art* had moved from a home-grown Russian focus to become an international magazine with frisson. Essays by Huysmans, whose fiction was forbidden in Russia, were later published in the magazine;[6] and Richard Muther was to extol the cult of evil as exemplified by Gustave Moreau.[7] Western artists introduced in the first year included Whistler, Degas, Rops and Vallotton.

The magazine's aesthetic breadth arose in part from the exuberance of youth. In this respect, it bears no comparison with anything then being published either in Russia or abroad. More practically, it emerged because the members of the World of Art group's editorial board had, in a sense, nothing in common except long-standing friendship.

Peculiarly Russian is the lack of rivalry between the group's members. Because of its high-school club background, this editorial board was unusual in that its members were on informal terms, calling each other by their diminutive first names (Diaghilev was Seryozha, Benois Shura, Somov Kostia, Bakst Levushka, Nouvel Valechka) and because, accustomed to collaborative ventures, the group naturally swapped art magazines, information, opinions and experiences.

Overall, each member of the magazine's editorial board had an equal opportunity for input and each pursued his own divergent interests. This lack of co-ordination inevitably led to an absence of any coherent policy governing the group's aesthetic approach. It also ensured a breathtaking spread of subjects for magazine features, illustrated (not always relevantly) by art from Bibiena to Hokusai.

World of Art attained its unique stamp through a combination of factors which can be identified as exclusively Russian. Some of them would appear to be negative. One such feature is an element of unself-consciously catholic enthusiasm for matters of the intellect. The magazine's literary section (run by Filosofov and Nouvel, joined briefly by the Russian Orthodox philosophical writers Merezhkovsky and Rozanov) expounded and appeared to espouse equally the philosophical theories of an overwhelming range of artists, critics and writers. They unashamedly sang the praises of Ruskin *and* Whistler; Zola *and* Baudelaire; Dostoevsky *and* Tolstoy.[8]

World of Art's aesthetic credo is expressed in Sergei Diaghilev's long article, 'Difficult Questions [*Slozhyne voprosy*]'. Split into four sections and running through two issues, the article, which one critic has described as 'an alloy of elements from the aesthetic of Kant and Schopenhauer, complicated by a Nietzschean individualism',[9] sets out the aims of art as being the search for beauty and the duty of the artist to find his individual self (*khudozhestvennoe ya*). Diaghilev further insisted on accepting all art non-judgementally.

The article begins with Michelangelo's motto, 'He who follows others will never outstrip them' and ends with the quotation from Nietzsche's *Thus Spake Zarathustra*, 'I go alone and you too will go alone'. In a cultural environment where a socially conscious form of realism had become the norm, tastes being for narrative, sentimental and patriotic art, this statement of Whistlerian aesthetics tinged with Wildean rebelliousness amounted to a cult of individualism.

From now on, the publications, pictures and exhibitions of World of Art members were dubbed 'decadent': a charge that infuriated Diaghilev and Benois, if only because it underestimated the seriousness and breadth of the group's aims. They were not promoting 'art for art's sake'. They claimed to be merely debunking art that was unworthy of the name.[10] The absence of a distinctive style is, of course, a weakness which invites misinterpretation.

The more recent labels of 'symbolism' and 'modernism' prove equally narrow definitions of the movement's aims and output, although elements of all the above tendencies can be traced in World of Art productions.

In the long run, the very openness of Diaghilev to all artistic phenomena would make for the unique creativity that became his

Konstantin Somov:
Ile d'Amour 1900
Cat. 81

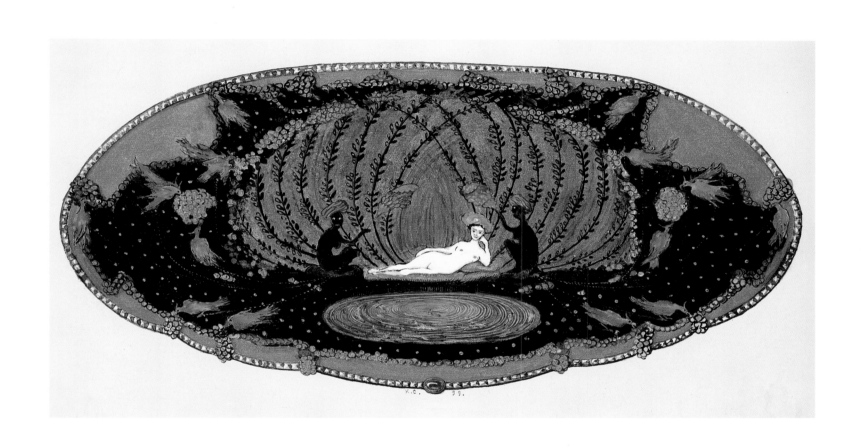

Konstantin Somov:
'Sultana': drawing for a snuff box 1899
Cat. 33

Léon Bakst:
Terror Antiquus *c.*1908
State Russian Museum, St Petersburg

trademark. He was not afraid to change his mind or to make mistakes. His editorials contain errors. Yet the innovations which began in Russian art from about 1915 had to some extent as their seedbed the ideas of Sergei Diaghilev's *World of Art*.

Another Russian quality is the polemical thrust of the magazine. This sits awkwardly with its alleged policy of universal tolerance. However, the butt of the magazine is always institutionalism. A distinct *World of Art* innovation is frank criticism in the magazine of the establishment arts institutions. A series of articles by different writers underlines the inadequacies of museums, both Russian and Western;[11] and several issues devote sections to the shockingly poor standard of student exhibitions at the Imperial Academy of Arts.[12] In a climate where the Academy of Arts was an extension of the court and, as such, the pre-eminent art college in Russia, this was dangerous stuff.

That institution had been reformed in 1893 by the influx into professional posts of members of the formerly dissident 'Wanderer' group. The hidebound attitudes that the new élite, too, had adopted had turned Diaghilev and Benois firmly against Repin and other artists they had once admired. Repin had correspondingly once admired the World of Art group and, initially, had contributed to the magazine, which he had described as 'A real art journal: Fresh! New! Talented!'[13] Forced to resign in solidarity with a colleague who had been lampooned, Repin then embarked on a painting, *Get Thee Behind Me, Satan*, which was thought to feature Diaghilev in the title role.[14]

Another criticism was implicitly levelled by *World of Art* at various stages against the establishment's official social policy. Léon Bakst had been dismissed from the Academy for antisemitic reasons;[15] while Grand Duke Vladimir Alexandrovich, Patron of the Academy, condoned, or at least did not actively oppose the events of Bloody Sunday which triggered the 'first Russian revolution' in January 1905. The savagery towards a peaceful peasant demonstration of the police platoon which the Grand Duke commanded was the cause of Valentin Serov's resignation from the Academy's teaching staff. (Vladimir Alexandrovich later became an important patron of Diaghilev's.)

Accompanying the magazine's overall polemical approach was an omniscient portentousness which, together with the marathon length of the articles, would never have been accepted today. This feature was not uniquely Russian. Indeed, many articles in *World of Art* were written by foreign writers, including Ruskin on the Pre-Raphaelites,[16] D.S. MacColl on Beardsley[17] and Nietzsche on Wagner.[18]

Both innovative and informative was the 'Arts Chronicle' section included in each issue, showing photographs of exhibits in contemporary Western European exhibitions (the Vienna Secession and Paris Salon are regularly included) and reproductions from the most recent issues of *Die Kunst*, *The Studio* and *The Magazine of Art*.

In view of the radicalism of the magazine's reinterpretation of the significance of art, its interest in specific works is surprisingly traditional, both in style and subject matter. Perhaps because *World of Art* had abjured the narrative and didactic in art, pictures reproduced there are overwhelmingly rural landscapes. Typical favourites are Levitan and Werenskiold.

Following the lead of thinkers as diverse as Ruskin and Wagner, World of Art activists clearly saw their theories best exemplified in the response by painters to nature: a theme enjoying a revival at the time.

Since *World of Art* represented every shade of opinion, it naturally contained elements both of Slavophilism and admiration for the West. Articles by Benois and Yaremich celebrate the (largely baroque) buildings of St Petersburg and Kiev built in Western idiom by such architects as Bartolommeo Rastrelli. Today's readers of the magazine, incidentally, can see in accompanying photographs of St Petersburg's Smolny Convent[19] and Kiev's St Andrew's Cathedral,[20] pristine examples of buildings later devastated in the Second World War and now visible only in reconstructed form.

Compared with other art magazines in Russia, *World of Art* paid little attention to the traditional Russian applied arts, though this area was well represented in the group's exhibitions.[21] Indeed, after its first number, the space devoted by *World of Art* to specifically Russian craftsmanship was minimal and most architectural photographs were confined to interiors of the Secession exhibitions. The other area avoided after the earliest issues was Russian neo-national painting.

The reason for both these phenomena was magazine politics. *World of Art* was funded by Savva Mamontov and by Princess Maria Tenisheva, both of whom ran crafts colonies, respectively at Abramtsevo (near Moscow) and Talashkino (near Smolensk). The two sponsors had agreed to support the venture on the understanding that it should be a low-priced publication dedicated primarily to the crafts and industrial design.

The slant, particularly for the crafts, was to be neo-nationalist and Muscovite. The stance, however, of most of the magazine's St Petersburg protagonists was eclectic. World of Art's core members were St Petersburgers and Westernisers. Except for Benois (who referred to the 'twin sisters of art and crafts') they were relatively indifferent to crafts, neo-nationalism and Muscovy.[22]

Support for the work of artists from Moscow was not, however, excluded by the World of Art group. The work of the Russian 'Impressionist', Konstantin Korovine, and of the Symbolist, Mikhail Vrubel, both of whom were associated with Abramtsevo and the Moscow tendency, were much admired; the former despite the group's suspicion of French Impressionism; the latter since the breadth of his creation appealed to the circle's holistic interests.

As well as paintings, Vrubel produced theatrical sets, furniture and ceramics. His colourful ceramic fireplace on the theme of Russia's

Valentin Serov:
Portrait of Savva Mamontov 1879
State Russian Museum, St Petersburg

national rivers [cat. 47] was exhibited at the 1900 *Exposition Universelle* in Paris; and *World of Art* devoted a long feature to his works, illustrated in forty reproductions in 1903.[23] Korovine's decorative panels for the Russian pavilion at the Paris *Exposition Universelle* appeared in the magazine of that same year.[24] Both exhibits were shown again at World of Art's 1901 exhibition at the Imperial Academy of Arts.

That these were essentially Mamontov's artists underlines the importance to *World of Art* of Mamontov's aesthetic philosophy, which was certainly an inspiration to Diaghilev. The former also ran a Private Opera Company, which specialised in Russian opera, when the Imperial Theatres were showing mainly Italian operas. It was through Mamontov that Chaliapin was truly launched and there is no doubt that Mamontov laid the ground that enabled Diaghilev to bring opera and, later, ballet, to Paris during the first decade of the twentieth century.

The magazine closed in 1904. This had a number of causes, apart from the drying up of funds. A number of the artists associated with the magazine had become involved in other work. From early 1905, an Imperial amnesty on political censorship heralded a rash of socialist satirical magazines, to which several of the group contributed. Diaghilev himself was now absorbed in the vast undertaking of the 1905 exhibition. Both these events were interpreted in the Soviet period as having strong political motivation. A more objective historical perspective could be applied here.

Except for Bilibin, Lanceray and, to an extent, Serov, World of Art artists were not primarily motivated by political ideals. However, in 1905, a phase of history was at an end in more senses than one. A new age was arriving, which artists were the first to sense.

DIAGHILEV AS THEATRE- AND ART-HISTORIAN

On the appointment in 1899 of Prince Sergei Volkonsky, who had recently been associated with the magazine, to the Directorship of the Imperial Theatres, World of Art members were variously engaged for theatrical work. Diaghilev became one of seven 'administrative assistants with special duties' at the Director's offices, Dmitry Filosofov earned a post at the nearby Alexandrinsky Drama Theatre; and World of Art artists began to work in the theatres of the two capitals as designers of sets and costumes.[1]

Diaghilev's post entailed editing the *Imperial Theatres Yearbook*, an annual report of the productions staged each season at the six public theatres of St Petersburg and Moscow. Benois in his memoirs describes Diaghilev as having become insufferable on his Imperial

Valentin Serov:
Portrait of Tsar Nicholas II 1900
Cat. 26

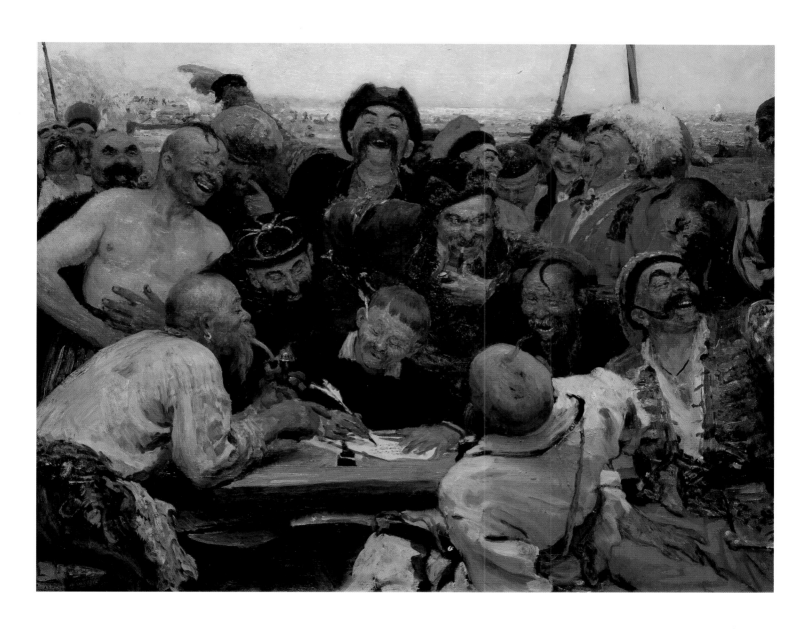

Ilya Repin:
Sketch for *Zaporozhian Cossacks* *c*.1880
Cat.77

appointment, which involved a move to an official apartment on St Petersburg's main embankment.[2] Diaghilev's tenure covered the theatre seasons 1898–9 and 1899–1900.

The year 1900 was the 150th anniversary of the Russian dramatic theatre and Diaghilev's second and last *Yearbook* was a resplendent two-volume jubilee edition, which quickly entered the ranks of rare books. To produce a publication on such a truly Imperial scale, its editor significantly exceeded his budget. It cost 30,000 roubles (then about £3,000), which represented an overspending of 10,000 roubles.[3] Although Diaghilev did not immediately observe it, this represented the beginning of a period of scandal associated with his employment at the Imperial Theatres.

The articles in the jubilee edition share the theme of innovation in Russia of all theatrical genres. An essay by A. Koptyaev about the ballet compositions of Alexander Glazunov,[4] for example, traces the new element of ballet music in the repertoires of Russian symphonic and operatic composers; the well-known critic and Ballets Russes supporter, Valerian Svetlov, writes illuminatingly of the classical origins of choreography in the dances described in Homer and Aeschylus.[5] This tradition was very soon to be revived, with the first visit to St Petersburg of Isadora Duncan in December 1904, and subsequently in the choreographic work of Michel Fokine. An essay on Wagner by Herman Laroche, the music critic and friend of Tchaikovsky's, who also wrote for *World of Art* magazine, shows the new Russian interest in theatre as a cosmic experience.[6]

Ballet, old or new, was overwhelmingly popular in St Petersburg, as is indicated by the number of performances staged (twenty-six in 1899–1900) as compared with opera (twenty-three). In Moscow, where Chaliapin was soloist that season, opera was more popular. The *Yearbook* is prolifically illustrated with photographs of performers in all the recent roles and also by invaluable historical portraits and early prints.

Alexandre Benois contributed to the *Yearbook* an essay on the classical architecture of the Alexandrinsky Theatre, which included illustrations by Somov and Bakst.[7] The latter, with Benois, Lanceray, Serov and Korovine, also made designs for the abortive production of *Sylvia* [see cat. 54], projected for 1901. Set to special ballet music by Léo Delibes, this ballet was for the World of Art associates an icon of Wagner's *Gesamtkunstwerk*.

In that year, Diaghilev was dismissed in connection with his involvement with *Sylvia*. When employees of the Maryinsky Theatre would not work under him as director of the new ballet production, Diaghilev refused to stand down at Volkonsky's request. He was sacked for defying the authorities. Diaghilev's artist associates demonstrated

Alexandre Benois:
Set design for the projected production of *Sylvia* 1902
Cat. 54

their support of him by boycotting work on productions at the Imperial Theatres.[8] They returned to their posts only after the resignation of Volkonsky himself, over a trivial issue concerning the costume of Mathilde Kshessinska, then *prima ballerina assoluta* of the Imperial Theatres.[9]

It is often said that World of Art 'rediscovered' the eighteenth century, an age which, during the nationalistic reign of Alexander III, had fallen from fashion because of its association with non-Russian architectural influences. However, Russian interest in eighteenth-century culture was already reviving when it began to receive attention in *World of Art* magazine. The innovation was a concern, fostered by Diaghilev himself, for accuracy of attribution, provenance and dating.

He made himself the authority on portrait painting of the eighteenth and early nineteenth centuries and, during the early 1900s, earned acknowledgment as such through his writings and by staging a unique exhibition. His discoveries and presentation of material began a new era in Russian art history.[10]

Early in 1900, Diaghilev began his research on the eighteenth- and early nineteenth-century portrait in Russia. With a view to compiling a complete catalogue of portraits in private collections throughout the land, he placed advertisements in one newspaper, *New Times* (*Novoe vremya*) and in two magazines: *World of Art* and *Art Treasures of Russia* (*Khudozhestvennye sokrovishcha Rossii*), a new magazine associated with the Society for Encouragement of the Arts and initially edited by Benois. He also sent six hundred letters to provincial land-owners. From the newspaper advertisement, he received one reply, from the magazine advertisements, twenty, and from the letters, twenty-eight replies. He then embarked on a project visiting archives, museums and provincial art collections that was to take him several years.

That same issue of *New Times* announced the forthcoming publication of Diaghilev's book, Volume One of *Russian Painting in the Eighteenth Century* [cat. 59], a monograph on the eighteenth-century portrait painter Dmitry Levitsky.

In view of the brilliance and acclaim of this volume (it won a gold medal from the Academy of Sciences) it seems surprising that Diaghilev did not continue the series on the history of Russian art, each volume of which was intended to highlight 'the ... apogee (of an age), abundant with dazzling talents'.[11] In fact, Diaghilev had three clear reasons for dropping the project: first, social unrest at the time made this rarefied subject unpopular and even dangerous; second, it proved uneconomic, and third, according to the familiar pattern, Diaghilev's interests changed.

Volume One, although researched by Diaghilev, contains the customary collaborative contributions from the World of Art members, with illustrations by Bakst, Lanceray and Somov. The book also contains a biographical article on Levitsky by V.P. Gorlenko, who had first filed this information in the Russian Archive in 1892.[12]

Levitsky, who never painted anything other than portraits, was the son of a priest and ecclesiastical painter from Kiev. Born in 1735, he received all his training in St Petersburg. After his election at the age of thirty-four as an Associate of the Academy of Arts, Levitsky exhibited there with a group of non-Russian portrait painters. His exhibit, a portrait of the architect Kokorinov (1769, State Russian Museum) won instant acclaim and he was easily selected as the most suitable painter to become portraitist to Empress Catherine II.

For the rest of his working life, Levitsky was Russia's top society portrait painter. His career coincided with the introduction in Russia of the full-length portrait. After his death (in 1822, at the age of eighty-seven and having lost his sight) Levitsky was quickly forgotten. His return to the Academy in 1808 did not long delay his replacement in society by Kiprensky and the painters of Romanticism. His work was not exhibited until 1862, when five of his Smolny Institute portraits were exhibited at the International Exhibition, London, where the Russian fine art section consisted of 125 exhibits.[13]

Diaghilev's approach to art history does not pretend to be analytical. None the less, his work on Levitsky breaks new ground. The first chapter of the Levitsky volume, after explaining the problems of compiling the book (owing to inaccurate records), demonstrates the fruits of three Diaghilev innovations: it gives a list of authenticated Levitsky works, whose whereabouts, at the time of writing, was unknown; it examines the attribution of existing works; and it finds that

three well-known portraits, previously attributed to Levitsky, are not by him at all. It also addresses the question of Levitsky's signatures. A list of them includes fifty-seven known Levitskys of early date and reveals thirty-five works published by Diaghilev for the first time.

These include the portraits of twelve Knights of the Order of St Vladimir, ascribed in a list at the Hermitage to two different artists (Borovikovsky and Argunov), although clearly being the hand of one author. Diaghilev found the document commissioning the twelve portraits in the Imperial archive. Intended for presentation to Tsar Paul for his palace at Gatchina, the portraits were ordered as a set and the artist named as Levitsky.

Dmitry Levitsky:
**Portrait of
Natalia Semyenovna Borshchova**
1776
State Russian Museum,
St Petersburg

Information provided for each portrait includes details of where and when the work was exhibited and of the copies extant. The end of the chapter consists of a chronology and a list of engravings after paintings by Levitsky.

Although Diaghilev did not proceed with his series on Russian eighteenth-century painting, he did complete some unique research which led to the discovery of the previously unknown eighteenth-century portrait painter Mikhail Shibanov.

In 1901 a portrait was reproduced in *Art Treasures of Russia*[14] of Catherine the Great's favourite, Alexander Dmitriev-Mamonov. A footnote gave biographical notes on the artist, allegedly one Shibanov. He was described as a serf of Catherine's one-time favourite, Prince Grigory Potemkin, a pensioner of the Academy of Arts, and a portrait painter. His works were said to have included *Empress*

Catherine II in Travelling Costume, *Prince Potemkin* and *Count Ivan Shouvaloff* (then President of the Imperial Academy of Arts and much painted and sculpted).

In *World of Art*, 1904,[15] this information is crucially updated in an article by Diaghilev entitled 'The Portraitist, Shibanov'. Based on the findings of his research in the Imperial Academy of Arts, Diaghilev's article reassesses two of the portraits mentioned above: of Dmitriev-Mamonov and of Catherine II, both painted in 1787.

Diaghilev starts with a new biography of this little-known artist. Here, he corrects mistakes by a nineteenth-century art historian, Petrov, who, in his tome *National Painting of the Last Century* (*Otechestvennaya zhivopis' za stoletie*) of 1862 had referred to Shibanov (also known at this time as Shabanov) as a pupil of Levitsky, who had later studied abroad.

After studying the biography of the alleged 'historical painter, Alexei Shabanov', Diaghilev developed a hunch, which led him to careful examination of the above two portraits ascribed to 'portrait painter, Shibanov'. He paid special attention to dating and scrutinised the signatures. His findings were quite surprising and led to the rediscovery of a forgotten artist.

In 1787, Alexei Shabanov (according to correspondence between the Russian Imperial Academy and its Italian scholars) was in Italy. He therefore could not have painted Catherine II or her favourite. Moreover, if a serf, he would not have been allowed to join the Imperial Academy. Finally, the portraits are not signed with the usual signature of the Shabanov who allegedly painted the portraits.

Diaghilev discovered that Mikhail Shibanov was another portrait painter of the same period. This man really was Potemkin's serf and did in fact paint both the Empress Catherine and Dmitriev-Mamonov. To this unknown artist, Diaghilev was also able to attribute the portraits of Potemkin and of Shouvaloff. Nowadays, Alexei Shabanov is an obscure footnote to the history of Russian art, whereas Mikhail Shibanov is a well-known artist and the author of two pictures at the Tretyakov Gallery familiar since 1917: *The Wedding Contract Feast* and *Peasant Lunch*. Had it not been for Diaghilev's research, he would probably have remained the alter ego of a minor portrait painter of the eighteenth century.

DIAGHILEV AND THE 'HISTORICAL EXHIBITION OF RUSSIAN PORTRAITS' 1905

In the arrangement of his historical portrait exhibition and its catalogue, Diaghilev engendered a new interest in portrait artists as well as their sitters, and a keen awareness of what portraits can tell us about our historic past. Ironically, through his activities in this field, Diaghilev himself exerted an influence on history. His climactic *Historical Exhibition of Russian Portraits* opened in St Petersburg in March 1905, in the thick of strikes, uprisings, violence and lootings. The first Russian revolution would have destroyed more of Russia's cultural heritage, had a large number of aristocratic family portraits not been in the exhibition at the time that estates were being torched throughout the Russian empire.

World of Art for 1902 contained Diaghilev's review of the Moscow exhibition, 'Works of an Earlier Age (*proizvedeniya stariny*)', which covered fifty years of portrait painting (1700-50). He compared this show unfavourably with one held in St Petersburg in 1870,[1] calling it 'dilettante': the catalogue he declared to contain 'more mistakes than ants in any anthill'.[2] A successful portrait exhibition, he observed, involves gargantuan preparation. As if to show what he meant, Diaghilev himself embarked upon two major portrait projects the same year: his Levitsky monograph and a retrospective exhibition of Russian portraits. In his memoirs, Benois describes Diaghilev's obsessive application to this and other augean projects as 'almost frightening at times', though showing marvellous 'energy, patience and firmness'.[3]

When the time came to begin collecting the exhibits, Diaghilev appointed an organising committee, with himself as Commissar. The exhibition's patron was Grand Duke Nikolai Mikhailovich, a connoisseur with funding potential, who helped in preparing the letters of inquiry and was already engaged in the production of a fully illustrated catalogue raisonné of Russia's portraits [cat. 60]. The Grand Duke also gained the financial support of his cousin, Tsar Nicholas II.

The *Historical Exhibition of Russian Portraits* opened on 6 March 1905 at St Petersburg's Tauride Palace and ran for over six months. The building had been commissioned by Catherine II from the architect Starov in 1783. It was intended as a gift to her ex-lover, Prince Grigory Potemkin, in recognition of his military services in Taurida, an area in the Crimea which he had won from the Turks. Potemkin, who was to die shortly after the palace was completed, never lived there, and the building fell into neglect for over a hundred years, until the time of Diaghilev's exhibition. Extensive restoration was therefore required before the show could be mounted, a feat that

Tauride Palace, St Petersburg:
Interior, eighteenth century
Courtesy Victor Kennett

Diaghilev was able to repeat effectively in Paris when he renovated the derelict Châtelet Theatre for the first appearance of dancers from the Russian Imperial Ballets.

Because Diaghilev was a freelance operator, the major museums in Moscow and St Petersburg did not lend to this exhibition. Nevertheless, the works finally hung in the exhibition numbered 2,226 and consisted of portrait paintings and sculptural busts.

The 1902 exhibition had been limited to the years 1700-50. Diaghilev's exhibition covered an historical span of 150 years and included a section on contemporary portraits. It attracted 45,000 visitors,[4] including members of the Imperial Family, who themselves played a consciously historical role in the event.

Tsar Nicholas II had, moreover, been gracious in lending items including furniture and precious objects from three Imperial palaces as well as plants from the Imperial hothouses.[5] These were selected and placed by the young artist Mstislav Dobuzhinsky. The overall décor was arranged by a committee of World of Art artists: Benois, Bakst, Lanceray and Shchuko. The new environment successfully recalled the glamour of the Catherine epoch. Benois remembers Bakst's 'Winter Garden' in the centre of the hall's colonnade, where the most important sculptures nestled among exotic plants and trellises.[6]

The exhibits were arranged by reign and grouped according to artist. Benois has recorded how this was done: 'In the centre of each group, under a special canopy, hung the portrait of the Emperor or Empress indissolubly identified with the epoch.'[7]

Dobuzhinsky recalls in his memoirs the success of the hall dedicated to the reign of Paul, whose canopy was made of black velvet. His overall assessment was contained in the observation: '... Everything here was *genuine* and everything was as it should be to suit the spirit of World of Art, which reigned there: restrained in style.'[8]

Critical reviews were mainly adulatory, a particularly constructive one being supplied by Baron N.N. Wrangel, who admired the contemporary section, which he analysed in detail. Less complimentary was the characteristically lengthy, demagogic review of Diaghilev's 'democratic' opponent, Vladimir Stasov,[9] who was anxious to show up the magnificent event as yet another product of Diaghilev's 'decadence'.

Stasov achieved this in two ways: first, by belittling the skills of the Imperial painters of the eighteenth century, whom he dismissed as empty flatterers, producing 'ballet masquerade art'; second, he denigrated the vast majority of the sitters, on the grounds that insufficient of them represented radical men of action or members of the lower classes.[10]

Stasov's obsessive list of sitters according to category has the opposite effect to the one he desired: it shows clearly that Diaghilev managed, against all the odds, to represent an impressive spread of classes, interests and occupations among the sitters. Apart from the 240 Imperial Family members and 300 aristocrats (representing, Stasov disapprovingly calculates, a good quarter of the show), there is an interesting spread of political and cultural activists, including liberals and nineteenth-century revolutionaries, such as Radishchev, Novikov and Chaadaev. The ecclesiastical ranks are also well filled and the only cultural area thinly represented is that of musicians (only three, one of whom was John Field, the Irish composer who lived in St Petersburg).[11]

Although Stasov tried to claim that no poor people were represented, it emerges from his own review that there was a good sprinkling of peasants, serfs and nursemaids, not to mention some colourful (though admittedly affluent) members of the merchant class. Considering that, in pre-revolutionary Russia, the upper classes commissioned the vast majority of portraits, this represents, for Diaghilev, quite a coup. Diaghilev's career as the begetter of grandiose projects had begun.

DIAGHILEV AND THE 1906 'EXHIBITION OF RUSSIAN ART' AT THE SALON D'AUTOMNE

By January 1906 Diaghilev had the measure of Paris, knew what to show there and how to market it. Indeed, he had been considering the question of suitable Russian material for exhibition in the West for some time. In a review of the Russian section of the Secession exhibition of 1896 in Munich, Diaghilev had written:

If Europe needs Russian art, then it needs its youth and spontaneity. And this is what our artists have not understood. They have, as it were, been ashamed to present to the court of Europe their nationality and have only tried to show that we too can paint like Western Europeans … But it has not once occurred to them to ask: Can we teach you something you don't already know? Can we say something new in European art or at least keep up with you? …[1]

The Western public had never seen an entire exhibition of Russian art that had not been selected and sanctioned by Russian officialdom. The Russian section of London's International exhibition of 1862 had consisted of 125 examples of painting, sculpture, prints and architectural drawings, all by top academicians and belonging to Imperial and other distinguished collections. Paintings there had included five portraits by Levitsky, which had been duly reviewed as examples of quasi-French art.[2] In 1897, the Wanderers had been shown in Copenhagen, Munich and Venice.

Even the Paris *Exposition Universelle* of 1900, which had shown some contemporary Russian art, had contained works by tendentious artists such as Repin and Vereshchagin. In Paris, examples of contemporary Russian fine and applied arts came from World of Art and Abramtsevo circles. Artists receiving medals there had included Vrubel and Serov. To Diaghilev, it seemed clear that the French should now view an entire galaxy of quality Russian culture.

On 19 April, Diaghilev wrote to Benois from Constantinople with news of a probable exhibition engagement at the Salon d'Automne. On 27 May, Benois informed Lanceray that Diaghilev had arrived in Paris. He was to stay there approximately six weeks, putting pressure on the French exhibition authorities, then returning to Russia to arrange the selection of works. The total organisation time for this exhibition, which was to fill twelve halls of the Grand Palais, was under two months.

During the summer and early autumn of 1906, the World of Art exhibitors Konstantin Somov, Anna Ostroumova-Lebedeva, Sergei Sudeikin and Anatoly Arapov were in touch with one another about the Paris show. According to Sudeikin's diaries,[3] Diaghilev commissioned

him, with Kuznetsov and Larionov, to collect the exhibits for Paris that were in Moscow, including two panels by Mikhail Vrubel from the house of his patron, A.V. Morosov.

Publicity was also in motion. In the new magazine, *Golden Fleece* (*Zolotoe runo*), the section 'News from Everywhere' contained the observation, 'Rumour has it that 1st October [old style year][4] will see an exhibition in Paris's Grand-Halle [sic] of Russian painting, embracing approximately all periods and all schools, from the reign of [Empress] Elizabeth to the present day …'

This announcement was in fact not entirely accurate: the Salon exhibition was to start earlier than the mid-eighteenth century and would consist of other media apart from painting. None the less, the publicity was invaluable, and Benois, on seeing it, was amazed by Diaghilev's organisational wizardry. The magazine further announced that the exhibition's patrons were to include 'the Parisian maecenas, Countess Greffulhe'. The most influential patron proved in the event to be Grand Duke Vladimir Alexandrovich, President of the Imperial Academy of Arts.

The project had obtained charitable status, donations were to be collected in aid of Russian war widows and orphans.[5] Diaghilev seemed to be having equal success with sponsorship. Benois wrote to Walter Nouvel, on 5 August: '… People are still saying here that Seryozha has secured from Moscow (from Meck?) 50,000 roubles, of which 20,000 are for the exhibition. Is this true?'[6]

Nouvel confirmed, on 12 August, that this was broadly accurate, although 30,000 roubles had been allocated to the exhibition and the rest was to go to charity: 'The exhibition will take place and work is on the boil in all directions.'[7] The main designer was to be Bakst and some decoration was to be provided by Golovine.

For this, his first Western project, Diaghilev formed a committee with himself as Commissar, Count I.I. Tolstoy as Chairman and the Russian Ambassador to France, A.I. Nelidov, heading an eminent coterie of rich and influential Russians with French connections. These contacts assured that the required funds and venue were secured.

The *Exposition de l'art russe* opened at the Grand Palais on 15 October 1906 and ran until 11 November. Of the 750 works, a significant number had been shown at the Tauride Palace exhibition of the previous year. Portraits of the eighteenth and nineteenth centuries were reinforced with suitable history paintings. As a retrospective, the show went back to the earliest Russian art, represented with a fine selection of icons from the distinguished Likhachev collection. Contemporary art predominated, in a section made up of works by artists shown in St Petersburg earlier the same year. As was customary, the last group of exhibits was of selected applied arts objects from the Imperial glass and porcelain factories.

Several Russian reviews appeared in issues 11 and 12 of *Golden Fleece*, the publication launched only that year. An article by Prince Shervashidze (who was also an exhibitor) describes in detail the décor of the display.[8]

Arbours and friezes abounded and each period of the exhibition was represented by a different coloured wallpaper: gold for the icon hall, silver for the petrine section and, for the eighteenth century, azure. An entire section was devoted to Catherine the Great, another to the nineteenth century from 1830 onwards, and the last section (occupying six halls – half the exhibition) was dedicated to contemporary art.

In the foreword to the catalogue, Diaghilev makes a short statement about values. 'Many names,' he declares, in a thinly veiled allusion to the Wanderers, 'once famous, have now lost their glory, some temporarily and others for ever … That will explain the intentional absence of several painters, who were too long considered in the West to be the only representatives of artistic Russia …'[9]

The contemporary section he describes as 'a faithful image of artistic Russia today, with its sincere training, its respectful admiration for the past and its ardent faith in the future.'[10]

The historical section he defines as 'a summary of the development of our art seen through modern eyes …'[11] Its presentation was governed by Diaghilev's personal interpretation of the history of Russian art, unchanged, in essence, since the days of 'Difficult Questions' in *World of Art*.

Artists of the nineteenth century who had produced both portraits and historical works, such as Karl Bryullov and Fyodor Bruni, or portraits and realist paintings, such as Ilya Repin and Nikolai Gué, were represented only as portraitists. Repin had one work only [see cat.77]; and the Wanderers as a school were ignored completely.

Some omissions were due to circumstances. Notwithstanding the success of his portrait exhibition of the previous year, Diaghilev was not permitted to borrow works from either of Russia's main museums: the Alexander III Museum (now the State Russian Museum) in St Petersburg and the Tretyakov Gallery in Moscow.

The exhibition catalogue essay was supplied by Alexandre Benois and is a subjective overview of the history of Russian art. Continuing themes already treated in his books, *A History of Russian Art in the Nineteenth Century* and *The Russian School of Painting*, Benois reveals a dislike of Academism, which he dismisses as a pathetic attempt to ape the classicism of Paris and Rome, and Realism, which, he claims, belongs with the 'purely literary'. On the other hand, he

explains concisely the aims of contemporary Russian art, which he describes unequivocally as a form of individualism, dividing it into two branches: St Petersburg (World of Art and its attendant historical nostalgia) and Moscow (a decorative faction descending from Vrubel).

Several Russian reviewers remarked on the subjective nature of the exhibition's selection. As usual, Viktor Stasov, who appreciated the aims of such an undertaking, reacted negatively to the exhibition's contents. Shortly before his death, he wrote: 'This, for me, was simply a frightful business! Such frightful things, generally, threaten our poor art!'[12]

His protégé, Ilya Repin, however, despite his own meagre showing there, writes about it with surprising warmth: 'At the moment there are two interesting exhibitions here: the French one and Diaghilev's; the latter is especially engaging: there are things which are interesting by virtue of their artistic merits and – by their impudence! Amazing! Yet all the names are there.'[13]

Interesting backstage insights are furnished in the personal journal of Alexandre Benois. 'The organisation of the exhibition,' he wearily records, 'followed the usual routine. Seryozha neglected everything, failed to pay essential visits, but sat for days rehanging pictures and tormenting the wallpaperers. As ever, right up to the last moment. Everything seemed chaotic, then suddenly got sorted out and properly ordered …'[14]

More cynical is Benois's aside about Diaghilev's mania for self advertisement: '… When there is an opportunity to swim among the grandees, Seryozha forgets everything and simply makes efforts to show himself off.'[15]

Critical acclaim was won by the icons, portraits by Levitsky and works by a range of contemporary artists, including Vrubel, who was hailed in *Le Figaro* as a genius.[16] All reviewers commented on the still-lifes of Larionov, the Breton landscapes of Jawlensky and the Symbolist works of Kuznetsov. Stylistically, the Fauve-like qualities of these works, particularly those by Larionov and Goncharova, indicated that the World of Art's era was over. It was the turn of the Russian avant-garde.

As a result of the exhibition, twelve of the artists, including Bakst, Benois, Vrubel, Roerich and Larionov, were elected as members of the Salon; while Diaghilev and his coterie of collectors from whom many of the works came, the Botkins, the Girshmans and Ivan Morosov, were elected to the status of Respected Members of the Salon d'Art.[17]

Diaghilev was invited to tour the show to Berlin, Vienna, Venice, Barcelona, Brussels, Munich and London. In the event, it travelled only to Berlin (accompanied by Diaghilev and Igor Grabar, who wrote the German catalogue) and to the Seventh Venice Biennale.

Diaghilev's aim to show Russian artists of significance can be judged in retrospect to have entailed a sound choice of enduring elements. The contemporary and historic heavyweights of his show are still considered the most significant in the history of Russian art. It is particularly interesting that even his contemporaries were selected by Diaghilev without error. A good number went on to join his ballet enterprises and many of them are known today. As Benois observed, when Diaghilev set about making his artistic selection, 'he made no compromises'.[18]

FRIENDS AND ENEMIES

In 1909, Elena Panaeva-Diaghileva read a newspaper review of the triumph in Paris of the stepson she was never to see again. Musing over his photograph, she remarked, in a letter to her sister-in-law, Anna Diaghileva-Filosofova: 'I don't think Seryozha has changed much since he was three …'[1]

Diaghilev's most curious physical feature, described in the memoirs of many associates, was his disproportionately large head: the reason, as he occasionally confided, why his mother survived his birth by only a few days.[2] Perhaps her death was the inevitable price for the advent of such a powerful personality. Diaghilev's intensity was apparent from an early age. His stepmother records that as a small boy, he showed such abnormal interest in everything that she took him to the doctor.[3] Alexandre Benois describes his tireless application as 'almost frightening'.[4] Both Igor Stravinsky[5] and Tamara Karsavina[6] refer to his phenomenal powers of concentration. His iron will was occasionally compared with that of Peter the Great, from whom, at grand moments, Diaghilev claimed to be descended.[7]

Soon after finding his niche in St Petersburg, Diaghilev affected a demeanour of foppish affectation. This was the outward manifestation of the snobbery which was to become the hallmark of the World of Art group, who seemed to be mocking everybody not in their immediate circle. For this they earned the dislike of many and aroused downright terror in some, such as Alexandre Golovine, who felt awkward in their company.[8]

From student days, Diaghilev was a shameless sycophant and a name-dropper. In his travels with Dmitry Filosofov, at home and abroad, the two would foist themselves unselfconsciously on celebrities, including Tolstoy,[9] Chabrier, Massenet, Dumas and Zola.[10] Diaghilev would seek their autographs, which he would flaunt on his return to St Petersburg.[11]

Diaghilev's literary name-dropping came near to home with his insistence on introducing Nanny Dunya as Arina Rodionovna (the name of Alexander Pushkin's nurse). This practice would always reduce the old lady to tears.[12] The self-consciously Pushkinesque pose is captured in Bakst's portrait of the two of them together [cat. 6]. When, in spring 1906, the painting was first exhibited in St Petersburg, the literary affectation was ridiculed by the crusty critic, Vladimir Stasov, a familiar sparring partner of Diaghilev's until his death later that same year.[13]

Diaghilev's relationships were neither exclusively personal nor professional, but straddled the two, providing ideal fuel for rifts of cosmic proportions. A number of his closest associations lasted many years, so adding to the pain of parting. Of his artistic associates, the only one who did not go back to World of Art days was the choreographer Michel Fokine.

Diaghilev and his cousin and, during the World of Art phase, inseparable companion Dmitry Filosofov, worked closely together in launching and running the magazine. They were smooth, often ruthless operators. One associate records how the pair repaid the critic Burenin for a derogatory review of a World of Art exhibition, by going round to his house, lurking in the street, and attacking him when he opened his front door. (The ploy had its effect. Burenin never again criticised the group adversely.)[14]

A similar thuggish incident at this period apparently earned Diaghilev the eternal enmity of World of Art painter Konstantin Somov. When Diaghilev and Filosofov were working for the Imperial Theatres, they would relay nuggets of court gossip to their editorial colleagues at the *World of Art* headquarters. These would invariably appear afterwards in a local newspaper. The cousins traced the leaks to Léon Bakst, whose brother was a journalist.

After due warning, which did nothing to staunch the flow of illicit column inches, the two gave Bakst a beating one evening in the corridor of the magazine's editorial offices. Bakst thought no more of the incident, and returned to work next day; but Somov appears to have witnessed the event and taken it badly. He wrote Diaghilev a bitter letter, resigning from *World of Art*'s editorial board.

Diaghilev, who greatly admired Somov 'as was shown by his attentions to Kostia [Somov] and the tone of his voice when he spoke to him', was seriously upset.[15] Attempts to prevail upon Benois and Nouvel to effect a reconciliation proved fruitless. Diaghilev, however, did not give up trying to win Somov back. Often without his permission and to Somov's frequent rage,[16] Diaghilev would include examples of his work in publications and exhibitions (including two programme covers in the *Imperial Theatres Yearbook* and several paint-

ings from Diaghilev's own collection in the *Exposition de l'art russe* of 1906) but they were never friends again. Hence Somov, whose work was ideally theatrical, never worked on Ballets Russes productions.[17]

Benois has a rider to this anecdote. He suggests that Somov had been seeking a rupture with Diaghilev for some time, for a 'purely personal, intimate reason'.[18]

Benois, who was at school with Somov and Filosofov, recalls in his early memoirs that the two had a crush on one another there and that Somov was excessively childish, 'always whispering and giggling, even when he was 18 and Dima [Filosofov] 16'.[19] In his later diaries, Benois recalls: 'Although the tenderness and quasi-lovesickness which had existed between Kostia and Dima were things of the past ... one cannot exclude the possibility that Somov bitterly resented the evident preference of his former closest friend for the newcomer.'[20]

There is no concrete evidence that the cousins had a homosexual relationship. Indeed, associates from the early World of Art period remember that the two professed horror of the practice.[21] However, in his writings, Benois implies that their friends took them

to be lovers. From the days of the Society for Self Improvement, the two trod the same paths of cultural creativity. In 1899, they were both engaged by the Imperial Theatres; and they were together when Diaghilev was sacked following his attempted production of Delibes's ballet *Sylvia*. A letter from Filosofov to Diaghilev's parents describes Diaghilev's reaction to his fate, which he had been disinclined to accept until he read the announcement in the court newspaper next day.[22]

It is an over-simplification to impute Diaghilev's dismissal from the Imperial Theatres to his homosexuality. Although Tsar Nicholas II almost certainly knew of his proclivities, Diaghilev was not unique in this respect, even within the context of the Imperial Theatres.[23]

The dismissal is far more likely to have arisen from Diaghilev's overbearing and, admittedly, affected manner. Benois remembers that 'during the first months at his new post ... Diaghilev's behaviour particularly annoyed and irritated the society of St Petersburg. Dressed in his smart, faultlessly fitting uniform, he had a way of walking through the stalls, his head in the air, which made tongues wag and gossip about him – often unfounded – spread like wildfire throughout the town.'[24]

With the stripping of rank symbolised by his flunkey's uniform, Diaghilev's hopes of Imperial preferment, indeed of employment generally, were dashed. Ultimately, this was the best thing that could have happened to Diaghilev. At the time, he shut himself up for several days in Dima's room, where he spent the time screaming and throwing cups at the wall; a scenario that, in later life, was to be repeated every time a young ballet protégé got married.[25]

This was the first and last time that Diaghilev was to take a professional reversal to heart. Where he harboured grudges in cases of emotional hurt, professionally he would never consider the possibility of defeat. Consequently, he almost always managed to win against heavy odds. When, after the successful *Saisons russes* of 1908, Diaghilev began planning his Paris Seasons of opera and ballet for the following year, he made a number of influential enemies in Russia, whose scheming he overlooked. In the case of Mathilde Kshessinska, he even indulged in a degree of cautious collaboration. On one occasion, in Paris, he had no hesitation in introducing her to Arnold Haskell as '*un adversaire bien digne de moi*'.[26]

Vladimir Teliakovsky, who succeeded Volkonsky as Director of the Imperial Theatres, made it hard for Diaghilev to find rehearsal space for his dancers following their return from their successful Paris début in 1909. Possibly Teliakovsky feared for his job. It is conceivable, though the evidence is circumstantial, that he also prevented Diaghilev's Company from performing in St Petersburg. The Ballets

Russes were never seen in their own country. In 1912, they were to have had their first St Petersburg Season, performing at the Narodny dom. This theatre burned down shortly beforehand.[27] Diaghilev did not seek another Russian engagement. In the final analysis, the rejection of Diaghilev and his ballets was Russia's loss.

In view of their grandiosity, an important component of Diaghilev's enterprises was finance. He was shrewd in drawing up budgets but his everyday attitude to money was characteristically dismissive.[28] Diaghilev's grandfather had given away his fortune and, at the time that Diaghilev first went up to university, his father went bankrupt.[29] However, money does not appear to have been a matter of serious personal concern to Diaghilev. He seems to have had sufficient for his own relatively modest needs; and, in the early stages, he funded his own exhibitions.[30]

His later enterprises required sponsorship and Diaghilev was obliged to make overtures to wealthy benefactors; a duty he found far from disagreeable. His natural snobbery and penchant for cultivating influential people came into its own here. With patrons and purely business associates, Diaghilev was both charming and unscrupulous. This tendency was recorded in the cartoon by Pavel Shcherbov of the *World of Art* sponsor, Princess Tenisheva, as a milch-cow [cat. 27].

Pavel Shcherbov:
Milking the Cow
Caricature of Diaghilev and Princess Tenisheva
Early 1900s
Cat.27
The cartoon includes the two-fish symbol and the skyline of turrets
from the cover of the *World of Art* magazine (see opposite)

This cartoon encapsulated the cause of an ugly confrontation between the Princess and the *World of Art* editors, Diaghilev and Benois.[31] Initially, she had taken Diaghilev into her confidence, believing his concerns to be her own, since he was a close associate of Benois, who had helped her to build up her art collection. When adverse criticism of her protégés, Repin and Vasnetsov, appeared in the magazine, Princess Tenisheva took it as a personal insult and a mockery of her principles, and temporarily withdrew her support. Diaghilev shamelessly wooed her again, with success. On the death of her wealthy husband in 1903, she took the opportunity to let funding drop definitively, having first tried imposing conditions that were impossible to keep.[32]

An indication that Tsar Nicholas II did not further penalise Diaghilev after the Imperial Theatres débâcle is that he continued for a short period to contribute 15,000 roubles annually to *World of Art*, having been alerted to its imminent doom by Valentin Serov, during an Imperial portrait sitting in 1900.[33] Whether the Tsar had ever read the magazine and, therefore, accepted its controversial and anti-establishment content, is uncertain.

The ballet patron with whom Diaghilev was closest was Misia Sert, a wealthy woman of Slavonic descent, rich, cultivated and extremely musical. At times, the ballet Company was in dire financial straits, the dancers had often to wait for their wages, and it was not uncommon for sets and costumes to be sequestered as collateral. The story of how Misia Sert had to go home to find money for the costumes before the curtain could rise on the first Paris performance of *Petrushka* on 13 June 1911 is often told. Through Misia, Diaghilev met a number of other Parisian patrons and collaborators. She was also his closest woman friend.

He was perhaps less fond and respectful of the impresario Gabriel Astruc, his opposite number in Paris. Astruc was incensed when he discovered that Diaghilev was arranging to bring Chaliapin for a second season to the Paris Opéra, when Astruc had different

World of Art
First issue, cover, 1898-9
Cat.12A

plans for the Opéra in spring 1909.[34] On the other hand, Astruc laid everything on the line to get the Ballets Russes for his new Théâtre des Champs-Elysées in 1913. Diaghilev drove a hard bargain. Astruc went bankrupt.

Several members of Diaghilev's Company describe the tremendous sense of freedom experienced in arriving in the West from Russia. It is reasonable to suppose that Diaghilev experienced it also. Freedom in Paris at the turn of the century included licence, exploited by renowned members of the gay community. Increasingly that scene was to centre on the Ballets Russes.[35]

Already in the 1890s, Diaghilev had made a point of being seen walking the streets arm in arm with the disgraced exile, Oscar Wilde.[36] He is reputed to have enjoyed innocent flirtations with gondoliers in Venice.[37] However, it would be wrong to define Diaghilev, despite his vanity and his monocle, as camp. It is impossible to imagine a man of his stature contributing to the scenario later described by Stravinsky in which Jean Cocteau and his friends swooned over every young man who appeared in a rehearsal room.[38] It is more probable that, like Stravinsky, Diaghilev found Cocteau palatable in small doses only, and would take him seriously if and when he was able to contribute a genuine project. Diaghilev's famous dictum, '*Etonne-moi*'[39] was probably a put-down, aimed at holding the tiresome sycophant at arm's length.

Diaghilev does appear, however, to have been suspicious, with some justification, of Cocteau's friendship with Nijinsky; but his rumoured attitude of insane jealousy at the friendship between Nijinsky and Auguste Rodin, then seventy-two years old, seems to have been ridiculous.[40]

Diaghilev was equally passionate in his professional jealousies. He made no effort to modify his morose attitude to the rival magazine, *Art Treasures of Russia*, which Benois edited in 1901. Stravinsky remembers feeling disappointment that Diaghilev could not share his joy at the success of the composer's independent, non-Diaghilev production, *The Soldier's Tale*.[41] Perhaps only more damning than Diaghilev's jealousy was his indifference, as described by Prince Shcherbatov with regard to his *Exhibition of Contemporary Art*, an interior design project which Shcherbatov set up with a handful of Diaghilev's artists both from Moscow and St Petersburg. Diaghilev was kind and gracious during the inaugural breakfast which launched the project. The exhibition, which was shown in apartments, first in St Petersburg and then in Moscow in the spring of 1903, was a resounding failure.[42]

With members of his Company, Diaghilev was notoriously tyrannical. His dictatorial behaviour can be dated to his earliest exhi-

bition days. As early as 1898 he announced that he would make his own selection of works for a large mixed exhibition of contemporary works to be shown the following year.[43] This was a process unimaginable until that moment, and heartily disapproved of by Vladimir Stasov.[44] The situation was reversed by a series of meetings called by World of Art's exhibiting artists in January and February 1900, and annually thereafter. They were held at *World of Art*'s editorial offices and attended by exhibitors both from St Petersburg's World of Art group and Moscow's Thirty-Six. At it, the artists insisted on drawing up a set of Society rules, limiting the powers of individuals. This was to be the only area of Diaghilev's enterprises where he would be overruled by his artists.[45]

Dancers of the Ballets Russes were later bound to Diaghilev by a contract which now seems draconian, even if those issued by the Imperial Theatres were worse.[46] Occasionally, there were murmurs of discontent about wages, which are recorded by Bronislava Nijinska and by Lydia Sokolova, but the dancers were too dedicated to their art to organise concerted opposition.[47]

Three major rifts occurred between Diaghilev and his associates during the ballet period. Alexandre Benois, Michel Fokine and Vaslav Nijinsky never recovered from their artistic rejection by the

Vaslav Nijinsky in *Don Quixote*, 1900s
Mander and Mitchenson Theatre Collection,
Beckenham

Mikhail Vrubel:
Pan 1899
Cat. 48

Mikhail Vrubel:
Swan Princess 1900
Cat. 49

impresario. The first two, in their memoirs, refer repeatedly and bitterly to Diaghilev's dismissive attitude to their work at the end of the pre-war period. Nijinsky, who was already insane by 1918-19, when he wrote his notebooks, refers to Diaghilev, his former lover, both obliquely and somewhat grossly at intervals throughout it.[48]

Although such a work cannot be taken as a reliable source, aspects of Nijinsky's notebooks do give an insight into the writer's character. Most revealing is the fact that Nijinsky seems not to have been homosexual by inclination. He simply needed a protector. His description of his first meeting with Diaghilev is interesting:

> I hated Diaghilev from the first days of our meeting, for I felt the power of Diaghilev. Lvov [Nijinsky's previous lover] introduced me by telephone to Diaghilev, who had me come to the Hotel Europe where he was living. I hated him because of his too assured voice, but I went to try my luck. I found luck, for I loved him straight away. I was trembling … I hated him but I pretended because I knew that my mother and I were starving.[49]

He also ventures:

> I used to see tarts in Paris when I was with Diaghilev. He thought I was going for a walk, but I was going to the tarts.[50]

He claims towards the end of their relationship to have spent the rest of his spare time masturbating.[51]

The leitmotif of Romola Nijinsky's biography of her husband is Diaghilev's alleged obsession with ruining Nijinsky following his marriage.[52] This seems improbable, if only because Nijinsky so swiftly attained his own ruin without outside intervention. Deep down, Nijinsky realised this. 'I knew all too well,' he confesses, 'that if I left Diaghilev I would die of hunger, for I was not sufficiently mature for life.'[53] Nevertheless, Nijinsky allowed himself to be lured into marriage by a virtual stranger; and life, predictably, defeated him.

It is plausible that Nijinsky expected, as his wife suggests, that Diaghilev would be understanding about his marriage and that the young 'Dieu de la danse' would continue to star in Ballets Russes productions.[54] At that time, it was hard to imagine the Company without him. Diaghilev's régisseur, Sergei Grigoriev, whom Diaghilev dragooned into signing a telegram of dismissal drafted by himself, reacted with a surprise that must have been shared by many. 'I thought that Nijinsky and Diaghilev's Ballet were indivisible,' he explained.[55]

Nijinsky had reckoned without Diaghilev's impetuous pride. Emotionally, Diaghilev could not do otherwise than dismiss him. Professionally, Diaghilev had begun to doubt Nijinsky's genius as a choreographer after his protracted agonies in creating The Rite of Spring. It is possible that Stravinsky was to some extent instrumental in this, since the latter states in his memoirs that, in rehearsing this ballet, Nijinsky showed himself to have neither training nor facility for music.[56] This view is loudly contradicted by Bronislava Nijinska, who gives several instances of her brother's musical abilities.[57]

Perhaps Diaghilev already intended getting rid of Nijinsky, just as Nijinsky, like his elder brother, was probably always destined to become insane. Jean Cocteau attests that, around 1912, Nijinsky became sulky and rude.[58] Nijinsky and his sister both imply that Nijinsky was feeling increasingly resentful of his dependence on Diaghilev and that Diaghilev had correspondingly tired of him by 1913, the year when Nijinsky was unprecedentedly allowed to travel without the impresario and promptly became engaged to the Company's pretty and aristocratic Hungarian groupie, Romola de Pulszky, on the boat to South America. Whatever the truth, the great dancer's career lasted scarcely ten years and his life as a rational being twenty-nine. After that, he was reduced to a husk of the awkward, inadequate youth that the overwhelming majority of his associates declare him to have been offstage.

Nijinsky was the only close associate whom Diaghilev dismissed. He did not part easily with his collaborators. In his biography of the impresario, Arnold Haskell demonstrates that Diaghilev engaged the majority of them repeatedly over many years. When they left him, he was always sorry and, more tellingly, he was always happy to take them back, without recriminations.[59] Even those who broke definitively with him continued to admire his work. In the final analysis, Diaghilev was dedicated to achieving the best possible artistic results with the best possible collaborators. As art was his life, his collaborators were also his closest friends. They ceased to be his friends when he could no longer work with them.

NOTES

Prologue
pp. 11–16

1. E.P. Subbotin, 'Sergei Diagilev – Gimnazist' in *Sergei Diagilev i Khudozhestvennaia kul'tura XIX–XX vv. Materialy pervykh diagilevskikh chtenii 17–19 aprelia 1987*, Perm, 1989, p. 15.
2. Ibid p. 14.
3. A. Laskin, *Neznakomye Diagilevy, ili konets tsitaty*, St Petersburg, 1994, p. 33.
4. Subbotin, op. cit. p. 13.
5. Laskin, op. cit. p. 34.
6. Alexandre Benois, *Reminiscences of the Russian Ballet*, London, 1941, p. 189.
7. Erté (Roman de Tirtoff), *Things I Remember: An Autobiography*, London, 1975, p. 48.
8. Laskin, op. cit. p. 85.
9. Ibid p. 88.
10. Ibid p. 85.
11. Alexandre Benois, *Vozniknovenie 'Mira Iskusstva'*, Leningrad, 1928, p. 9.
12. Laskin, op. cit. p. 113.
13. Alexandre Benois, *Memoirs*, 2 vols (trans. Moura Boudberg), London, 1960–4, vol. II, p. 79.
14. Ibid p. 166.
15. Ibid p. 169.
16. Ibid p. 178.
17. Laskin, op. cit. p. 101.
18. Ibid p. 102.
19. Ibid p. 117.
20. Benois, *Memoirs*, op. cit. p. 80.
21. Letter to Michel Fokine, Lunacharsky Theatre Library, St Petersburg, Arkhiv L.D. Krupitskogo, R 12/53.
22. Letter from Mikhail Nesterov, Tretyakov Gallery Archive, 100/124, 9 iii 1897.
23. Arnold Haskell (in collaboration with Walter Nouvel), *Diaghileff. His Artistic and Private Life*, London, 1935, pp. 160–1.

24. Dokladnaia zapiska Diagileva S.P. Ministru Narodnogo Prosveshcheniia 15/11/1905, Russian Museum Archive, f137 ed. khr. 942.
25. M. Fokine, *Protiv techeniia: vospominaniia baletmeistera*, Leningrad, 1981, pp. 229–30.
26. Bronislava Nijinska, *Early Memoirs*, Durham and London, 1992, p. 324.
27. Benois, *Reminiscences*, op. cit. p. 319.
28. Serge Lifar, *Serge Diaghilev. His Life. His Work. His Legend. An Intimate Biography*, London, 1940, p. 332.
29. Benois, *Reminiscences*, op. cit. pp. 382–3.
30. E.V. Paston, 'Khudozhestvennye printsipy mamontovskogo teatra' in *Materialy pervykh diagilevskikh chtenii, op. cit.* p. 28.
31. Benois, *Reminiscences*, op. cit. p. 68.

The World of Art Group
pp. 16–26

1. Ilya Repin, Letter from Paris, in G.Yu. Sternin, *Khudozhestvennaia zhizn' Rossii na rubezhe xix–xx vv*, Moscow, 1970, p. 128.
2. Alexandre Benois, *Vozniknovenie 'Mira Iskusstva'*, Leningrad, 1928, p. 10.
3. Alexandre Benois, 'Khudozhestvennye Eresi' in *Zolotoe runo*, vol. I, no. 2, Moscow, 1906–7, pp. 80–8.
4. See D.V. Sarabianov, *Russian Art: From Neoclassicism to the Avant-Garde*, London, p. 226.
5. See Somov's Letter to A.A. Mikhailova, 28 April 1932, in *Konstantin Andreevich Somov, Mir khudozhnika*, ed. Yu. N. Podkopaeva and A.N Sveshnikova, Moscow, 1979, p. 395.

6. *Mir iskusstva*, vol. IX, no. 1, 1903, pp. 1–24.
7. S.P. Yaremich, 'K.A. Somov' in *Iskusstvo*, no. 12, Kiev, 1911.
8. *Konstantin Andreevich Somov*, op. cit. p. 6.
9. Ibid.
10. 'Pis'ma iz Miunkhena', in *Mir iskusstva*, vol. VII, nos 1–6, 'Art Chronicle' 1902, pp. 96–8.
11. Janet Kennedy, *The Mir iskusstva group and Russian Art 1898–1912*, New York and London, 1977, p. 177.
12. N.N. Pruzhan, 'Kartina L.S. Baksta "Drevnii Uzhas"' in *Soobshcheniia gos. russkogo muzeia*, issue X, Moscow, 1974.
13. Alexandre Benois, *Russkaia shkola zhivopisi*, St Petersburg, 1904, p. 94. However, Benois already admires Bakst's theatre designs, commenting favourably on his work for *The Fairy Doll*, 1903.
14. Benois, 'Khudozhestvennye Eresi', op. cit. p. 88.

The *World of Art* Magazine
pp. 26–31

1. Alexandre Benois, *Vozniknovenie 'Mira Iskusstva'*, Leningrad, 1928, p. 42.
2. Ibid p. 8.
3. Illustrations and other references to the most recent issues of the following Western magazines were regularly included in *World of Art*: *Die Kunst*, *The Magazine of Art*, *The Studio*. Perhaps surprisingly, *La Revue Blanche* was not represented.
4. Benois, *Vozniknovenie*, op. cit. pp. 23–5.

5. Paintings by Gauguin are reproduced in *Mir iskusstva*, vol. XII, nos 8–9, 1904, pp. 217–22; in the same volume, a reproduction of a work by Van Gogh appears on p. 250. Cézanne is mentioned by Benois in vol. V, 1901, p. 35 as one of the artists excluded from the French Pavilion at the World Fair. In his editorial, 'Poiski Krasoty', Diaghilev refers to the Impressionists as 'incomprehensible' and their work as 'wild smearing which disguises trickery and carelessness'. *Mir iskusstva*, vol. I, no. 1, 1899, pp. 37–49. Reproductions of works by Degas, however, occur in the first volume (no. I, pp. 200–2) and proliferate in vol. X, no. 12, 1903, pp. 248–54.
6. *Mir iskusstva*, vol. II, nos 13–24, 1899, pp. 61–8.
7. *Mir iskusstva*, vol. I, no. 1, 1899, p. 53.
8. Janet Kennedy, *The Mir iskusstva group and Russian Art 1898–1912*, New York and London, 1977, p. 113.
9. V.N. Petrov, *Mir iskusstva*, p. 352. In Kennedy, op. cit. p. 64.
10. Benois, *Vozniknovenie*, op. cit. p. 30. It was Repin who originally coined the phrase 'Art for art's sake', when propounding his anti-establishment manifesto. For a glimpse of the later rift between Repin and the World of Art group, see items of correspondence: 'Po adresu Mira iskusstva' in *Mir iskusstva*, vol. I, nos 3–4, 1899, p. 21; and 'I. Repinu' in *Mir iskusstva*, vol. III (literary section) nos 1–2, 1900, pp. 24–7.
11. 'Temnitsy iskusstva', *Mir iskusstva*, vol. III, nos 1–4, 1900, pp. 1–24, pp. 34–48, pp. 163–74.
12. 'Uchenicheskaia vystavka', *Mir iskusstva*, vol. II, nos 13–24, 1899, p. 21; and vol. XII, nos 8–9, 1904, pp. 149–54.
13. G.I. Chugunov, *Valentin Serov v Peterburge*, Leningrad, 1990, p. 101.

14. Sergei Makovsky, *Portrety Sovremennikov*, New York, 1955, pp. 191–220.
15. Charles Spencer, *Léon Bakst*, London, 1973, p. 17.
16. *Mir iskusstva*, vol. IV, nos 13–24, 1900, pp. 73–96, 97–128.
17. *Mir iskusstva*, vol. III, nos 1–2, 1900, pp. 73–84, 97–120.
18. *Mir iskusstva*, ibid, nos 3–6, 1900, pp. 59–63.
19. *Mir iskusstva*, vol. VII, no. 1, 1902, pp. 16, 62.
20. *Mir iskusstva*, vol. IX, no. 1, 1903, pp. 31, 49.
21. Each exhibition contained a section devoted to the applied arts. In 1903, members of the group attempted an exhibition of interior design, organised by Prince Shcherbatov (*Mir iskusstva*, vol. IX, 1903, p. 221 and Sergei Shcherbatov, *Khudozhniki v ushedshei Rossii*, New York, 1955, pp. 158–73).
22. Kennedy, op. cit. p. 115.
23. *Mir iskusstva*, vol. X, nos 10–11, 1903, pp. 1–24, 143–74, 188–90.
24. *Mir iskusstva*, vol. IV, nos 13–24, 1900, p. 101.

Diaghilev as Theatre- and Art-Historian
pp. 31–36

1. See 'Iskusstvo', *Mir iskusstva*, vol. II, nos 3–5, 1899, pp. 62–8, 68–89, in which Volkonsky writes on art and the nature of perception. He also planned a competition involving the design for a house, to be judged by World of Art artists featured in the magazine.
2. Alexandre Benois, *Memoirs* (trans. Moura Boudberg), vol. II, London, 1960–4, p. 182.
3. Arnold Haskell (in collaboration with Walter Nouvel), *Diaghileff. His Artistic and Private Life*, London, 1935, p. 146.
4. Sergei Diaghilev (ed.), *Ezhegodnik imperatorskikh teatrov*, 2 vols, 1898–9, and 1899–1900, St Petersburg, supplement 2, pp. 49–59.

5. Ibid supplements 1–3, pp. 119–120.
6. Ibid supplements 1–3, pp. 60–81.
7. Ibid vol. I, pp. 171–80.
8. A. Benois, *Memoirs*, op. cit. vol. II, pp. 194–202.
9. The incident, in which the ballerina was fined for wearing an incorrect costume, is described both by Kshessinska and Volkonsky. It is interesting to compare the two versions of the story. See Matil'da Kshesinskaia, *Vospominaniia*, Moscow, 1992, pp. 80–2 and Prince Sergei Wolkonsky, *My Reminiscences* (trans. A.E. Chamot), 2 vols, London, 1925, vol. II, pp. 98–113.
10. N.V. Naumenko, 'Diagilev – istorik russkogo portreta' in *Sergei Diagilev i khudozhestvennaia kul'tura XIX–XX vv. Materialy pervykh diagilevskikh chtenii 17–19 aprelia 1987*, Perm, 1989, pp. 110–21.
11. Diaghilev, *Russkaia zhivopis' v VIII veke. D.G. Levitskii*, St Petersburg, 1902, p. 2.
12. V.I. Gorlenko, 'D.G. Levitskii'/Russkii arkhiv – book 10, 1892, in N.V. Naumenko, op. cit. pp. 204–22.
13. *International Exhibition 1862*, Official Catalogue of the Fine Art Department, published by the Society of Arts, London, 1862, p. 227.
14. *Les Trésors d'art en Russie* (Russkie sokrovishcha), 7 vols, 1901–7, is the most important reference source for buildings and art collections of the period. The first volume was edited by Benois. The portrait of Dmitriev-Mamonov is reproduced there in no. 9, plate 71. The corresponding biography by S. Noakovsky can be found on p. 88.
15. Diaghilev, 'Portretist Shibanov' in *Mir iskusstva*, vol. XI, no. 3, 1904, pp. 125–36.

Diaghilev and the *Historical Exhibition of Russian Portraits*
pp. 36-37

1. Sergei Diaghilev, *Mir iskusstva*, vol. VII, 1902, part 3: Chronicle, pp. 32-4.
2. Ibid.
3. Alexandre Benois, *Reminiscences of the Russian Ballet*, London, 1941, p. 233.
4. N.V. Naumenko, 'Diagilev – istorik russkogo portreta' in *Sergei Diagilev i khudozhestvennaia kul'tura IX-XX vv. Materialy pervyh diagilevskikh chtenii 17-19 aprelia 1987*, Perm, 1989, p. 114.
5. Russian Museum Archive (Dobuzhinsky), f 115/392 21.XII.1904 and III.1905.
6. Benois, *Reminiscences*, op. cit. p. 237.
7. Ibid p. 233.
8. M.V. Dobujinsky, *Vospominaniia*, Moscow, 1987, p. 224.
9. V.V. Stasov, 'Itogi nashei portretnoi vystavki' in *Izbrannye sochineniia*, ed. P.T. Shchipunov, 3 vols, Moscow, 1952, vol. III, pp. 304-14. The first champion of Ilya Repin, Stasov favoured tendentious art.
10. Ibid.
11. Ibid.

Diaghilev and the 1906 *Exhibition of Russian Art*
pp. 38-40

1. I.S. Zilberstein and V.A. Samkov, *Sergei Diagilev i russkoe iskusstvo. Stat'i, otkrytye pis'ma, interv'iu. Perepiska. Sovremenniki o Diagileve*, 2 vols, Moscow, 1982, vol. I, p. 56.
2. F.I. Buslaev, 'Kartiny russkoi shkoly zhivopisi, nakhodivshiesia na Londonskoi vsemirnoi vystavke, *Sovremennaia letopis*', 1863, in *Sergei Diagilev i khudozhestvennaia kul'tura XIX-XX vv. Materialy pervykh diagilevskikh chtenii, 17-19 April 1987*, Perm, 1989, p. 120.

3. TsGALI f 2350 op 1 ed khr 173, in A.V. Tolstoi, 'O russkoi vystavke 1906 goda v Parizhe', *Sovetskoe iskussvoznanie*, 1981, pp. 279-90.
4. See *Zolotoe runo*, vol. I, no. 6, p. 97. (In the twentieth century, the Russian Orthodox calendar is thirteen days behind the Western one.)
5. Presumably the result of losses in the Russo-Japanese war of 1904. This exhibition was a conscious attempt, following her humiliating defeat in that war, to regain respect for Russia in the West.
6. A.V. Tolstoi, 'O russkoi vystavke 1906 goda v Parizhe', *Sovetskoe iskussvoznanie*, 1981, pp. 279-90. Baron V.V. von Meck was a dress designer and an associate of Prince Sergei Scherbatov's. Recent research in Moscow has shown that he helped to fund Diaghilev's enterprises 1898-1906.
7. Ibid.
8. *Zolotoe runo*, vol. II, nos 11-12, 1906-7, p. 130.
9. *Exposition de l'Art Russe*, catalogue, Salon d'Automne, Paris, 1906. Foreword by Diaghilev, p. 7.
10. Ibid.
11. Ibid.
12. Letter to Ilya Repin in *Perepiska so Stasovym*, vol. III, pp. 144-5. Also quoted by Valerii Dudakov in 'Diagilevskaia vystavka v Parizhe i russkoe iskusstvo "Serebriannogo veka"', *Tvorchestvo*, no. 1, 1992, pp. 57-9.
13. Repin, letter from Paris, in G.Yu. Sternin, *Khudozhestvennaia zhizn' Rossii na rubezhe XIX-XX vv*, Moscow, 1970, p. 128.
14. Russian Museum Archive, f 137, ed khr 64, p. 163.
15. Ibid pp. 163-4.
16. Tolstoi, op. cit.
17. Valerii Dudakov, 'Diagilevskaia vystavka', op. cit.
18. Zilberstein and Samkov, op. cit. vol. I, p. 405.

Friends and Enemies
pp. 40-46

1. A. Laskin, *Neznakomye Diagilevy, ili konets tsitaty*, St Petersburg, 1994, p. 22.
2. Bronislava Nijinska, *Early Memoirs*, Durham and London, p. 255.
3. E.P. Subbotin, 'Sergei Diagilev – Gimnazist' in *Sergei Diagilev i Khudozhestvennaia kul'tura XIX-XX vv. Materialy pervykh diagilevskikh chtenii, 17-19 aprelia 1987*, Perm, 1989, p. 12.
4. Alexandre Benois, *Reminiscences of the Russian Ballet*, London, 1941, p. 233.
5. Igor Stravinsky, *An Autobiography*, London, 1975, p. 28.
6. Tamara Karsavina, *Theatre Street*, London, 1988, p. 211.
7. Alexandre Benois, *Vozniknovenie 'Mira Iskusstva'*, Leningrad, 1928, p. 36.
8. Sergei Shcherbatov, *Khudozhniki v ushedshei Rossii*, New York, 1955, p. 137.
9. I.S. Zilberstein and V.A. Samkov, *Sergei Diagilev i russkoe iskusstvo. Stat'i, otkrytye pis'ma, interv'iu. Perepiska. Sovremenniki o Diagileve*, 1982, vol. II, p. 7.
10. A. Laskin, op. cit. p. 110.
11. Ibid p. 108.
12. Ibid p. 117.
13. V.V. Stasov, 'Nashi nyneshnie dekadenty' in *Izbrannye sochineniia*, ed. P.T. Shchipunov, 3 vols, Moscow, 1952, vol. III, pp. 315-21.
14. Sergei Makovsky, *Portrety sovremennikov*, New York, 1955, pp. 191-220.
15. Alexandre Benois, *Memoirs* (trans. Moura Boudberg), 2 vols, London, 1960-4, vol. II, pp. 185-8.
16. Letters from Somov to Diaghilev, TsGALI, Moscow, f 869, op. 1, ed. 30.

17. Somov, however, did appreciate performances of the Ballets Russes, which he attended in Paris from 1923. Shortly after Diaghilev died, he wrote to his sister of his shock. See letter to A.A. Mikhailova, 26 August 1929, in *Konstantin Andreevich Somov. Mir khudozhnika. Pis'ma. Dnevniki. Suzhdeniia sovremennikov*, ed. Yu. N. Podkopaeva and A.N. Sveshnikova, Moscow, 1979, p. 357.
18. Benois, *Memoirs*, op. cit. vol. II, p. 187.
19. Benois, *Memoirs*, op. cit. vol. I, p. 274.
20. Benois, *Memoirs*, op. cit. vol. II, p. 188.
21. Serge Lifar, *Serge Diaghilev. His Life. His Work. His Legend. An Intimate Biography*, London, 1940, p. 32.
22. Laskin, op. cit. p. 125.
23. Richard Buckle claims that Prince Volkonsky was homosexual. See Richard Buckle, *Diaghilev*, London, 1979, p. 48.
24. Benois, *Reminiscences*, op. cit. p. 205. Although the Russian court appears to have fostered unusually lax attitudes to heterosexual morality, homosexuality was not condoned.
25. Laskin, op. cit. pp. 126-7.
26. Arnold Haskell (in collaboration with Walter Nouvel), *Diaghileff. His Artistic and Private Life*, London, 1935, p. 239.
27. Bronislava Nijinska, op. cit. p. 407.
28. *Sergei Diaghilev*, sale catalogue for the collection of Max Reinhardt, Sothebys, July 1969, pp. 252-3.
29. Pavel Diaghilev was declared bankrupt on 9 October 1890. It was announced in the financial publication *Birzhevye vedomosti*. See Laskin, op. cit. p. 49.

30. See letter to Apollinari Vasnetsov and others, 20 May 1897, Tretyakov Gallery Archive, f 11/561, ed. khr. 1, p. 2. (Diaghilev had come into his mother's inheritance in 1893 when he reached the age of twenty-one.)
31. The ensuing scandal was described by Somov in a letter to his father in 1899. See *Konstantin Andreevich Somov*, op. cit. pp. 66-7.
32. See L.S. Zhuravleva, '"Dalos' mne eto ne bez bor'by"' *Prometei* no. 14, 1987, pp. 70-3. Tenisheva stipulated that Nikolai Roerich be appointed editor of the magazine.
33. G.I. Chugunov, *Valentin Serov v Peterburge*, Leningrad, 1990, pp. 76-7.
34. Astruc, Letter to Emile Enoch, 14.12.1909, in 'Diaghilev Ballets Russes. Dossier comprenant 125 documents provenant des Archives de Gabriel Astruc 1909-14', Archive de l'Opéra, Bibliothèque Nationale, Paris.
35. Lynn Garafola, *Diaghilev's Ballets Russes*, Oxford, 1989, pp. 373-4.
36. Richard Buckle, *Diaghilev*, op. cit. pp. 37-8.
37. Sergei Makovsky, op. cit.
38. See Charles Spencer, *The World of Serge Diaghilev*, London, 1974, p. 67.
39. *The Journals of Jean Cocteau*, London, 1957, p. 52.
40. See Catherine Lampert, *Rodin. Sculpture and Drawings*, London, 1986, p. 234.
41. Stravinsky, *An Autobiography*, op. cit. p. 79.
42. S. Shcherbatov, *Khudozhniki v ushedshei Rossii*, op. cit. pp. 158-73. The exhibition is illustrated in *Mir iskusstva*, vol. IX, nos 5-6, 1903, pp. 221-52.
43. Tretyakov Gallery Archive, Letters, May 1897, op. cit.

44. See V.V. Stasov, 'Vystavki 1897-8. Russkikh i Finliandskikh khudozhnikov', in *Izbrannye sochineniia*, op. cit. pp. 215-28.
45. *Pravila vystavki zhurnala Mira iskusstva*, St Petersburg, 24 February 1900 and 17 February 1901.
46. Archive of the Lunacharsky Theatre Library, St Petersburg, dance contracts. Arkhiv L.D. Krupitskogo, r 11/17.
47. Richard Buckle (ed.), *Dancing for Diaghilev. The Memoirs of Lydia Sokolova*, London, 1960, p. 116. At times, Diaghilev could not pay his artists. The dancers were generally stalwart about this, especially as, in principle, he paid top rates. Nijinsky claims in his memoirs that Diaghilev had always been in debt to him and still owed him a substantial sum.
48. See 'Lettre à Serge Diaghilev. A l'Homme' in Nijinsky, *Cahiers* (unexpurgated version), Paris, 1995, pp. 296-300.
49. Ibid pp. 142-3.
50. Ibid p. 142.
51. Ibid p. 141.
52. Romola Nijinsky, *Nijinsky* and *The Last Years of Nijinsky*, London, 1980, p. 257.
53. Nijinsky, *Cahiers*, op. cit. p. 211.
54. Romola Nijinsky, op. cit. p. 249.
55. S.L. Grigoriev, *Balet Diagileva 1909-1929*, Moscow, 1993, p. 84.
56. Stravinsky, *An Autobiography*, op. cit. p. 40. Stravinsky later qualified this statement, admitting 'of course he was musical'.
57. Bronislava Nijinska, op. cit. pp. 121-2. Nijinska admits that Nijinsky did not conform to conventional discipline, and played by ear.
58. *The Journals of Jean Cocteau*, op. cit.
59. Arnold Haskell, op. cit. p. 273.

Diaghilev as Musician and Concert Organiser

Diaghilev developed a passion for music from an early age, and it was a passion which was to remain with him for the rest of his life. He came from an intensely musical family. Both his father (who was reputed to know Glinka's *Ruslan and Lyudmila* by heart) and his step-mother possessed fine singing voices, while his uncle Ivan, proficient on both the cello and piano, was the driving force behind a small amateur orchestra which was formed as the natural outcome of the family's musical activities in Perm, the provincial city where Diaghilev spent the latter part of his childhood. Music-making (which some-times extended to domestic performances of whole operas) was so natural a part of all their daily lives, in fact, that Sergei and his brothers, even as small children, would apparently quite unconsciously whistle tunes from Beethoven symphonies or Schumann quintets as they walked about.[1]

It was Diaghilev's stepmother, the cultivated and debonair Elena Panaeva, born in 1851, whose musical influence was the most formative on the young boy. Her sister, Alexandra Panaeva-Kartseva, was an opera singer of some renown, who had studied with Pauline Viardot and performed at La Scala, and such was their father's de-votion to Italian opera, meanwhile, that he set up his own theatre for its production in 1888, as a counter measure against the aggressive promotion of Russian music in the Imperial Theatres instigated by Alexander III.[2] The tastes of Diaghilev's aunt and stepmother were

Pyotr Ilyich Tchaikovsky *c.*1890
Central State Archive of Cinema and Photo Documents,
St Petersburg

more eclectic. While *Rigoletto* and other masterpieces from the Italian repertoire may have been family favourites, the sisters also shared a deep love of Russian music, which in the 1870s was highly unfashion-able among the concert-going public, and the preserve of a small minority. They may perhaps have been unaware of the genius of Mussorgsky, whom Diaghilev encountered as a child when the com-poser came to accompany his aunt on the piano, and who only began to achieve recognition after his death in 1881; but Tchaikovsky, to whom Alexandra was distantly related by marriage, was revered. The composer himself held her performances of his songs in high regard, and Diaghilev was always fiercely proud of having once been taken as a child to meet 'Uncle Peter' at his estate in Klin, outside Moscow.[3] When his interest in music deepened during his adolescence, it was Tchaikovsky who became his first love. Precisely because of the powerful emotional impact Tchaikovsky's music made on him, and the charges of vulgarity levelled against it by the sophisticated élite in whose company he moved in Paris, Diaghilev subsequently tried to dismiss his infatuation with it as a youthful enthusiasm, but, as with Wagner, who became his other great musical idol, he was penitent about once again acknowledging its great hold over him at the end of his life.[4]

Music was a constant backdrop during Diaghilev's early child-hood years in St Petersburg, and continued to be so after his family moved to Perm, when he was ten years old. Their home quickly became the centre of cultural life in the town, and throughout the winter season, the scene of many lively impromptu musical performances. Diaghilev was allowed to stay up late when local musicians came over to rehearse for the charity concerts the family organised each winter, and also whenever his uncle Ivan sat down at the family Bechstein to play duets with the local German teacher, who gave him his first piano lessons.[5] Diaghilev was never an outstanding pianist, but certainly a highly competent one, to judge from the fact that he was able to per-form the first movement of the Schumann piano concerto while still in his teens, and it was due to his superior pianistic skills that he was able to persuade the Comtesse de Greffulhe, President of the Société des Concerts Français, to support his endeavours in organising a Season of Russian music in Paris in 1907.[6]

By the time Diaghilev moved back to St Petersburg in the autumn of 1890 in order to go to university, music had become his chief interest, and although officially enrolled as a student of Law, it was in the opera house and the concert hall that he continued

Maryinsky Theatre, St Petersburg with the monument to Mikhail Glinka *c.*1910–15
Central State Archive of Cinema and Photo Documents, St Petersburg

his real education.[7] The new friends he made through his cousin Dmitry Filosofov took seriously his intentions of pursuing a career as a musician, but found his tastes initially rather unsophisticated. Alexandre Benois, for example, was already a committed Wagnerian by this time, having attended the first performances of the *Ring* staged in St Petersburg the previous year by a German touring company, and he was also a devoted follower of Tchaikovsky, who was at last beginning to come into vogue with the Russian public.[8] Diaghilev's veneration of Glinka and Borodin, meanwhile, combined with a rather indiscriminate enthusiasm for Italian opera (the heyday of which was now passing), struck him as being rather provincial, and even *mauvais ton*,[9] although Diaghilev's high esteem of Mussorgsky, of whose works he had a sound knowledge long before they were appreciated by a wider public, already speaks eloquently for the quality of his aesthetic judgement.

Whatever naïveté marked the eighteen-year-old Diaghilev's musical inclinations when he first arrived in St Petersburg soon disappeared. That summer he travelled for the first time to Europe, where he was swept away by hearing for the first time a Wagner opera performed in Vienna ('power, passion, and temperament' was what he most admired in music, according to Walter Nouvel),[10] and he became a regular habitué of the Maryinsky Theatre, Russia's most important opera house, immediately upon his return. Despite the opulence and grandeur of its productions, the Maryinsky was a conservative institution, artistically speaking, due to the fact that it was run by government bureaucrats, as were all the Imperial Theatres. Prejudice meant that there was little opportunity for Diaghilev to hear much Wagner there until the turn of the century, for example, apart from old warhorse productions of *Tannhäuser* and *Lohengrin*,[11] but at the end of 1899, three years after his first trip to Bayreuth, he was finally able to attend a performance of the first Russian production of *Tristan und Isolde* which, together with *Die Meistersinger*, would always remain his favourite operatic work.[12] Despite a general lack of approbation among the opera-going public, he correctly greeted its appearance in the Maryinsky repertoire in the pages of his journal *World of Art* as an event of the first magnitude (this was his first piece of music journalism),[13] and he went on to follow the production of the *Ring* which followed with close, but not uncritical, attention. The 1890s were a time of transition for the Maryinsky, as for all other musical institutions, and if Diaghilev was unable to indulge his new-found passion for Wagner to any great degree at this time (although this situation soon changed), he was at least able to acquaint himself with works by Russian composers. Not only were there now several composers with solid reputations, whose operas were no longer discriminated against in favour of the Italian repertoire, but the conservatoires of St Petersburg and Moscow (Russia's first institutions of professional musical training, both founded in the 1860s) were also now producing talented composers who were able to compete on an equal footing with their French and Italian counterparts, and their music was doing much to enrich Russian musical life. After years of struggle, Russian music was finally coming of age, and Diaghilev was able to attend two important premières during his first winter in St Petersburg alone: the first performance of Borodin's *Prince Igor*, completed after the composer's death by Rimsky-Korsakov and Glazunov, and Tchaikovsky's *Queen of Spades*, which followed soon afterwards.[14] It was at this point that Diaghilev's passion for Tchaikovsky began in earnest.[15] As well as the operas and ballets, Diaghilev particularly loved Tchaikovsky's symphonies, and was present at the first performance of the *Pathétique* (no. 6), conducted by the composer shortly before his death in 1893. Such was Diaghilev's depth of feeling for Tchaikovsky that he went immediately to pay his last respects upon hearing he had died, and was the first to lay a wreath at the composer's feet.[16]

During his student years, Diaghilev continued the family's musical traditions with his new friends, meeting most frequently with Walter Nouvel to sing through operas and play through scores (still an indispensable way of discovering and enjoying music in the pre-recording age)[17] and organising private chamber concerts. And to further his career as a professional musician, Diaghilev now began to take singing lessons with Antonio Cotogni, a baritone who sang with the Italian opera. He also embarked on a course in music theory with Nikolai Sokolov at the St Petersburg Conservatoire. With all the characteristic self-confidence, ambition and fearlessness that had given him the courage to pay calls on Tolstoy, Zola and Verdi, Diaghilev soon decided it was time to take his musical compositions to show Rimsky-Korsakov.[18] The latter's frank response was discouraging, but Diaghilev's wounded vanity did not prevent him from later boasting that he had once taken composition lessons with Rimsky-Korsakov. The failure of a concert to which he invited his friends, and at which he was prominent not only as a soloist, but also as a composer, spelled the final end to his career as a practising musician. The programme included a duet he had written for the 'Fountain Scene' in Pushkin's *Boris Godunov*, but the resulting music, performed by him and his aunt, Alexandra Panaeva-Kartseva, displayed an unholy mixture of Italianate melody and the inevitable influence of Mussorgsky, and was not well received.[19] Diaghilev made one last valiant attempt to forge a career in music by becoming a member of the venerable Russian Music Society, in the hope of injecting some life into its frequently stale concert programmes. The Society had been organising the capital's most important orchestral concerts since 1859, and was in dire need of reform by the end of the century, but here too Diaghilev was unsuccessful.[20] He decided to turn his energies instead to art.

Although professionally Diaghilev's attention was now taken up with the organisation of exhibitions and the production of the *World of Art* magazine, his interest in music certainly did not wane, nor did it cease to figure in his activities. Apart from the highly informed reviews of the Maryinsky Theatre's Wagner productions that he himself contributed to *World of Art*, Wagner and other musical subjects were the focus of further articles published in the magazine,[21] and the consummate musical knowledge he had by this time acquired can have been no hindrance during his tenure at the Imperial Theatres, although his autocratic style certainly was.[22]

Music once more played an integral part in Diaghilev's activities in 1907, when his plans to acquaint Western Europe with Russian culture became more ambitious. If Russian composers had fought a hard battle for recognition in their own country, then overcoming the fierce prejudices against their music in Europe presented an even greater challenge. Very little Russian music was performed in Paris and the other major capitals (certainly no operas, which represented its finest achievements), and, although Tchaikovsky had become world famous by the time of his death, Russian composers were more often than not treated with condescension.[23] After organising a successful exhibition of Russian art in Paris in 1906, Diaghilev decided the time had come to change the situation, rightly believing that Russia now had a unique musical tradition of its own which deserved to be better known and respected. His timing was impeccable, for Russian music was now ready to be exported. The success of the five 'historic concerts' which took place at the Paris Opéra in May 1907 was not only due to Diaghilev's supreme entrepreneurial genius and indefatigable energy, but also to the authority of his aesthetic judgement in knowing exactly which pieces of music should be performed, based on a profound knowledge of the repertoire, and a sure vision of what was needed to lend a sense of occasion to the whole enterprise.

Diaghilev's organisation of the concerts was nothing short of brilliant. To ensure that they made the greatest possible impact, he needed to count on securing the very best performers and some high-level support. In Paris, he won over the influential Comtesse de Greffulhe, simply by sitting down at the piano and playing her excerpts from the pieces he knew and loved. In Russia he obtained the patronage of wealthy businessmen by promising them an entrée to the Imperial Court, and that of the government by agreeing to include in the programme of one of the concerts the Second Symphony of Alexander Taneev, who was head of the Tsar's private chancery, and an amateur composer.[24] This was his one compromise. To all his sponsors Diaghilev offered not merely five concerts of wonderful music, with performances by Russia's leading singers, including Chaliapin, Litvine, Cherkasskaya and Smirnov, but an almost theatrical spectacle, which would include the performance of whole acts from operas and soloists and chorus, six different conductors (three of whom would also be the composers of the music they were conducting), and a carefully produced and handsomely illustrated programme featuring articles, autographs, set designs, pictures of the artists in their roles, and specially commissioned portraits of the composers by artists such as Bakst and Serov. It was a huge undertaking, and Diaghilev was under no illusion as to the problems he faced in co-ordinating all the various sponsors, performers, administrators and composers. 'Don't forget that I have to convince Grand Duke Vladimir that our enterprise will be useful from a national point of view, the Minister of Finance that it will be profitable on the economic side, and even the Director of Theatres that it will bring benefit to the Imperial stage! And there are so many others! And it's so difficult!' he wrote in one of the many letters he sent to Rimsky-Korsakov at the beginning of 1907, in which he cajoled the composer to come to Paris to conduct his music.[25] Nothing on this scale had ever been tackled, and, as the critic Alexander Ossovsky commented in an article in March 1907: 'One has of course to be filled with a genuine love of one's national culture in order to take on a project of such difficulty.'[26]

In the end Rimsky-Korsakov agreed to make the journey, and the first of the five concerts featured extracts from his opera *Christmas Eve*, as well as Tchaikovsky's Second Symphony, excerpts from Glinka's *Ruslan and Lyudmila*, conducted by the famed Arthur Nikisch, and Borodin's *Prince Igor*. But the night belonged to Fyodor Chaliapin, who was making his European début. He created a sensation, and the applause for him was so prolonged that Nikisch, due to conduct the next item in the programme, walked out in impatience.[27] The first concert was attended by a glittering audience of Russian and French nobility, and pronounced an outstanding success, as were the remaining concerts, despite the presence of a few dissenting voices who seem to have had an axe to grind.[28] The other great discovery for the Parisian audiences was Mussorgsky's *Boris Godunov*, excerpts from which were performed at the second concert. Claude Debussy was among those on whom this opera made a very deep impression.[29]

Rimsky-Korsakov and Borodin were also popular.

In putting together balanced programmes for the five concerts, which were intended to be a representative survey of Russian music from Glinka to Scriabin, Diaghilev demonstrated both his expertise and his exquisite taste. A major goal was to introduce the music produced by the five nationalist composers of the Balakirev circle (although very little by Cui, the weakest of the group, much to the latter's indignation),[30] since it was so little known, and Diaghilev chose particularly to emphasise the masterpieces that Rimsky-Korsakov, Borodin and Mussorgsky had contributed to the operatic repertoire. He also introduced Russia's newest talents, however, among them Scriabin, Rachmaninov and Glazunov, who all came to Paris to take part. Tchaikovsky was the one composer who already had a reputation outside Russia, and his relative familiarity, combined with the fact that the French tended to criticise his music as too sentimental, was what probably led Diaghilev to represent him to a lesser degree, and with more unusual works.

Now that Russian music has become such a staple of concert and opera repertoires all over the world, it is difficult to imagine a time when it was still completely unknown outside its native country, but as Serge Lifar has pointed out, the fact that his concert programmes do not now seem anything out of the ordinary is entirely Diaghilev's great achievement.[31] The success of the 1907 concerts paved the way for the next stage of his plans, which was to present complete productions of Russian operas, none of which had ever been performed in Paris or any of the other great capitals. If Peter the Great had opened for Russia a window onto Europe at the beginning of the eighteenth century, Diaghilev was now opening for Europe a window onto Russia at the beginning of the twentieth, and it was a cultural venture of inestimable significance.

1. Serge Lifar, *Diagilev i Diagilevym*, Paris, 1939, pp. 26, 30.
2. Arnold Haskell, in collaboration with Walter Nouvel, *Diaghileff: His Artistic and Private Life*, New York, 1935, p. 12.
3. Lifar, op. cit. p. 27.
4. Ibid pp. 27-8.
5. Ibid p. 30.
6. Richard Buckle, *Diaghilev*, London, 1979, p. 95.
7. Buckle, op. cit. p. 16.
8. I.S. Zilberstein and V.A. Samkov, eds, *Sergei Diagilev i russkoe iskusstvo*, 2 vols, Moscow, 1982, vol. II, p. 221.

9. Buckle, op. cit. pp. 16, 24.
10. Haskell, op. cit. p. 28.
11. R. Bartlett, *Wagner and Russia*, Cambridge, 1995, pp. 59-65.
12. Lifar, op. cit. p. 47.
13. See Lifar, op. cit. p. 48.
14. Buckle, op. cit. p. 20.
15. Haskell, op. cit. p. 28.
16. Buckle, op. cit. p. 23.
17. Haskell, op. cit. p. 28.
18. Lifar, op. cit. p. 55.
19. Buckle, op. cit. p. 27.
20. Lifar, op. cit. p. 56.
21. See Lifar, op. cit. pp. 89, 105, 116-17.
22. See Buckle, op. cit. p. 61.
23. See Zilberstein and Samkov, op. cit. vol. I, p. 408.

24. Zilberstein and Samkov, op. cit. vol. I, p. 410.
25. Zilberstein and Samkov, op. cit. vol. II, p. 100.
26. Zilberstein and Samkov, op. cit. vol. I, p. 411.
27. Buckle, op. cit. pp. 97, 99.
28. See Zilberstein and Samkov, op. cit. vol. I, p. 411.
29. François Lesure and Roger Nicholas, ed., *Debussy Letters*, London, 1987, p. 179.
30. Zilberstein and Samkov, op. cit. vol. II, p. 414.
31. See Lifar, op. cit. p. 163.

Diaghilev and the Artists of the Saisons Russes

'Many are the names which Diaghilev wrote, with his own hand, in the book of fame,' the ballerina Tamara Karsavina writes with gratitude.[1]

Diaghilev's most valuable quality was his ability to act as a creative 'prompt' to an artist, musician, choreographer, singer or dancer. He was not a creator, but he was indispensable to those who were. He could give advice which revealed the essence of a problem, the potential of a created image. Pierre Vorms, author of the book on the artists of the Diaghilev ballets, wrote that Diaghilev 'gave flesh and blood to the ideas of others, knew how to draw out the best of which an artist was capable'.[2] Everyone who came into contact with him through their work experienced it. Stravinsky said that much of his music was inspired by Diaghilev. Observing the production in progress, he could alter forms, co-ordinate the various elements in order to make of the ballet an integral whole.[3] Karsavina writes that a few words, thrown off in passing by Diaghilev, seemed 'to illuminate a clear image or a new concept in the darkness like a ray of light', that 'with a simple remark he could draw aside the curtain before you and fire your imagination'.[4] As an organiser, however, he was despotic and ruthless. In pursuit of his aims all means were good. In this bold and irrepressible spirit the features of a Don Quixote and a patron of an earlier age coexisted happily with those of an American businessman, Benois writes.[5]

Diaghilev's incontrovertible authority over his artists was based on and maintained by their awed trust in him, their faith in his artistic perception and their conviction that he could find a way out of any difficult situation. Where was Diaghilev to seek artists for his enterprise if not among those connected with Benois and the World of Art group? Their paintings were composed as though framed by a proscenium arch, their favourite characters were the 'masks' of the *commedia dell'arte*.

While he was still in Russia, Diaghilev made an attempt to attract his World of Art associates into the theatre. During the short period (1899–1901) in which Prince Volkonsky was Director of the Imperial Theatres, Diaghilev secured the commission for himself and a group of artists to stage the ballet *Sylvia*. Benois [cat. 54], Bakst, Lanceray, Korovine and Serov collaborated to produce sketches for the settings and costumes. But the work, begun so auspiciously and with such enthusiasm, was suddenly terminated. Diaghilev, becoming entangled in the intrigues of the court department and refusing to submit to their rigorous demands, behaved too arrogantly and was dismissed. Soon afterwards, as the result of a dispute with the prima-

Mathilde Kshessinska, early 1900s
State Museum of Theatre and Music,
St Petersburg

ballerina Kshessinska, the all-powerful favourite of the Imperial family, Volkonsky himself was obliged to retire. He was replaced by Vladimir Teliakovsky, previously the director of the Moscow theatres. The latter already knew and appreciated the abilities of Konstantin Korovine and Alexander Golovine, having invited them to work at the Bolshoi Theatre, and was inclined to sympathise with the idea of a renewal in theatrical thinking. It was thanks to him that the first works of Benois and Bakst were seen on the stages of the Hermitage and Maryinsky Theatres. Benois was not satisfied with these early attempts – the settings for *Love's Revenge* and *Twilight of the Gods*. Oddly enough, it was Diaghilev who reviewed the Wagner opera; Benois could only agree with the severe criticism of the man who had been, so recently, his obedient pupil. As for Bakst, the series of costume sketches for the pantomime *The Heart of a Marquise* and the ballet *The Fairy Doll* had already shown him to be an exceptional master of his art, who had broken with the customary stereotypes. His contribution to the production of Euripides' *Hippolytus* and Sophocles' *Oedipus in Colonus* at the Alexandrinsky Theatre, which foreshadowed,

Alexandre Benois:
Le Pavillon d'Armide: **Set design for Scene 2** 1907
Cat.107D

Alexandre Benois:
Le Pavillon d'Armide: **Backcloth design** 1907
Cat.107A

in many respects, his use of images in the cycle of ballets on classical themes staged for the *Saisons russes*, soon gave further proof of his talent.

Benois and his friends had been inveterate theatre-goers since their childhood. Their views on theatre had been formed in the audience. Fervent admirers of Stanislavsky, they burned with the desire to see the art of living truth influencing the musical stage, where their own interests lay. Years later Diaghilev would say that the principles of the Moscow Arts Theatre were reflected in the aspirations of the *Saisons russes*. The friends wholeheartedly shared the Russian audiences' enthusiasm for the star of Italian ballet, Virginia Zucchi, who had toured in Russia; they were enraptured not only by her virtuosity but by the natural simplicity of her mime and gesture. As lovers of the ballet, they had been forced to accept the low standard of its music, and the score of Delibes's *Coppélia* was greeted with delight. As Benois said, he 'heard, rather than saw' the performance. They loved *Giselle* with its lyrical music by Adam and its 'unhappy ending', a rarity in the ballets of that time.

But it was the appearance of Tchaikovsky's ballet *The Sleeping Beauty* which Benois called the 'turning point' in the history of ballet.

He insisted that if *Sleeping Beauty* 'had not aroused the group of young people to a passionate enthusiasm which became a kind of madness',[6] the *Saisons russes* would never have materialised. The music was not ballet-music in the conventional sense. It possessed the dramatic tension, the profundity characteristic of a symphony. That same year, 1890, saw the first performance of *The Queen of Spades*. Again, the music of Tchaikovsky, combined with the Pushkin theme and set in St Petersburg during the age of Catherine, the beloved eighteenth century, produced a powerful impression.

Fired with the desire to create a ballet similar to *The Sleeping Beauty*, Benois wrote a libretto to the music of Tcherepnine. Its subject, largely based on a short story by Théophile Gautier, revived images of theatre at the court of the French monarchs. But *Le Pavillon d'Armide* was not performed until 1907, when it was premièred at the Maryinsky Theatre. Owing to the events of 1905 and Benois's absence abroad, the score had lain untouched until then.

It was while he was working on the production of *Le Pavillon d'Armide* that Benois first met Fokine, and gained an ally in the struggle for the renewal of the art of ballet. World of Art and the Imperial Theatres finally parted company over this production.

The Sleeping Beauty in performance, 1890
State Museum of Theatre and Music, St Petersburg

Ivan Bilibin:
Boris Godunov: Costume design for Boyar's Wife 1908
Cat.93

Alexandre Golovine:
Portrait of Chaliapin as Boris Godunov 1908
State Russian Museum, St Petersburg

The break, when it came, was immediate and long-lasting; conflict with the administration during work on the ballet was so extreme that co-operation had become impossible.

The situation was summed up by Diaghilev: 'This must be shown to Europe!' All efforts were now directed towards the organisation of the foreign Seasons.

At Benois's apartment, or more frequently in Diaghilev's modest little flat, the 'staff' of the enterprise gathered around the table with its simmering samovar. They discussed plans and budgets, composed scenarios, put forward bold, innovative ideas, conducted endless stormy debates. 'Each one of them had his own ideas,' Fokine recalled. When he was working out the movements for a new ballet with the artists in the rehearsal hall, 'the entire World of Art' stood at his shoulder.[7]

Ballet, in the West, was in decline; it had lost its importance as a serious genre. However unlikely it now seems, the organisers doubted that the ballet would succeed, and resorted to 'well-tried weapons'. Diaghilev's enterprise, soon to be known as the Ballets Russes, took opera as its starting point.

On 6 May 1908, at the Paris Opéra, Mussorgsky's *Boris Godunov*, with Chaliapin in the main role, was performed in all its

operatic glory to the Paris audience. The settings were the work of Golovine [cat. 95 A–B], with the exception of the Polish act designed by Benois [cat. 92]. In order to show Paris the genuine Russia of the sixteenth and seventeenth centuries, Diaghilev and Benois, with the help of the artists Bilibin [see cat. 93] and Stelletsky, had scoured the villages and St Petersburg's markets and antique shops for ancient artefacts, old-fashioned utensils, shawls that had lain in the trunk for centuries, *sarafans* and *kokoshniks*, the traditional headdress of the Russian peasant woman. Chaliapin's performance, full of tragic power, his extraordinary voice, a chorus which could not only sing but also act, scored a triumphant success. 'Alps crossed. Paris taken,' Chaliapin joked, in a telegraph message to a St Petersburg friend.[8] Benois and Diaghilev experienced 'a total sense of victory'. It inspired them in their preparation for the following season; they had already decided to stake their reputations on the ballets which were to dominate the programme.

The intrigues of the Russian authorities prevented Diaghilev from making the Paris Opéra his base. This season was to open at the Châtelet Theatre, a bleak, barn-like building with a badly equipped stage. By the beginning of the tour, however, all that was changed. K.F. Valtz, 'wizard and magician', the technical director of the Bolshoi

Alexandre Golovine:
Boris Godunov: **Set design** 1908
Cat. 95B

Theatre, specially invited by Diaghilev, had transformed it beyond recognition. Working with feverish haste, overcoming the obstacles which arose daily, he seemed to Diaghilev ubiquitous. His energy forced the complex and cumbersome machinery of the theatre into action and overcame the opposition of its staff, who watched the proceedings with hostile suspicion.

Hundreds of articles and books have been written about the triumphs of the first Ballets Russes Seasons. Those who took part in them or were present at them recount how every evening something like a miracle occurred; audience and performers breathed as one. Leading figures in France were eloquent in their praise of the music, the dancers and the artists. Romain Rolland, Rodin, Debussy, Ravel, Mirbeau, Prévost, Anatole France, Maeterlinck and many others called the Russian tour 'the discovery of an unknown world', a new era in the art of musical theatre and ballet.

Teliakovsky, stunned by the success of the enterprise, hastened to announce, in some confusion, that Diaghilev, in showing Paris these performances from the Imperial stage, was fully supported in his work by the administration. But it had not been possible to see in St Petersburg what Paris saw. The productions were given new settings, new costumes, the choreography was reinterpreted, the music changed. There were no officials in Diaghilev's 'artistic administration'. Its members, totally dedicated to art, behind whom, as Benois said, stood 'the whole of Russian culture', chose the brightest and best from the enormous reservoir of talent in Russia, among them, of course, artists from the Imperial stage. Performers, artists, ballet-masters were enabled to give substance to their creative ideas. Thus, Fokine, as choreographer for the *Saisons russes*, fulfilled his dream of purging classical ballet of its tendency towards 'acrobatics', its 'demonstration of muscular strength', of the primitive, conventional gesticulation, reminiscent of a sign language for the deaf. In his view the gesture and body-movement of the dancer should express emotion, one should feel the 'movement of the soul', the music should cease to be a mere accompaniment to the dance.

The settings for the operas chosen from the Imperial Theatres remained unchanged; they were the work of Korovine and Golovine, who had blazed the trail for the members of the World of Art in their search for integrity of form within a production. Benois and Diaghilev admired Korovine's impressionistic style, which merged organically with the music. He himself liked to call his colours 'the chords of form'. The whole gamut of colour in his settings and costumes revealed a fascinating unity. In the infinitely changing play of light on stage, its range seemed inexhaustible. Creating costumes for the stage, Korovine not only enriched them with historical, ethnographic details, but assisted at the birth of a new 'plastique'. In ballets on a Russian theme the traditional tutu was replaced by the *sarafan*, in ballets with an 'Eastern' subject by wide oriental trousers.

Diaghilev had known Golovine since 1898. It was he who responded with an approving article to the latter's first appearance in the world of theatre as the designer for Koreshchenko's opera *The House of Ice* [see cat. 56]. In St Petersburg he often visited Golovine's studio, up in the attics of the Maryinsky Theatre, where the friends of the

Alexandre Golovine:
Set design for the opera
The House of Ice
1901
Cat. 56

artist had formed their own club. Both Korovine and Golovine might have been more closely connected with the *Saisons russes* but for their friendly relations with Teliakovsky, who, according to Benois, was Diaghilev's 'worst enemy'.

The first ballet Seasons had already shown what opportunities for a synthesis of the arts lay in attracting important painters to the theatre. In 1909 *Le Pavillon d'Armide*, *Cléopâtre*, *Les Sylphides*, the *Polovtsian Dances* from *Prince Igor* and *Le Festin* were triumphantly successful. In 1910 *Carnaval*, *Schéhérazade* and *The Firebird* were added to the repertoire.

Valentin Serov:
Poster for the *Saisons russes*:
Anna Pavlova in *Les Sylphides* 1909
Cat.115

The ballets created by the members of Diaghilev's group occupied the major part of the programme. According to Jean Cocteau, the performances moved audiences to ecstasy and 'shook France'. Serov's posters depicting Pavlova's ethereal Sylphide [cat. 115] were torn from the walls and carried off as souvenirs. By the end of the tour admirers were already avidly awaiting the return of the Company, declaring that 'Spring won't be spring without the Ballets Russes'. Most of the productions won recognition from the public and, as a rule, remained in the repertoire. Only a very few of them were not destined to survive. This instant acclaim was an indication that the essential reforms achieved by the *Saisons russes* were long overdue. Noverre had sug-

gested to his contemporaries that music should give ballet its soul, while the stage should clothe the music in living flesh and blood. Hugo had already attempted his own reforms in the spirit of Romanticism. But in recent years theatre had moved away from serious painting. Genuine artists very rarely designed settings, isolated attempts soon came to nothing and the achievements of Impressionism had not found their way onto the stage.

In the productions of Diaghilev's Company the idea of an harmonious unity between all aspects of a musical performance was not always perfectly realised, but each production was created in the name of this idea. The creative history of every one of them deserves description and analysis, but the main events must suffice.

Le Pavillon d'Armide, from which, according to its creator, Benois, 'everything started', received the first ovations. The performance was interrupted by wild applause, uncontrollable as a bursting dam. In those days the whole Company, including Diaghilev, felt bewitched, as though they themselves had suddenly been transported to the enchanted gardens of Armida. The well-known critic Levinson wrote that Benois's love for the age of Louis XIV was encapsulated in this ballet like 'a yearning for the fatherland'.[9] The gardens of Armida [see cat. 107D] resembled Versailles, each formally clipped tree was a frozen madrigal. At the same time the critics pointed out that a pre-

Alexandre Benois:
Le Pavillon d'Armide:
Costume design for Armida's Slave 1907
Cat.106E

Léon Bakst:
Set design for *Schéhérazade* 1909
Musée des Arts Décoratifs, Paris

occupation with detail worthy of the meticulous Menzel, the German painter and critic, added a certain mosaic-like quality to the colourful impression. Both Benois and Fokine had overloaded the production with 'effects'.

Cléopâtre, which introduced Bakst to the French public, laid the foundations of his popularity; *Schéhérazade*, in 1910, increased it enormously. Bakst's vision of scenic spectacle had no precedent. He was not concerned with historic-ethnographic objects. Sensing the stylistic features of various epochs he transformed them, unpre-dictably and fantastically. Arrayed in the costume he had designed for her, Ida Rubinstein's Cleopatra looked like a copy of some graphic vision by Aubrey Beardsley. Antiquity was turned into a search for a modernist style, refined, almost grotesque. The audience, dazzled by the magnificent spectacle of *Schéhérazade*, applauded. The vibrant play of colour in the settings and costumes seemed to embody the Eastern theme of the music, as it faded in a diminuendo or trembled in a high register with a kind of passionate languor. Processions of oda-lisques [see cat. 119B] in dark-red and green veils, swarthy mulattos, negroes in gold and silver brocade, formed groups overflowing with colour in scenes of unprecedented splendour. The sketches for

Schéhérazade were immediately bought for the Musée des Arts Décoratifs, Paris. Critical opinion saw the ballet as a genuine musical drama, and Bakst was acknowledged the unsurpassed master of ballet costume. Dress-designers borrowed the cut of the odalisques' costumes, turbans and skirts resembling oriental trousers became fashionable, 'haute couture' filled its salons with low divans, heaped with bright cushions.

The soft pastel tones of the ruined cemetery by moonlight in the settings by Benois for *Les Sylphides* [see cat. 105] and *Giselle* com-plemented the lyrical quality of these romantic ballets. In *Le Spectre de la Rose*, *Carnaval* and *Papillons* Bakst adopted a different approach to Romanticism. He combined, in the costumes for those ballets, a dreamy lyricism with the naïve forms of the 'Biedermeier' style. His images were not disembodied abstractions, but acquired concrete, life-like features, which in no way detracted from their charm. The French critics failed to appreciate the costumes for *Carnaval*, although for the accuracy with which they reflect the music and style of an epoch they deserve to be counted among Bakst's best work.

In the history of the *Saisons russes*, one of the greatest triumphs was that of the *Polovtsian Dances*, staged by Fokine. They were the

From design by Nikolai Roerich:
Prince Igor: **Costume for Polovtsian Warrior** 1909
Cat.113A

Borodin's score. The music alone inspired both choreographer and artist, and the images they created merged on stage into a work of powerful inner unity. The wild surge of the dancers towards the footlights, the riot of contrasting red, blue and green costumes [cat. 113A–C], flaring up in ceaseless movement against the background of a coppery-golden sky stretched out above the scorched, boundless steppe [cat. 112] – everything stemmed from a single frenzied rhythm of ever-increasing intensity which produced an extraordinary state of tension in the audience.

Diaghilev's enterprise constituted a magnetic centre. More and more new talents were drawn into its orbit, those who had something new to contribute to the sphere of art. In 1910 Stravinsky, at that time a young and unknown composer, became one of its defining figures. Diaghilev commissioned him to write the music for *The Firebird*, a ballet based on a Russian tale, adapted by Fokine. The settings and costumes were taken from sketches by Golovine [cat. 125A–C, 126], with the exception of the three main characters, whose costumes were designed by Bakst. The dissolving visions of flowers, trees and palaces in the secret garden of Koshchei [see cat. 126], created by Golovine, were considered to be among the best settings of the Diaghilev Seasons. The brilliance of the orchestration, the colourful mosaic of Stravinsky's music, seemed to acquire substance in the fantastical patterning of branches in the enchanted garden. The outlines of the towers and cupolas of Koshchei's castle gradually appeared in the fading light of dusk, as a vision of the mysterious kingdom arose. Suddenly, like a flash of light, the Firebird, with its coruscating plumage, flew across the stage. Reviewers wrote that there was a striking coincidence between the colours and rhythms of the settings and nuances of the orchestral texture. The bird seemed borne aloft by the music. It was as though they saw in Golovine, Fokine and Stravinsky a single creative mind.

The main event of the 1911 Season was the ballet *Petrushka*. Benois, Fokine and Diaghilev were united in its creation by a passionate enthusiasm. The markets, the St Petersburg squares at Shrovetide, Petrushka, the hero of the fairground booths, were all cherished memories from childhood. Benois and Diaghilev knew how to captivate Fokine with that unfamiliar music, which 'assaults the ear while it comforts the soul'. Fokine saw this ballet as the one in which his reforms were most fully implemented. Musicologists consider the score to be the summit of Stravinsky's creative genius. Nijinsky, beneath the unprepossessing exterior of the clumsy ranting clown, revealed a tragic humanity. The art of ballet was raised to the powerfully psychological grotesque. Benois's love for his theme conveyed a lively fascination for the folk festivals of nineteenth-century St Petersburg and the charac-

creation of the Diaghilev enterprise and were not performed on the Imperial stage until 1909. Both Fokine himself and Diaghilev remembered them with pride. The success of the first night exceeded all expectations. As the dance ended the public poured towards the stage, breaking through the orchestra rail. The choreographer and the designer Roerich had had no preparatory discussions about the Polovtsians and their way of life, and they were unprovided with any information or materials. Fokine worked directly and only from

Alexandre Benois:
Petrushka: **Set design for The Fair** 1911
Cat.142A

ters of the fairground booth. His colours were fresh and bright and he found new approaches to composition in his work on these settings [cat. 142A–D]. *Petrushka* took its place in the world repertoire. Benois was to design the décor for more productions, worldwide, than any other artist of his day.

The success of Diaghilev's enterprise had exceeded the wildest expectations of its creators. But by 1912 there were already indications that this particular phase in its history was nearing fulfilment. Performances were no longer greeted with the unanimous approval of previous Seasons; each première presented the public with something new and unexpected, strange, unfamiliar, even challenging to 'educated' taste. Changes were taking place in the Diaghilev milieu.

There was a noticeable cooling in his attitude towards Benois and Fokine. It seemed to Diaghilev that their art was already outmoded, although both masters were still in their prime. The aesthetic of the World of Art itself was beginning to feel dated. The romantic world of the nineteenth century, the poeticisation of the past, the themes of Gautier, misty symbolism – all of it had outlived its revival, and like the self-sufficient colourful 'formlessness' of Impressionism, lost its fascination. Diaghilev had his finger on the pulse of the times; now he was listening to new voices. Stravinsky was closely involved with the Company. He accompanied it on tour, always attended rehearsals and promoted the forging of stronger links with French musical circles by every means within his power. From 1912 to 1914 ballets were performed to the music of Western composers, among them Debussy, Ravel and Florent Schmitt. Jean Cocteau, poet and artist, herald of Surrealism, worked closely with the Company, writing libretti, designing posters [cat. 146, 147] and advising. 'Jean, surprise me!' was Diaghilev's constant cry.

The search for the new did not always meet with success. Not every ballet remained in the repertoire. Some were not sufficiently innovative, others 'surprised' but failed to delight. Audiences were unmoved by *Salomé*, for instance. The settings [cat. 164] and costumes by Sudeikin, with their heady mixture of exotica and erotica, looked like carbon copies of Bakst. The choreography of *Le Dieu Bleu* was unexciting; the beauty of Bakst's costumes [cat. 132A–C, 139A–C] could not compensate for the lifeless dances. The ballet *Jeux* only lasted for a few performances, though not on account of any weakness in its aggressively contemporary choreography which, before startled audiences, pushed the genre to its limits and beyond. As Diaghilev

Jean Cocteau:
Poster for Ballets Russes:
Tamara Karsavina in *Le Spectre de la Rose* 1911
Cat.146

said, the ballet might well have dated from 1930, not 1913. The artists, dressed for tennis, with rackets in their hands, danced against the background of a contemporary urban landscape [see cat. 137]. A tall town-house was visible between the trees surrounding the court.

The main hope of the 1913 Season was Stravinsky's *Rite of Spring*, the libretto of which was created by the composer in collaboration with the artist Roerich. The ballet – 'scenes from pagan Russia' – showed the games and dances, the ritual worship of the earth, awakening from the frozen torpor of winter, performed by members of the tribe, magicians and shamans. The ancient world was a subject on which Roerich was an unrivalled expert. But he was far from being a mere provider of archaeological data concerning pagan Russia. His images and the style of his painting inspired the composer, while one could sense the oppressive, commanding rhythms of Stravinsky's music in the artist's settings [cat. 162A–C], even though they lacked the dissonances characteristic of the music. These rhythms can be felt in the reluctant movement of the clouds, drifting like slow waves, and in the gently sloping lines of the hills. Stravinsky maintained that his music was 'an objective construction', that it contained nothing descriptive. But the architectonic quality is also the strongest feature of Roerich's painting. There is descriptiveness, but it is subordinated to the pressure of emotional tension, the inspirational power of the mysterious atmosphere which foreshadows the approaching terrible events. His stylised, recherché costume sketches [cat. 161A–D, 163] show no sign of that harsh, brutal quality suggested by the music. Nevertheless, the clumsy provocative display of Roerich's young men [see cat. 161A] reveals an awareness of harmonic dissonance, even a certain prompting in the direction of the choreographer. With their feet encased in thick-soled bast slippers and their wide canvas shirts, they presented an unusual image, which coarsened the 'plastique' of the dance without making it uncouth or ponderous.

Nijinsky, the ballet's choreographer, tried to embody mechanical rhythms in the dance. Levinson wrote that the performers moved 'as if under hypnosis, elbow to elbow, feet turned inwards, dully repeating persistent movements whose monotony remained undisturbed by the sudden spasmodic shocks of the music'.[10] Customary perceptions of beauty were rejected. Paradoxically, it was Bakst who actively assisted Nijinsky in this search for a new approach to choreography.

The Rite of Spring was the signal for radical change; it was seen as the manifesto of anti-romantic art. It is common knowledge that the première was accompanied by unprecedented scenes. The audience hissed and whistled and it took all Diaghilev's efforts to carry the performance to its conclusion. Protests and insults were directed at both choreographer and composer, although within a year Paris would accord a rapturous reception to a concert performance of this same music. The staging of the production had in no way departed from the accustomed forms, but even the décor provoked a mixed response. The son of the composer Rimsky-Korsakov declared the music to be unworthy of Roerich's magnificent settings, while Jean Cocteau, theoretician of artistic rebellion, praised Stravinsky and Nijinsky for rescuing art from Impressionism and called Roerich a mediocre artist whose décor had weakened the innovative nature of the ballet. Jacques-Emile Blanche, in his review of Roerich's work, made associations which had not previously figured in criticism of the *Saisons russes*; he wrote that the décor was immersed in a 'Cézanne-like' atmosphere, and that the Virgins made one think of Gauguin.

The performance of *La Légende de Joseph* in 1914 could hardly be termed a ballet. It contained almost no dancing; this was replaced by processions of a ritual nature. The designer of the décor was the Spaniard, José-Maria Sert, the costumes were by Bakst. The work was based on an idea suggested by Benois, several years earlier, of

creating a ballet in the style of Veronese. Bakst surpassed himself. Using the characteristic motifs of the costumes, the sinuous baroque line of figures in silhouette, so familiar in the paintings of Veronese, he created something of his own, varying every shade of red, investing it with a tense, tragic resonance. Asafyev called the decorative virtuosity of this baroque piece 'stunning'; in the artist's hunger for ever new combinations of colour and texture, in the frenzied masquerade, he saw the brilliant sunset of a talent.[11]

Gordon Craig considered that this 'feast for the eyes' destroyed the spiritual content of the *Saisons russes*, although he admitted their powerful fascination.[12]

The last pre-war season made it abundantly clear that the World of Art period of the Diaghilev enterprise was at an end. The contradictions in its practice and in its attempts to find a future direction had been laid bare. Its artists had shown the significant role of painting in the achievement of an harmonious unity between all the components of a musical performance. Painting was no longer a mere background. It had become an active participant in the performance. But in claiming a self-sufficient supremacy, it had led to the destruction of synthesis.

In 1914, for the first time, members of the artistic avant-garde were invited to take part in the *Saisons russes*. The production of *Le Coq d'Or* heralded the beginning of a new stage in their history – its designer was Natalia Goncharova. Benois never overcame his hostility to the work produced by the Diaghilev enterprise in the period 1915 to 1929; that the services of Natalia Goncharova were enlisted on his initiative is one of the ironies of fate.

Translated from the Russian by Mary Hobson

Natalia Goncharova:
Le Coq d'Or:
**Costume design for the
Russian Woman** 1914
Cat.155A

1. T.P. Karsavina, *Teatral'naia ulitsa*, Leningrad, 1971, p. 186.
2. P. Vorms, *Serge de Diaghilew et la décoration théâtrale*, 1955, p. 9.
3. 'Diagilev, kotorogo ia znal', in *Igor' Stravinskii – publitsist i sobesednik*, Moscow, 1988, pp. 163-4.
4. T.P. Karsavina, op. cit. p. 187.
5. *Aleksandr Benua razmyshliaet*, Moscow, 1968, p. 500.
6. Alexandre Benois, *Reminiscences of the Russian Ballet*, London, 1941, p. 127.
7. M. Fokine, *Protiv techeniia: Vospominaniia baletmeistera. Stat'i. Pis'ma*, Leningrad-Moscow, 1962, p. 233.

8. Telegram to P.G. Shcherbov, 26 May 1908 from the album, *Fedor Ivanovich Shaliapin*, vol. 1. *Literaturnoe nasledstvo Pis'ma*, Moscow, 1976, p. 423.
9. A. Levinson, 'Russkie khudozhniki-dekoratory' in *Stolitsa i usad'ba*, Petrograd, 1916, 1 May 1916, no. 57, pp. 12-15.
10. A. Levinson, *Staryi i novyi balet*, p. 80.
11. B.V. Asafyev (Igor Glebov) 'Russkaia zhivopis'' in *Mysli i dumy*, Moscow, 1966, p. 131.
12. V. Botsianovskii, 'Gordon Kreg o russkom balete' in *Ezhegodnik Imperatorskikh teatrov*, 1913, issue VII, p. 103.

Léon Bakst:
Boris Godunov:
Set design for Act III
*c.*1913
Cat.90

IRINA VERSHININA # *Diaghilev and the Music of the Saisons Russes*

Diaghilev's contribution to music is universally acknowledged. In monographs dedicated to the *Saisons russes* in Paris it is referred to, in passing, as an established fact; the ballet or décor usually attracts the major share of attention. And yet Diaghilev's special gift as an 'inspirer', a term frequently used by Western writers to describe him, was no less apparent in the sphere of music than in that of choreography or design.

Diaghilev's influence on the music of the *Saisons russes* manifested itself in various forms, reflecting the various facets of his creative gift. 'An entrepreneur of genius', as Lunacharsky called him, he discovered new musical talents, among them that of Stravinsky; his selection of works for the historic Russian concerts or his arrangement of the opera and ballet programmes for the *Saisons russes* reveal the taste and flair of the man who had organised the exhibitions; while in the numerous examples of his work on the musical scores of both operas and ballets one recognises the hand of a professional and the skill of an experienced editor. The quality which gave a unity of purpose to everything Diaghilev undertook, however, was his extraordinary ability to reveal or inspire just those elements in a composer's creativity, or in a particular work, which pointed to the way ahead, elements that were evidence of that art which, at whatever period it is conceived, lives and develops in the cultural context of its day. This is why he singled out Mussorgsky from the classical Russian composers whose works were performed during the season, and Stravinsky from the other contemporary composers. Stravinsky, for whom, in his own words, 'only the truth of the present' and the vital necessity of 'knowing and serving it' existed.[1]

Although a single aesthetic aim guided Diaghilev in his staging of both operas and ballets, the genres presented different musical problems. It will be useful to consider them separately.

OPERA

The historic concerts of 1907 had been, in their way, a 'reconnaissance in force'. The battle, as we know, was won; the brief but recherché 'anthology' of Russian classical music was received by the Parisians with lively interest and even, on occasion, rapturous enthusiasm. The Russian press, guarded and a little jealous, keeping a wary eye on Diaghilev's enterprise, graciously declared him to be 'the quartermaster of our music'. The ground was prepared for the offensive. The way was paved for Russian opera to make its appearance

at the Paris Opéra. The two operas chosen by Diaghilev for this historic début were Mussorgsky's *Boris Godunov* and Rimsky-Korsakov's *Sadko*. Both provided that essential quality, a vivid national originality. They were chosen, moreover, for their contrasting genres; an historical, psychological drama and an opera based on a traditional Russian heroic poem, something unknown in the West. Problems connected with the staging of *Sadko* immediately became apparent, and plans for the production were abandoned. Only *Boris Godunov* remained in the programme for the tour.

It was Diaghilev's first experience of preparing a musical production, and his role went far beyond that of 'quartermaster'. As always, he undertook the management of the whole enterprise. He attracted the best singers from the Maryinsky Theatre under the leadership of Chaliapin; engaged the entire chorus of Moscow's Bolshoi Theatre with their chorus-master, Ulrich Avranek; invited the well-known director, Alexander Sanine, who had had great success with his crowd scenes on the dramatic stage; concerned himself with the finding of an excellent conductor, Blumenfeld; and entrusted the décor to a group of superb artists, including Golovine, Yuon, Yaremich and Benois. And yet all this was only the beginning. Now Diaghilev needed to communicate his own vision, his own conception of a musical production to this great assembly of artistic talent. He began by making a careful study of the original score of *Boris Godunov* (published in 1874), and comparing it with the published edition by Rimsky-Korsakov, the version established in the repertoire of the Maryinsky Theatre.

The most effective and dramatically significant moments immediately caught Diaghilev's attention: the Clock Scene, cut from Rimsky-Korsakov's version, and the Scene at Kromy, omitted in the St Petersburg production. Both were included in the Paris production, and subsequently in numerous other productions of *Boris Godunov*, both in Russia and in the West. Diaghilev found the second scene of the Prologue, the Coronation, particularly successful from a theatrical point of view. 'The Coronation Scene must be staged so that the French are staggered by the grandeur of it all,' he wrote to Rimsky-Korsakov[2]. He even asked the composer to write forty extra bars into the score, which the latter, obligingly, did, in order to prolong the procession of the boyars and the priests. He felt that the sorrowful monologue of Tsar Boris, heard against this festive, ceremonial background, would emphasise his isolation. At one stage Diaghilev considered sacrificing the first scene of the Prologue, and beginning

Boris Anisfeld:
Sadko: **Costume design for the Golden Fish** 1911
Cat. 89C

the opera at this point. He was afraid that the long interval between
these two scenes, essential for the change of scenery and the redis-
position on stage of about 300 performers, chorus and extras, would
dissipate the enthusiasm of his audience. Fortunately he abandoned
this idea, and kept both scenes, separating them by interposing the
scene in the Chudov monastery. This disturbed the logic of the plot,
but introduced an element of contrast; the crowd scene was now
followed by a solo.

The Polish act, too, was transposed. Diaghilev wished it to
precede the scene in the Tsar's palace, with Boris and Shuisky. Having
restored the scene at Kromy which, in the original version, was the
crowning point of the opera, Diaghilev made the last scene the death
of Boris, foreseeing its full theatrical impact when played by Chaliapin.
He was right. Benois confirms that the Death Scene was 'the best
finale' for the opera.[3] It made a convincing conclusion to the psychological drama of Tsar Boris.

Sadko in performance, 1911
Bibliothèque Nationale, Paris

Alexandre Golovine:
The Maid of Pskov: **Set design for City Council of Pskov Kremlin** 1901
Cat.94B

Like many Russian operas in subsequent productions by Diaghilev, *Boris Godunov* did not escape serious cuts. In the Polish Act, the scene in Marina's apartments was omitted, an alteration which has since been observed in numerous productions. Apart from that, Diaghilev left out the scene in the tavern, considering that its coarseness might well shock a Paris audience. Those French composers who admired Mussorgsky tried to dissuade Diaghilev, and various people expressed their disapproval while the production was still in rehearsal. It is thought, however, that these cuts, and later those in *Khovanshchina*, were also made for purely practical reasons.

Diaghilev's thinking was firmly based on his own assessment of his audiences' attention span. He made a careful time-study of each performance, taking into account the number of minutes required for changes of scene. Not one of the operas in his repertoire, beginning at eight o'clock in the evening, was to end later than a quarter to midnight. It is, of course, possible – and here we are on the somewhat shaky ground of supposition – that Diaghilev excluded the scene in the inn because he considered that its rich, individual flavour, unashamedly proclaiming its genre, falls short of the general stylistic level of the score, and detracts from the main dramatic confrontation between Tsar Boris and his people.

Rimsky-Korsakov's editing was similarly criticised. The original score of *Boris Godunov* had been well known in Paris since the 1880s; it was frequently performed in the circle of Mussorgsky's admirers. This criticism did not pass unnoticed; Diaghilev took it into consideration when he began his preparatory work on *Khovanshchina*. However, even in its edited form, Mussorgsky's music scored a triumph.

The première of the opera on 20 May 1908 was a tremendous success. It was said to be a masterpiece, comparable only to those of Shakespeare. '*Boris Godunov*,' the critic of *La Liberté* wrote, on the day after the première, 'commands, like the works of Shakespeare, an intense awareness of the past, an all-embracing universality, realism, richness, profundity, a mercilessly disturbing quality, artistry and that same unity of the tragic and the comic, that same supreme humanity.'[4] The Russian artists proved to be worthy of this music. Chaliapin shook the audience with the tragic power and the striking realism of his performance in the Death Scene. In the Clock Scene he reduced them to a state of terror. Several members of the audience stood up in their places, trying to make out, in the depths of the stage, the apparition to which Chaliapin, as Boris, was feverishly pointing.

'The greatness of Chaliapin lies precisely in his art as a tragic singer and the miraculous way in which he blends his singing with his acting,' Paul Dukas wrote.[5] Louis Schneider, in *Le Théâtre*, seconded

Valentin Serov:
Portrait of Chaliapin 1905
Cat.100

him: 'Chaliapin is beyond praise as a singer, and beyond praise as an actor. He is equally great in his uniting of these two arts.'[6] Robert Brussel, in the pages of *Le Figaro*, commented on the striking artistic simplicity of his interpretation: 'The most passionate, intense scenes became perfectly natural – there was so much conviction in his performance.'[7] The remainder of the soloists were scarcely inferior to Chaliapin. Smirnov, the young man, possessor of a remarkable tenor voice, still relatively unknown in Russia, to whom Diaghilev had entrusted the role of the Pretender Dimitri, was particularly good.

The crowd scenes were greeted with enormous enthusiasm by both audience and critics. 'The singers in the Russian chorus amazed us with their power, the purity of their intonation, the flexibility of their performance. They act as magnificently as they sing,' Pierre Lalo wrote in *Le Temps*.[8] 'Each member of the chorus, each extra is an actor,' the critic of *Le Matin* wrote, developing the same theme. 'Each has his role, carefully studied and contributing to the general picture, so splendidly put together by the producers.' The credit was due, in fact, to Sanine, who continued to lead the chorus himself, appearing on stage during performances, now in the costume and make-up of an officer of the law (in Scene 1), now as a distinguished boyar (in the Coronation Scene, and in the meeting of the *Duma*).

A chorus that could both sing and act magnificently was such an amazing phenomenon to the habitués of the Paris Opéra, that after Scene 1 of the Prologue its members, for the first time in the history of that theatre, received an ovation.

The success of *Boris Godunov* encouraged Diaghilev. It had prepared the ground for the organisation of the annual *Saisons russes* in Paris. It was assumed, of course, that these Seasons would consist of operatic performances. Diaghilev intended to prepare, for the 1909 Season, an 'anthology' of Russian classical opera. Glinka's *Ruslan and Lyudmila*, Serov's *Judith*, Borodin's *Prince Igor*, Rimsky-Korsakov's *The Maid of Pskov* (retitled *Ivan the Terrible*) and, once again, *Boris Godunov*. These plans were unexpectedly changed. Friends and colleagues of Diaghilev persuaded him to show French audiences, in addition to the operas, the new Russian ballet, and four one-act ballets were added to the list of operas. Insufficient funds, however, were available for this vast project. Diaghilev was refused a subsidy by the authorities and was obliged to make extensive cuts in the operatic repertoire. The only opera to be performed in its entirety was *The Maid of Pskov*, with Chaliapin in the role of Ivan the Terrible. The première was a success with both audience and press, but it was not the triumph that *Boris Godunov* had been in the previous year. A single act was staged from each of the remaining operas. The brilliant overture and first act of *Ruslan and Lyudmila*, musically perfect and structurally the most satisfying; the third act of *Judith*, the climax of the drama, with its original 'duel' between Judith and Holofernes, brilliantly performed by Chaliapin and Felia Litvine; and the second act of *Prince Igor*, culminating in the *Polovtsian Dances*. *Boris Godunov* was not included.

In the years between 1910 and 1912 opera disappeared altogether from the repertoire of the *Saisons russes*.

The Season of 1913, which opened in the Paris Théâtre des Champs-Elysées and continued in London's Drury Lane Theatre, included three operas. New productions of *Boris Godunov* and *Khovanshchina* were taken to Paris, and *The Maid of Pskov* was added to the London programme. *Boris Godunov* was received with the former enthusiasm, but it was *Khovanshchina* which attracted the most attention. Among musicians the production gave rise to a bitter controversy, with Diaghilev at its centre. This time he had allowed his creative initiative free rein; he presented not only his own conception of the opera, but, in essence, his own 'edition' of the score.

He had been thinking about *Khovanshchina* since 1909. In the

winter of that year, on his return to St Petersburg, Diaghilev, in his own words, 'spent hours in the Public Library studying the manuscript'. Comparing it with the published score, edited by Rimsky-Korsakov, he came to the conclusion that 'there is scarcely one page of the original manuscript without numerous important corrections and alterations made by Rimsky-Korsakov'.[9] It was then that he conceived his bold plan. He would restore the passages cut by Rimsky-Korsakov, revive the original version of those episodes which the latter had retained but which had undergone significant editing, and he would order a new orchestration.

In 1912 Diaghilev commissioned Stravinsky to reorchestrate the opera and to compose a final chorus. Mussorgsky had not managed to finish *Khovanshchina*. He left only a rough sketch of the chorus, based on the original Old Believers' melody. It was not long before Ravel joined forces with Stravinsky. They decided that Stravinsky would orchestrate Shaklovity's aria, 'The lair of the Streltsy is sunk in sleep', and compose the final chorus; Ravel would undertake the remainder of the work. In the autumn Diaghilev commissioned designs for the production from the young artist Fedor Fedorovsky; early in 1913 he secured the services of Sanine as director, Pokhitonov as chorus-master, Emile Cooper as conductor and, of course, Chaliapin, who was to sing the role of Dosifei.

Press reports concerning the forthcoming production drew angry protests from admirers of Rimsky-Korsakov. A.N. Rimsky-Korsakov, the son of the composer, called Diaghilev's project 'an act of vandalism'. It displayed a disgraceful lack of respect for the memory of his father and his selfless work. Ravel was obliged to answer him in an open letter, in which he assured his critic that the wish to acquaint the public with Mussorgsky's original score did nothing to diminish the importance of Rimsky-Korsakov, for whom he himself, Stravinsky and Diaghilev felt the most sincere affection and respect.

Further complications arose in connection with Chaliapin, who would only agree to appear if the entire part of Dosifei were to be performed in the Rimsky-Korsakov version, with the exception of the final chorus. Moreover, he refused to accept Diaghilev's suggestion that Shaklovity's aria should be included in his part, since Diaghilev considered it more appropriate to the character of Dosifei than to the 'arch-villain', as Mussorgsky himself described Shaklovity. Diaghilev was forced to concede the point. The aria was cut.

This new version of the opera proved to be something of a compromise. Based on the orchestral score of Rimsky-Korsakov, it contained manuscript interpolations orchestrated by Ravel, and a manuscript score of the final chorus composed by Stravinsky. The introduction of new episodes – a number of choral scenes from

Acts I and II had been restored – meant that the future performance would exceed the allotted time-span. Diaghilev was faced with the necessity of making further cuts. The five-act opera was reduced to four acts. He removed the whole of the second act – the princes' quarrel, Martha's divination – and the second scene of the fourth act, the departure of the exiled Golitsyn and the pardoning of the condemned Streltsy.

Opponents of the production saw Diaghilev's actions as impermissible and arbitrary. But the cuts that he had made related directly to his conception of the opera. His artistic flair prompted him to emphasise the innovative nature of *Khovanshchina* as a choral piece. It was precisely this aspect of Mussorgsky's opera which had remained undervalued by his friends and contemporaries. Vladimir Stasov had warned him: 'In its present form there is too great a predominance of choruses in your opera, and too little action for individual characters.'[10] Rimsky-Korsakov's editing 'corrected' this 'deficiency'; he underlined the intrigue which connected the principal characters, not allowing it to dissolve into the lengthy development of the drama with its massive crowd scenes. In Diaghilev's version, on the other hand, the chorus was a powerful force which absorbed the 'individual characters' and subordinated them to its will. Despite the vivid and colourful personalities of the soloists, the choruses of Streltsy and Old Believers were no less important.

In place of a religious-political tragedy, as Karatygin described Rimsky-Korsakov's edition of the opera, Diaghilev offered the Paris audiences pages from the chronicles of Russia, relived through the music of Mussorgsky, in which 'choral' images, united by the tragic experience of this turning point in Russian history, played the dominant role.

The theme of the Old Believers acquired a new scale, a new significance in Diaghilev's version; perfectly consistent with the musical logic, it was fully developed in Stravinsky's new chorus, based on the themes Mussorgsky had written for them. This was a very different finale to that in Rimsky-Korsakov's edition. If we may judge from Mussorgsky's letters to Stasov, it corresponded more closely to the original idea of its creator. The audience at the Théâtre des Champs-Elysées did not see the powerful scene showing the self-immolation of the Old Believers, or the triumphant arrival of Peter's troops to the sound of the popular Preobrazhensky march. Pavel Lamm, who studied Mussorgsky's manuscripts in the 1920s, came to the conclusion that Mussorgsky had evidently 'decided not to stage the self-immolation scene and end the departure of the Old Believers on a diminuendo'.[11] This is precisely how the finale appeared in the Paris production of *Khovanshchina*. The ascetic tones of the Old Believers'

melody, sung first by the alto *a capella*, to which other voices and then the orchestra were gradually joined ('the Old Believers go to their death … not all at once, but in groups,' Mussorgsky wrote to Stasov),[12] rose to a crescendo, reached fortissimo in the tutti and began to diminish. The sound of the chorus gradually died away; the performers left the stage slowly, descending through the trap, while the violins played a scarcely audible tremolo in a high register.

In spite of the extensive cuts, for which Mussorgsky was criticised not only by Rimsky-Korsakov but by Lunacharsky (the latter wrote of the 'scandalously shorn appearance' of the opera), the historic significance of Diaghilev's 'edited version' is undeniable. It was the first step on the path to the true Mussorgsky, taken two decades before Asafyev began his public campaign in the same cause, and Lamm embarked on his exhaustive study of the manuscripts.

The 'choral opera' was unknown in Europe. It became the Russian chorus's 'benefit performance' on the stages of Paris and London. '*Khovanshchina* had an extraordinary success,' Fedorovsky remembered. 'Apart from Chaliapin, the artiste Petrenko and the singers Domaev and Zaporozhets, the chorus of the Streltsy made a great impression. The chorus always have such a remarkable performance of "Come out to us, our father and leader" that the French audiences rose to their feet, applauded wildly and demanded three encores. They regarded it as the ultimate in vocal artistry.'[13] 'The first act was greeted by a storm of applause. The final *a capella* chorus so delighted the audience that it had to be repeated. I don't think that a chorus has ever had such a dazzling success,' Lunacharsky confessed.[14] 'The prayer of the Streltsy' from *Khovanshchina*, 'Oh Lord, preserve us from the enemy', was repeated three times at each performance and was encored at concerts,' Pokhitonov tells us.[15] 'It is the entirely new and remarkable quality of the choral singing which makes an overwhelming impression and, more than anything else, distinguishes Diaghilev's Company from all the other companies we have ever heard in London,' wrote the critic of *The Times*.[16]

In the last pre-war Paris Season Diaghilev presented two more operatic productions: Rimsky-Korsakov's *Le Coq d'Or* and Stravinsky's *Le Rossignol*. Both were successful although, paradoxically, they revealed that Diaghilev was becoming less interested in opera as a genre than in ballet. The fact that *Le Coq d'Or* was staged as a ballet indicates the future course of a musical theatre based on the interaction of vocal score and dance – Stravinsky's *Pulcinella*, *Le Renard* and *Les Noces*. *Le Rossignol* did not find a permanent place in the repertoire, although later Stravinsky, at Diaghilev's request, wrote the score for a ballet using material from the opera.

In that pre-war period the greatest achievements in the sphere

Alexandre Benois:
Le Rossignol: **Costume design for the Palace Marshal** 1914
Cat.143B

Alexandre Benois:
Le Rossignol: **Costume design for Mademoiselle Briand** 1914
Cat.143D

Alexandre Benois:
Le Rossignol:
Set design for the Emperor's Bedroom 1914-17
Ashmolean Museum, Oxford

Alexandre Benois:
Le Rossignol:
Set design for the Throne Room 1914
Ashmolean Museum, Oxford

of opera remained *Boris Godunov* and *Khovanshchina*. On one occasion, in 1906, when Diaghilev was still preparing himself for the task ahead, he said that he wished 'to nurture Russian painting' and 'present it to the West, extol it in the West'. In the *Saisons russes* of 1908 to 1914 he succeeded in 'extolling in the West' the least traditional aspects of Mussorgsky's great opera and, above all, the choral nature of that composer's dramatic art.

MUSIC FOR BALLET:
THE RENEWAL OF THE GENRE

If the operatic productions of the *Saisons russes* were intended to 'open the eyes' of Europe to the inimitable originality and intrinsic worth of Russian classical opera, to present it as an integral part of world music, to show that, besides Wagner's *Tristan*, there was also *Boris Godunov* and *Khovanshchina*, then the ballets laid claim to something more. According to Diaghilev, they were to show the world 'a new musical theatre', as yet unknown both in Russia and in Europe.

After the Season of 1910, Diaghilev attempted to define the 'essence and the secret' of this new kind of ballet: 'We wanted to find an art form in which the whole complexity of life, all its feelings and passions, would be expressed, not rationally in words and concepts, but elementally, visually, incontrovertibly.' 'The secret of our ballet lies in rhythm,' Bakst said, echoing him. 'We have found it possible to communicate not feelings and passions, as in drama, and not form, as in painting, but the actual rhythm of feelings and form. Our dances, our settings, our costumes – they are all so exciting because they reflect that most elusive and secret thing – the rhythm of life.'[17]

For some reason neither Diaghilev nor Bakst mentioned music in this interview. But surely the direct expression of 'the elusive and secret rhythm of life' is indeed the true vocation of music, hence its special new function in ballet. The exponents of 'free dance' were the first to understand this: Loïe Fuller, Maude Allan and, above all, Isadora Duncan. The latter rejected the ballet music of the nineteenth century. Her improvisations were based on the music of Bach, Gluck, Beethoven and Chopin, music not intended for dance but possessing a rich variety of rhythmic content, unfettered by the metric formulae laid down for each genre in classical ballet. A polka for the entrance of the ballerina, for instance, a waltz for the solo variations, a gallop for the final 'ballabile'. 'So far only geniuses have understood rhythm,' Duncan explained. 'That is why I have drawn my dance from their works.'[18]

The rejection of the traditional 'music for dance' in favour of the variety of style and genre in classical and contemporary instrumental music was fundamental to Fokine's ballet reforms. Diaghilev subsequently maintained that the ideas for the renewal of ballet, including those concerning its music, were his own. Fokine had merely been successful in putting them into practice. Naturally, an indignant Fokine refuted this claim. *The Dying Swan*, danced to the music of Saint-Saëns, and *Chopiniana*, which laid the foundations for one of the main trends in twentieth-century ballet, were created *before* his acquaintance with Diaghilev; even in their collaboration Fokine remained a somewhat independent artist. But it is unjust to deny Diaghilev, as Fokine does, his influence on the reforms in the sphere of music for the ballet.

Diaghilev insisted from the outset that the ballet music in his productions should be of a consistently high standard. In order to ensure this he allowed himself 'editorial rights' over the musical score, as he had in the case of the operas. The degree of intervention varied. In *Chopiniana*, for instance, which he immediately renamed *Les Sylphides*, Keller's orchestration of the Chopin pieces did not suit him. He commissioned a new orchestration from several composers, amongst them Liadov, Glazunov and Stravinsky.

The renaming of the ballet was no empty formality. It related directly to the content. Diaghilev felt that it was necessary to intensify the lyrical atmosphere of the piece. He insisted that the Prelude in A major, a miniature with the intimate quality of chamber music, should replace the animated ceremonial Polonaise, also in A major.

Léon Bakst:
Portrait of Isadora Duncan 1907-8
Cat. 53

Les Sylphides:
A scene with the set by Alexandre Benois 1909
State Museum of Theatre and Music, St Petersburg

Léon Bakst:
Daphnis and Chloë: **Set design for scene** I 1912
Cat.136A

Nikolai Roerich:
The Rite of Spring:
Costume designs 1913

Maiden
Cat.161C

Maiden
Cat.161B

Youth
Cat.161A

Old Man
Cat.161D

The Mazurka in C major op. 33 performed by Nijinsky, the only variation for male dancer, was replaced by the elegant Mazurka in C major, op. 67, close to the earlier work in spirit, but stronger melodically.

The changes made by Diaghilev to Arensky's score for the ballet *Une Nuit d'Egypte* were far more radical. Having decided to stage the ballet as a choreographic drama, with a tragic finale, and having made Cleopatra the central figure, he ensured that the most powerful moments in the scenario would be supported by equally powerful music, written for the genre. The striking entrance of Cleopatra was danced to music from Rimsky-Korsakov's opera-ballet *Mlada* ('The Vision of Cleopatra'). The *pas-de-deux* for the Slave and the Slave-girl, specially created by Fokine for Nijinsky and Karsavina, was performed to the music of the 'Turkish Dance' from Act IV of Glinka's *Ruslan and Lyudmila*. Glazunov's 'autumn' bacchanal from his ballet *The Seasons* was used for the final orgiastic ensemble, while the touching scene in which the maiden Ta-Hor (Anna Pavlova) mourns her lover, slain by Cleopatra, was accompanied by the 'Dance of the Persian Girls' from *Khovanshchina* (here used to express a languorous yearning).

Anna Pavlova in *Une Nuit d'Egypte c.*1908
State Museum of Theatre and Music, St Petersburg

In each case these borrowed passages fulfilled their function. They provided a decorative accompaniment which intensified the visual impact of the scene. In this sense Diaghilev, in spite of justifiable accusations of an impermissible musical eclecticism, had done what he set out to do. Similarly, if we accept the view formed at the time by Benois, Diaghilev managed to introduce these alien episodes into the musical fabric of Arensky's score so skilfully, to contrive the joins so expertly, that the seams were scarcely noticeable in this 'recomposed' ballet; it even achieved a certain degree of musical integrity. Later, however, in his memoirs, Benois called it 'musical vandalism'.

Rimsky-Korsakov's music for the ballet *Schéhérazade* was more successful as a 'decorative accompaniment'. Diaghilev used the second and fourth sections of the symphonic suite of the work, leaving out the third section as less suited to interpretation in dance; the first section was played as an overture. The performance drew angry protests from Rimsky-Korsakov's widow and children. They were upset that the music should have been used at all in connection with an unrelated scenario, particularly one of such a violent nature. Nevertheless Sergei Prokofiev testified to the 'successful correspondence' between the Fokine-Bakst production and the music.[19] Stravinsky, too, wrote to Rimsky-Korsakov's son Vladimir of 'the glorious spectacle which transports one into the great music of *Schéhérazade* in a way that could not be bettered'. It is clear that the music itself permitted this kind of free interpretation which yet remained faithful to the romanticised oriental spirit imprinted on the score.

Borodin's *Polovtsian Dances* occupied a very special place in the 1909 Season. This choreographic finale of Act II in *Prince Igor* overshadowed the operatic part of the performance and was widely perceived as an independent work. French criticism declared these dances 'the best ballet in the world' (E. Lalo) and drew attention, perceptively, to the main innovation, the musical derivation of their imagery. The *Polovtsian Dances* were the musical-choreographic embodiment of the mass element in dance. Borodin had created a collective image of the Polovtsians, of such monolithic thematic content, on such a scale of symphonic generalisation and unity of form, that it was time to speak of a 'new type of musical composition for the ballet', revealing no trace of the traditional balletic divertisse-ment. 'Where did I get my steps from? I would say – from the music,' Fokine recalled, and added '... if the Polovtsians didn't dance like that, then, given Borodin's music, they should have done'.[20]

This approach to music as a source of imagery, the basis upon which the choreography was to be built, became the distinguishing aesthetic aim of the Diaghilev ballet. 'For us it was the music which provided ballet with its centre of gravity,' Benois emphasised. 'The organic combination of an archaic monumentalism in the use of thematic material and the character of its orchestral dynamics (overtones of the occult), with the refinement of its melodic line in the depiction of the principal characters in this pastoral romance, proved to be a profound and unique example, presented during the *Saisons russes*, of a classical theme communicated in symphonic terms.

Contact with Debussy was established immediately after the first Season of ballet. It appears from Diaghilev's letters that he was planning a ballet based on Venice in the eighteenth century. The composer himself was to undertake the libretto, while a reworked version of *Les Masques*, written for pianoforte, would provide the music. In 1912 the possibility of a ballet to the music of the symphonic nocturne, *Fêtes*, was discussed. But finally Diaghilev decided to use the symphonic prelude *L'Après-midi d'un faune* to create, in collaboration with Nijinsky and Bakst, the ballet of that name. This was an entirely new approach to the classical theme, without ensembles or the traditional Fokine 'bacchanal'. In contradistinction to the décor of Bakst, which claimed the choreography for its own, so to speak, now

Boris Frodman-Kluzel:
Prince Igor: **Adolph Bolm as Polovtsian Warrior Chief** *c.*1909
Cat.109

L'Après-midi d'un faune:
Vaslav Nijinsky as the Faun *c.*1912
Bibliothèque Nationale, Paris

moment had arrived when one listened to the music and, in listening to it, derived an additional pleasure from seeing it. I think this is the mission of ballet.'[21] In the Borodin-Fokine *Polovtsian Dances* this mission was brilliantly accomplished.

The success of the first ballet season did not obscure the urgent need for new ballet scores; composers were the breath of life to Diaghilev's enterprise. His first choice was Maurice Ravel. He commissioned the music from the latter for a 'classical' ballet which was to be based on the Hellenistic love story of *Daphnis and Chloë*. Benois, who expected nothing more than graceful trifles from the composer of the *Rapsodie Espagnole* and the piano pieces, could not understand why Diaghilev did not approach the composer of *L'Après-midi d'un faune*. But evidently something in Ravel's music suggested to Diaghilev its possible plastic interpretation; the elegantly shifting rhythms, perhaps, the vivid dynamics, the elasticity of his style. Diaghilev's intuition did not betray him. *Daphnis and Chloë*, with its strikingly dictating and dominating the rhythm of plastique and pose, now releasing it, the music of Debussy sounded somehow especially free; it did not become a decorative accompaniment to the angular choreographic picture full of restrained expression. On the contrary, it breathed life into it, and spoke to the listening, watching audience of that 'elusive and secret rhythm of life' concealed in the lingering and controlled movements of Nijinsky's faun [cat. 159, 166]. The only original opus which Diaghilev commissioned was the ballet *Jeux*, staged by Nijinsky in the 1913 Season.

In an extremely full programme, the 'novelties' of Russian music, Mussorgsky's *Khovanshchina* and Stravinsky's *Rite of Spring*, were the centre of attention. Debussy's miniature ballet remained in the shadows. He himself could not entirely accept Nijinsky's choreography, which did indeed puzzle a number of people. The ballet was not revived in subsequent Diaghilev Seasons. The score, however, possessed great merit. Stravinsky considered it a 'masterpiece of orchestration'. Debussy said that the symphonic poem came to him when Diaghilev introduced him to the scenario. 'He talked to me about a scenario ... created for that elusive thing of which, as I understand it, a balletic poem should consist.' Here was 'everything necessary to summon rhythm to life in a musical atmosphere'.[22] It is clear that in this instance, too, Diaghilev assumed the role of 'inspirer'.

Diaghilev's greatest achievement in the music of the *Saisons russes* was his 'discovery of Stravinsky'. He was determined to include an original Russian ballet in the programme for 1910. The libretto based on a fable from Russian folklore already existed; the ballet was to be called *The Firebird*. The choice of Liadov was a natural one. Diaghilev rightly considered the composer of the descriptive orchestral pieces *Kikimora*, *Baba-Yaga*, *The Enchanted Lake* and numerous arrangements of Russian folksongs to be 'our first, most interesting and outstanding musical talent'.[23] But Liadov was slow to begin work on the piece, and it became clear that it would not be ready in time. At one point Diaghilev considered Glazunov: 'If we can't have Liadov we'll have to ask Glazunov, but the former would be so much pleasanter!' he wrote to Benois. For a while Nicholas Tcherepnine worked on *The Firebird*, but finished by composing a symphonic work, *Le Royaume Enchanté*, having 'suddenly lost interest in ballet', according to Benois. At that point Diaghilev, not without some prompting from Asafyev, began to think seriously about the as yet unknown young composer, Igor Stravinsky.

In the winter of 1909 Diaghilev had heard Stravinsky's *Scherzo Fantastique* for orchestra at one of Siloti's concerts. The work sounded extraordinarily fresh and new. The unusual rhythms, the brilliant variations of timbre and colour, the general impression of a strong

Jean Cocteau:
Stravinsky at the piano, playing *The Rite of Spring* 1913
Cat.148

creative individuality which distinguished the orchestral writing, caught Diaghilev's attention. Intuition showed him the work's potential as a score for a ballet. A performance of Stravinsky's symphonic miniature, *Feu d'artifice*, which he heard in company with Fokine, only served to reinforce his first impression. Fokine agreed with him wholeheartedly. 'This music burns, it blazes, it throws off sparks. It is what I need for the fiery image of the ballet.'[24]

The decision was taken and Stravinsky received the commission. Once again, Diaghilev's intuition had not failed him. The quality that he had heard in the orchestral colour of *Scherzo fantastique* was further developed in the resonant images of Koshchei's kingdom and above all in the image of the miraculous bird.

The Flight and the Dance of the Firebird were examples of the new musical approach to the traditional entrée and solo variation of the ballerina. The musical fabric of these episodes, deprived of a strong, distinct melody, seemed to arise from an elemental interweaving of texture and harmony, from the spontaneous movement of orchestral timbres. Only the sharp, rhythmic pizzicato of the cellos secretly ordered and directed this shimmering tremulous sound, imparting to it the suggestion of a fantastical dance. A feeling for gesture, for the rhythmic movement of the human body, an ability to subordinate the music to the practical problems of staging, were already in evidence in this first ballet; they were, without a doubt, one

Alexandre Benois:
Petrushka:
**Set design for
Petrushka's Room** 1911/1921
Cat.142B

Alexandre Benois:
Petrushka:
**Set design for
The Moor's Room** 1911/1921
Cat.142C

83

of the strengths of Stravinsky's musical-theatrical talent. Audiences at the Paris Opéra saw in *The Firebird* 'a miracle of the most ravishing balance between movement, sound and form'.[25] It was a completely new realisation of the World of Art's *Gesamtkunstwerk*.

The extent to which the young composer was immediately able to grasp the spirit and character of Diaghilev's ideas is extraordinary. *The Firebird* was, in its way, a 'musical encyclopedia' of the fundamentals and achievements of the Russian classics, a masterly embodiment of Diaghilev's 'anthological principle' within one work. Rimsky-Korsakov, Tchaikovsky, Borodin, Mussorgsky, Liadov, Glazunov were all reflected in the sound-structure of the ballet; from all their original, disparate, creative individualities Stravinsky had been able to catch the common characteristics of a 'single Russian style', to convey the essence of a whole musical epoch.

Diaghilev was also responsible for the staging of Stravinsky's second ballet. We do not know what the composer might have done, finally, with his *Konzertstück* for piano and orchestra, if Diaghilev

The Firebird:
Tamara Karsavina as the Firebird
and Michel Fokine as Ivan Tsarevich, 1912
Bibliothèque Nationale, Paris

had not persuaded him to use the existing material for a complete choreographic drama. In a letter to Benois, Diaghilev calls the *Konzertstück* 'The Cry of Petrushka', and mentions another piece, the 'Russian Dance', declaring both fragments to be 'in the fullest sense of the word, works of genius'.[26] He had even given the future ballet its name. For the first time in the history of world musical theatre there appeared on stage, touched by the Diaghilev magic, *a powerfully characterised lyrical hero* (author's italics).

The score of *Petrushka* brought genuine innovation to the genre of ballet music. Everything in it was new, from the unusual main leitmotif – Petrushka's bitonal fanfare – to the equally unusual and witty orchestral interpretations of the most hackneyed popular tunes. The brilliant theatricality of the music, combined with Stravinsky's characteristic 'personification' by means of orchestral timbre, did not prevent him from composing a score which resembled a symphony in four movements. 'I did not make a suite out of *Petrushka*. It can be played as a symphony – all four "scenes" one after another,' he wrote, in connection with a concert performance of the ballet.[27] Both the first and last street scenes, in which the celebrating crowd is contrasted with the mysterious world of the puppets, are associated with a sonata-like allegro. The intervening scenes comprise, in a mixture of genres, the lyrical and scherzo movements of a symphony. Petrushka, alone in his room, presents the scherzo element, while the Moor's solo scenes parody the lyrical mood.

Diaghilev had an extremely high opinion of this score. Only the last notes of the finale caused him, at first, some hesitation. Unlike *The Firebird*, the final cadence of *Petrushka* is not in the principal key of the work. The pizzicato of the last two bars tends to suggest an indeterminate tonality, as if warning us that the spirit of 'the eternal, unhappy hero of all fairgrounds in all countries'[28] has not died, and that everything may well begin all over again. Diaghilev was afraid that audiences would not understand such an unusual ending to a ballet. However, the unvarying success of every performance dispelled his doubts and inspired him with fresh confidence in Stravinsky's musical thinking.

The first sketches for *The Rite of Spring* momentarily shook that confidence. When the composer played Diaghilev the opening of 'Spring Divination', in which the same complex chord, with varying rhythmic accentuation, is repeated fifty-nine times, Diaghilev was baffled. 'Confused and annoyed, but not wishing to offend me,' the composer recalled, 'he said something extraordinarily insulting. "And is this going to go on for long?" I answered, "Right to the end, my dear chap!" He was silent, understanding that my answer was a serious one.'[29]

As he got to know the music for the ballet, especially when Nijinsky began to rehearse, Diaghilev became more and more enthusiastic. He envisaged something on a huge scale and insisted on employing 'a gigantic orchestra'. This enabled Stravinsky to make free use of harmonies which were 'more complex than ever'. But the most important discovery, of which the composer was particularly proud, was 'the new language of the rhythm'.[30] Endlessly varied and smoothly flowing in the mysterious Spring Rounds, elemental, as though charged with muscular energy, in the men's games of war, powerfully commanding in the inevitable, measured tread of the ritual processions, tragically convulsive in the final sacrificial dance of the Chosen Virgin – this 'new rhythm' drew to the surface and made almost visible that 'mysterious rhythm of life' of which Bakst spoke at the dawn of the *Saisons russes*.

The noisy scenes of the opening night, 29 May 1913, were foreseen neither by Diaghilev nor by the creators of the ballet. Subsequent performances, in both Paris and London, met with a calmer reception and a sympathetic press. However, Diaghilev decided not to revive the Nijinsky production, feeling that it was 'better to let the thing lie for a while ... the public is not ready for it'.[31] He did not include *The Rite of Spring* in the repertoire until 1920, then only in Massine's version, and after its complete acceptance on the concert platform.

The *Saisons russes* renewed the genre of ballet music. The changes were radical. They enabled the composer to create new forms of symphonic programme music; the symphonic suite, the symphonic scene and the symphonic poem indicate the variety of genres introduced. At the beginning of the twentieth century many composers began to write ballets specially for the Diaghilev enterprise. After Stravinsky came Prokofiev, whose balletic creativity was similarly inspired by Diaghilev. Tcherepnine, too, was a regular participant in the Seasons, both as conductor and composer; he wrote his ballets *Narcisse* and *The Red Mask* for Diaghilev. Now the composers from the Rimsky-Korsakovs' 'enemy camp' were eager to contribute something to the *Saisons russes*. Shteinberg arranged one of his own pieces from the cycle 'Metamorphosis' for the ballet *Midas*. French composers who worked for Diaghilev, apart from Debussy and Ravel, included Paul Dukas, Reynaldo Hahn, Florent Schmitt; later they were joined by Manuel de Falla. Even the venerable Richard Strauss was unable to resist a commission from Diaghilev, and composed his only ballet, *La Légende de Joseph*.

By 1914 Diaghilev's strategy for 'conquering Europe' had succeeded. The day was won. And not by the quartermaster, but by the 'Generalissimo', as his friend Benois called him. It was the name

that Mussorgsky had given to Vladimir Stasov, the ideological leader of the 'Mighty Handful' or, as they are sometimes known, 'The Five'.

Lunacharsky, describing the pre-war season, wrote from Paris: 'Russian music has become a clearly defined concept, characterised by its freshness, its originality and, above all, its outstanding instrumental mastery.'[32]

Such were the achievements in music of the *Saisons russes* of 1908 to 1914, whose source was the intuitive genius of Diaghilev and his rare gift as an 'inspirer'.

Translated from the Russian by Mary Hobson

1. Igor Stravinsky, *Khronika moei zhizni*, Leningrad, 1963, p. 250.
2. Zilberstein and Samkov, *Sergei Diagilev i russkoe iskusstvo*, vol. 1, Moscow, 1982, p. 103.
3. Alexandre Benois, *Moi vospominaniia* vol. 2, book 5, Moscow, 1980, p. 490.
4. A. Gozenpud, '"Boris Godunov" M.P. Musorgskogo vo Frantsii 1876-1908' in *Vospriiatie russkoi kul'turoi na zapade: ocherki*, Leningrad, 1975, p. 240.
5. Paul Dukas, 'Boris Godunov' in *Stat'i i retsenzii kompozitorov Frantsii*, Leningrad, 1972, p. 330.
6. A. Gozenpud, op. cit. p. 246.
7. Ibid p. 247.
8. Ibid p. 245.
9. Zilberstein and Samkov, op. cit. vol. 1, pp. 221-2.
10. M.P. Mussorgsky, *K piatidesiatiletiiu so dnia smerti: 1881-1931. Stat'i i materiali*, Moscow, 1932, p. 483.
11. Pavel Lamm, 'Ot redaktora' in *M.P. Musorgskii: Polnoe sobranie sochinenii* vol. 2, Moscow, 1931, Editor's Foreword.
12. Modest Mussorgsky, *Literaturnoe nasledie*, book 1: *Pis'ma, biograficheskie materiali i dokumenty*, Moscow, 1971, p. 16.
13. Fedor Fedorovsky, *Zagranichnaia poezdka 1912 [1913] v Parizh na 'Russkii sezon'*, MSS O/R GTS TM im. Bakhrushina f. 467 ed. khr. 2.
14. Anatolii Lunacharsky, 'Russkie spektakli v Parizhe' in A. Lunacharskii, *O Muzyke i muzykal'nom teatre*, vol. 1, Moscow, 1981, p. 149.

15. Daniil Pokhitonov, 'Vospominaniia o F.I. Shaliapine' in *Fedor Ivanovich Shaliapin*, vol. 2, Moscow, 1977, p. 244.
16. 'Novosti Sezona', 25 June 1913.
17. Zilberstein and Samkov, op. cit. vol. 1, p. 214.
18. Isadora Duncan, 'Chem dolzhen byt' tanets' in Serge Lifar, *Tanets*, Paris, 1939, p. 126.
19. N. Ia. Miaskovsii, *Stat'i. Pis'ma. Vospominaniia*, vol. 2, Moscow, 1964, p. 309.
20. M. Fokine, *Protiv techeniia. Vospominaniia baletmeistera. Stat'i, Pis'ma*, Leningrad-Moscow, 1962, p. 233.
21. Alexandre Benois, 'Khudozhestvennye pis'ma: russkie spektakli v Parizhe' in *Rech*, 25 June-17 July 1909.
22. Claude Debussy, 'Igry' in *Debiussi K. Stat'i. Retsenzii. Besedy*, Leningrad, 1964, p. 199.
23. Zilberstein and Samkov, op. cit. vol. II, Moscow, 1982, p. 110.
24. M. Fokine, op. cit. p. 256.
25. V. Svetlov, *Sovremennyi balet*, St Petersburg, 1911, p. 11.
26. Alexandre Benois, *Moi vospominaniia*, op. cit. p. 521.
27. Igor Stravinsky, op. cit. p. 469.
28. Ibid p. 72.
29. *I. Stravinsky: Publitsist i sobesednik*, Moscow, 1988, p. 10.
30. Ibid.
31. I.F. Stravinsky, *Stat'i i materialy*, Moscow, 1973, p. 477.
32. Anatolii Lunacharsky, op. cit. p. 182.

Ballets Russes first season: rehearsal 1910
Tamara Karsavina, centre; Igor Stravinsky, second from left, seated at the piano;
Michel Fokine leaning against piano, with score
State Museum of Theatre and Music, St Petersburg

Diaghilev's Ballets Russes: The First Phase

During the second half of the nineteenth century the art of ballet declined so much in the West that it all but disappeared, whereas in Russia it flourished in the Imperial Theatres, supported exclusively by the patronage of successive emperors and under the tutelage of the great 'classical' choreographer and teacher Marius Petipa, who worked in St Petersburg from 1847 until his death in 1910. He was largely responsible for creating the Russian dancer with the impeccable technique for which the Russians became, and still are, famous. But by thriving on its very success, ballet became trapped in outmoded convention.

Alexandre Benois first enthused Diaghilev about ballet when he took him to a performance of his *Pavillon d'Armide* at the Maryinsky Theatre in 1907, after which Diaghilev said to him: 'This must be shown to Europe'.[1] In 1850-1 Richard Wagner had stated in *The Work of Art of the Future*: 'The supreme work of art is the drama. Given that it can be perfect, it can, however, only exist when all the arts contained in it reach the highest perfection.' This is the idea of the *Gesamtkunstwerk* or synthesis of all the arts. Wagner had invented the music drama, but with Diaghilev, surprisingly, it was through ballet that he achieved his *Gesamtkunstwerk*. His sympathies were instinctively directed more towards opera, but he recognised from Benois's example that there was greater potential in ballet for creating the complete work of art. In a letter written in 1928, Diaghilev described his conversion to ballet while preparing for the 1909 Season in Paris: 'From Opera to Ballet is but a step. At that time there were more than 400 ballet dancers on the roster of the Imperial Theatres. They all had a remarkably good training, and they danced the traditional classical ballets.... I could not help observing, however, that among the younger members of the St Petersburg ballet, a sort of reaction to the classical tradition, which Petipa so jealously preserved, was beginning to make itself felt. From that moment, I began wondering whether it would be possible to create a number of short new ballets, which besides being of artistic value, would link the three main factors, music, decorative design, and choreography far more closely than ever before.'[2]

Diaghilev was not a creative artist, but he created the climate and the conditions in which the creative artists around him could work. The chosen medium, the theatre, is probably the most fickle because, by its very nature involving so many people in a single enterprise, it is constantly subject to compromise. The art of the theatre depends upon the skill of the impresario in minimising the compromise. Diaghilev was an impresario of genius. He was a master (often infuriating and

Le Pavillon d'Armide 1907
Hulton Deutsch Collection Limited, London

intractable) who manipulated the strands of theatre into a new form. The art of the theatre also depends upon luck, and Diaghilev was lucky in the group of people gathered around him.

Benois, although accustomed and attached to Petipa's 'classical' ideals of ballet, had been affected by Michel Fokine, his young choreographer of *Le Pavillon d'Armide*, who, considering those ideals to be old-fashioned, sought to modernise ballet by liberating it from the constraints of its rigid rules of mime and movement. Fokine later described the situation as he had found it and what was his own innovative idea: 'A story was taken and twisted by the choreographer until it would show off the most difficult *pas* of his *danseuses* to the best advantage.... The simple fact that the dance ought to be used not as an attraction interpolated in the ballet but as an actual means of telling the story, which is the basis of my reforms, was most unacceptable in the early days of the present century.'[3] As a revolutionary young student at the Imperial School, Fokine had submitted to the Director of the Imperial Theatres in 1904 a libretto for a ballet based on Longus' *Daphnis and Chloë* together with a plan setting out in detail his rules for the reform of ballet of which the following are the most pertinent: 'In the ballet the whole meaning of the story can be expressed by the dance.... The ballet must no longer be made up of "numbers", "entries" and so forth. It must show artistic unity of conception ... the ballet must have complete unity of expression, a unity which is made up of harmonious blending of the three elements – music, painting, and

plastic art.'[4] Fokine had reached the same conclusion as Diaghilev, only earlier. But *Daphnis and Chloë* was thrown into a cupboard along with the notes.[5] Fokine, undeterred, began to experiment with his ideas, using fellow students. It was ballet's good fortune that among the students were a number of young dancers who were of incomparable talent, and in sympathy with Fokine's ideas: among them Anna Pavlova, Tamara Karsavina, Vaslav Nijinsky and Adolph Bolm. The male dancer was beginning to be of equal, if not of more importance, than the ballerina.

Developing his ambition to 'show Russian art to the West', after his exhibitions and concerts, Diaghilev had first presented opera in Paris in 1908, a production of Mussorgsky's *Boris Godunov*,[6] introducing Fyodor Chaliapin in the title role. But with a choreographer who shared Diaghilev's artistic aspirations, with such talent available among dancers, with Russian composers providing suitable music, and with painters like Alexandre Benois and Léon Bakst, already experienced in working for the theatre designing sets and costumes, it was natural to include ballet as well as opera in the second Russian programme for Paris in 1909. Besides, ballet was also much cheaper, and logistically easier, than opera. Diaghilev hoped that his programme would again be subsidised by the Emperor. He therefore thought it prudent to include in his company Mathilde Kshessinska, *prima ballerina assoluta*[7] of the old school, ex-mistress of the Tsar, married to Grand Duke Andrei Vladimirovich, and extremely influential. But when she discovered that she was only to dance one role, Armida, she refused to accept the engagement and used her influence at court to have any intended subsidy withdrawn.[8] By withholding the subsidy from Diaghilev, Grand Duke Sergei Mikhailovich spitefully hoped that the Emperor 'would send the ballet company of the Imperial Theatres to Paris with Kshessinska at the head',[9] thus thwarting Diaghilev's plans. A more crucial factor, however, in the Emperor's sudden withdrawal of vital subsidy was the death, in February 1909, of Grand Duke Vladimir Alexandrovich, who had for some time been Diaghilev's loyal supporter. Diaghilev sensibly ignored all the court intrigues, and hastily approached his French impresario Gabriel Astruc for financial help in order to salvage the Season. Without Astruc the whole enterprise would have collapsed before it had even begun. Primarily a concert promoter, he nevertheless saw the artistic potential in Diaghilev's ideas. His whole life was inspired, as Robert Brussel wrote in an obituary, 'by the genuine ideals of journalism: to circulate quickly, with clarity, precision and truth new ideas which can create a change of opinion'.[10] Astruc wholeheartedly backed Diaghilev's ideas, and therefore quickly arranged, with the help of the Russian Embassy in Paris, adequate guarantees from financiers and bankers including Basil Zaharoff, Baron Henri de Rothschild, and the Banque de Paris et des Pays-Bas.[11] The project could continue.

In establishing the programme for the first Season of ballet, Diaghilev relied for the most part on a repertory of ballets, choreographed by Fokine, which had already been 'tried out' in St Petersburg. *Le Pavillon d'Armide*, based on a story by the French writer Théophile Gautier but with music by the Russian composer Nicholas Tcherepnine, opened the first evening on 18 May 1909,[12] a gala occasion which Astruc ensured, with his flair for publicity, that no member of Parisian society could afford to miss. He even filled the front row of the dress circle with pretty girls, alternately blonde and brunette. The expectation was eager. Richard Buckle wrote of the *pas de trois* in the second scene: 'The conquest of Europe by Russian dancing and the reign of Diaghilev as Director of the Ballets Russes can be said to begin at the moment Nijinsky takes the stage with his two partners.'[13] Tamara Karsavina, who was one of the partners (Alexandra Baldina was the other), remembered how 'Nijinsky should have walked off the stage to reappear in a solo. On that night he chose to leap off. He rose up, a few yards off the wings, described a parabola in the air, and disappeared from sight. No one in the audience could see him land; to all eyes he floated up and vanished. A storm of applause broke; the orchestra had to stop…. Once all reserve was thrown away, the evening worked up to a veritable frenzy of enthusiasm.'[14] Yet the response to *Le Pavillon d'Armide* was nothing compared to that given to the second ballet, the *Polovtsian Dances* from Alexander Borodin's opera *Prince Igor*. The passionate frenzy of Borodin's music and its interpretation by equally energetic and barbaric dancing, led by Adolph Bolm as the Chief Warrior, startled the Parisian audience into unbounded admiration. Fokine himself claimed it was one of his most important works showing the 'expressiveness of a group dance'.[15] Diaghilev, thereafter, could hardly afford to leave it out of his programmes.

Another Fokine ballet from the first season which Diaghilev had to revive almost every year in response to public demand was *Les Sylphides*. Diaghilev, deliberately recalling the famous romantic ballet of the 1830s, *La Sylphide*, gave this title to a ballet first performed in 1907 and revised for a charity performance in 1908. It was originally called *Chopiniana*, and used Chopin's music orchestrated by Alexander Glazunov.[16] A plotless ballet of intensely romantic feeing, it is the first instance of pure interpretation of music through movement, requiring immaculate technique on the part of all the dancers.

Cléopâtre was Diaghilev's new title for *Egyptian Nights*, first performed in 1908, which he agreed to include in the first Season provided it was strengthened musically. With his unerring sense of what was right (or wrong) he had pinpointed the two weaknesses of the ballet. Although it remained something of a musical hotch-potch,

Cléopâtre was another sensation. It introduced the startlingly exotic and blazingly colourful scenery [cat. 104] and costumes [cat. 103A–B] of Léon Bakst, the dancing of Anna Pavlova, Fokine himself, and, in the title role, Ida Rubinstein.[17] Bakst, who had already worked with Rubinstein, persuaded Diaghilev, against his better judgement, to cast her as Cleopatra. Very rich, besotted with the theatre but not trained as a dancer, she had nevertheless been taught privately by Fokine. Diaghilev did not regret his casting, as Rubinstein, not having to dance much, thrilled with her curiously androgynous sexual appeal. Benois, however, was not charmed by her 'in spite of her marvellous beauty. There is something mysterious about her, but she is cold and chilling. There is something intoxicating and refined about her, but in my view, depressing.'[18] The last item was a suite of dances from operas and ballets already familiar to the dancers, presented under the general title *Le Festin*, scrambled together because a new, purely Russian work had not materialised. Diaghilev, provocatively, had also wanted to present the purely French *Giselle* but this, too, had to be postponed.

The 1909 Season was an artistic triumph but a financial failure, a pattern that was repeated more or less every year. Diaghilev was left

Prince Igor: Adolph Bolm as the Polovtsian Warrior Chief, 1909
Hulton Deutsch Collection Limited, London

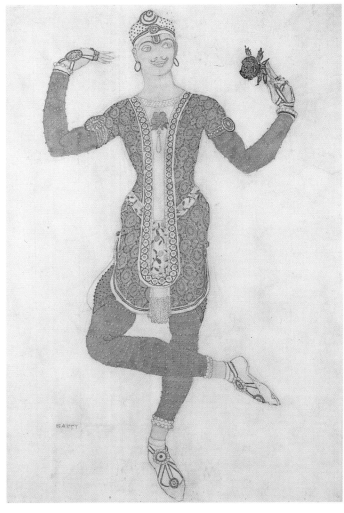

Léon Bakst:
Le Festin: **Costume design** 1909
Cat. 102

in debt to Astruc, who sequestered the scenery, costumes and props. Astruc then made a deal with Baron Raoul Gunsburg, a director of the Société de Monaco, who agreed to buy most of them for 20,000 francs but release them if Diaghilev repaid the debt by a certain date. Diaghilev found the money, as he always did, and the enterprise continued. In fact, Diaghilev never craved personal gain, so he did not see why any of his artists should be concerned about money, although he did make reasonable contracts with all his dancers except Nijinsky. He needed money exclusively for his productions. Since box-office receipts were never enough to cover costs, he would skip lightly from financial crisis to financial crisis, and, using his charm, would beguile rich, usually titled, ladies of Paris and London to subscribe to boxes for the season and part with necessary cheques. Among his most loyal supporters were Princesse Edmond de Polignac (née Winnaretta Singer), Comtesse Greffulhe, Lady Cunard and Lady Ripon. A friend who was always ready to help Diaghilev with a desperately needed cheque was Misia Edwards.[19] Known as the 'Godmother of the Russian Ballet', Diaghilev's relationship with her was as with a sister. According to Jacques-Emile Blanche, the painter of flamboyant portraits of both Nijinsky and Karsavina, 'it was her taste that decided whatever Diaghilev undertook, and he never embarked on a production without her sanction'.[20] Doubtless Blanche credited her with too much artistic authority, but there is no doubt that she was very influential in keeping Diaghilev financially afloat.

The first programme in many ways set the pattern for the choice of ballets in subsequent seasons. The exotic, spectacular and 'oriental' (that is, East of Suez rather than East of Calcutta) style set by Fokine with *Cléopâtre* was continued by him with *Schéhérazade* and *Les Orientales* in 1910, *Le Dieu Bleu* and *Thamar* in 1912. Fokine's romantic style of *Les Sylphides* was followed by *Carnaval* in 1910, *Le Spectre de la Rose* in 1911 and *Papillons* in 1914. The barbaric *Polovtsian Dances* foreshadowed *The Rite of Spring* of 1913. An innovation in 1911 was Bakst's Greek style with *Narcisse* [cat. 131A-J, 138] followed by *L'Après-midi d'un faune* and *Daphnis and Chloë* [cat. 135A-C, 136A-B] in 1912.

Schéhérazade has always been considered to be the epitome of the Ballets Russes. The first night on 4 June 1910 at the Grand Opéra (the company had graduated from the somewhat dilapidated Châtelet Theatre of the year before) was an occasion of the utmost artistic importance because *Schéhérazade* changed the way people considered the art of ballet. Nothing like it had ever been seen before. It was not just the dancing of Rubinstein as Zobéide, Nijinsky as the Golden Negro and Alexis Bulgakov as the Shah that was astounding, it was the whole production – music, décor, costumes, lighting – all combined

Léon Bakst:
Le Dieu Bleu: **Set design** 1911
Cat.133

into forty minutes of pure and overwhelming sensation, that made it so memorable. Good taste kept a fine balance between the exotic and the erotic and preserved its oriental Russian-ness from degenerating into kitsch. A critic wrote: 'Go and see the amorous orgy of the negroes and the sultan's wives, see the voluptuousness of the dances, the passionate frenzy of the gestures, attitudes, and intertwinings; compare these with the various scenes of orgy in our ballets; you will soon realise on which side lies the superiority.'[21] So instantly popular was this ballet that, with its repercussions in fashion and interior design, Diaghilev could have kept his company going profitably for years by always including *Schéhérazade* in his programme. But he chose not to. That was not his style. Diaghilev was never interested in profit, he was interested in art.

The promised 'purely Russian work' had to wait for the second season in 1910, when only ballets were presented. Diaghilev now made his greatest musical discovery. He commissioned the young Igor Stravinsky to compose a ballet on the theme of the Russian folk tale *The Firebird* after he had heard his *Feu d'artifice* at a concert. (Liadov, who had initially received the commission, only ever got as far as buying the music paper.) The first performance was on 25 June 1910; Tamara Karsavina created the Firebird, Fokine was Ivan Tsarevitch, his wife Vera the Tsarevna, and Bulgakov played the evil magician Koshchei.

Stravinsky followed the fantastical Russian-ness of *The Firebird* in 1910 with the burlesque Russian-ness of *Petrushka*, the story of the puppet with human feelings, in 1911. Written and designed by Alexandre Benois [cat. 141A–C, 142A–C], the ballet is set in St Petersburg during the Butter Week Fair around 1830. Fokine created a choreography in which the crowd at the Fair is never treated as a single *corps de ballet* but as groups of individuals with their own personalities. The choreography for the four main protagonists, Petrushka, the Ballerina, the Moor and the showman, played respectively by Nijinsky, Karsavina, Alexander Orlov and Enrico Cecchetti, also reflects their characters. In *Petrushka*, dance is not used as an end in itself but as a means of psychological expression. It is not really a ballet, and succeeded primarily because Nijinsky was able convincingly to interpret Stravinsky's and Fokine's intentions. Stravinsky himself paid 'heartfelt homage to Vaslav Nijinsky's unsurpassed rendering of the role of Petroushka [sic]. The perfection with which he became the very incarnation of this character was all the more remarkable because the purely saltatory work in which he usually excelled was in this case definitely dominated by dramatic action, music, and gesture.'[22]

Nijinsky was a dancer whose art appears to be inexplicable. No single description among the volumes of praise seems adequate.

Henri Gaudier-Brzeska:
The Firebird: **Tamara Karsavina and Adolph Bolm** 1912
Cat.124

Even his own famous (though alleged) response about his elevation: 'I jump, I stay up there for a while, and then I come down', does not explain the secret of his art. Yet the contemporary comments to the effect that not only was his technique so perfect as to be unnoticeable, but also that he could by turn transform himself, and not by make-up alone, into the essence of a rose in *Le Spectre de la Rose*, or a faun in *L'Après-midi d'un faune*, or a straw puppet with a heart in *Petrushka*, persuade one to believe that indeed there was never another dancer like Nijinsky. Diaghilev, keen to promote him as a choreographer as well, encouraged him, with Bakst's help, to arrange the choreography for *L'Après-midi d'un faune* and hoped he would replace Fokine. More than a hundred rehearsals over a period of nearly two years were needed for this twelve-minute work and, although Nijinsky's ideas for the movements based on profiles on Greek friezes and vase painting were revolutionary, the dancers found them almost impossible to execute. Louis Vuillemin was obviously unaware of the dancers' difficulties but acknowledged the aptness of the choreography. 'M. Nijinsky is one of the most sensitive, intelligent and musical artists. At first sight the gestures and attitudes of the nymphs and Faun are strange, but they work like a charm. They follow and reflect, if I may venture to say so, every modulation, sweep, flight and reticence of the music.'[23] On the first night, the final moment of the ballet, when Nijinsky as the Faun made love to a scarf discarded by one of the nymphs, scandalised the audience. Diaghilev mischievously mistook the boos for cheers and ordered the ballet to be repeated immediately.

Nijinsky's other two ballets, *Jeux* and *The Rite of Spring*, caused even greater difficulties for the dancers. The first performance of *The Rite of Spring* on 29 May 1913 created a riot in the audience, caused not by Nijinsky's choreography but by Stravinsky's music. Stravinsky, disgusted by the demonstrations, remembered that 'during the whole performance I was at Nijinsky's side in the wings. He was standing on a chair, screaming "sixteen, seventeen, eighteen" – they had their own method of counting to keep time.'[24]

Jean Cocteau:
**Poster for
Ballets Russes:
Vaslav Nijinsky**
in *Le Spectre de la Rose*
1911
Cat.147

Petrushka: Tamara Karsavina, Vaslav Nijinsky,
Alexander Orlov and Enrico Cecchetti 1911
Bibliothèque Nationale, Paris

Although *The Rite of Spring* was only performed eight times, Nijinsky's genius as a choreographer was soon acknowledged. As Karsavina pointed out: 'In these two works of his, Nijinsky declared his feud against Romanticism and bid adieu to the "beautiful".'[25] However, instead of replacing Fokine, he was dismissed by an enraged Diaghilev when in 1913 he suddenly married a Hungarian girl, Romola de Pulszky. Fokine had to be recalled to choreograph Richard Strauss's *La Légende de Joseph* in 1914, in which the title role was played by the young Léonide Massine, who would shortly replace Fokine as the Company's main choreographer and initiate the second era of the Ballets Russes.

As early as 1895 Diaghilev had announced that he had found his true vocation: to be a patron of the arts. Until 1914 Diaghilev was essentially a patron of Russian art and Russian artists.[26] Usually through sensible discussion and civilised argument, though sometimes after violent tantrums and bitter quarrels, the 'impossibiliste'[27] Diaghilev nurtured the talents of his artists, the choreographer Fokine, the composer Stravinsky, the designer Bakst, the dancers Nijinsky, Karsavina and all the others until they blossomed as no other group of artists ever had before. Together they reinvented the art of ballet and ensured its continuance. Many of the ballets in their original form are still in the repertory of major dance companies throughout the world.

Léon Bakst:
Jeux: **Set design** 1913
Cat.137

On 29 April 1993 I was in the Royal Opera House in Stockholm when the curtain went up on the first performance of a revival of *Schéhérazade* in the original set which had been stored there, unused since 1914. When the curtain rose up to reveal Bakst's famous harem set of blues and greens, and reds and pinks, and yellow and gold, and the thrilling dancing began, the whole audience burst spontaneously into clamorous applause. I understood why. The effect made the spine tingle, and I appreciated what the audience must have felt at the Opéra in Paris in 1910.

1. Quoted in Alexandre Benois, *Reminiscences of the Russian Ballet*, London, 1941, p. 266.
2. Quoted in Serge Lifar, *Serge Diaghilev*, London, 1940, pp. 176–7. Lifar did not say to whom this letter was addressed.
3. Quoted by The Sitter Out in *The Dancing Times*, December 1921, p. 178.
4. Cyril W. Beaumont, *Michel Fokine and His Ballets*, London, 1945, p. 23.
5. *Daphnis and Chloë* was eventually and reluctantly produced by Diaghilev in 1912 with Nijinsky, Karsavina and Bolm, and sets and costumes by Léon Bakst. Fokine, exasperated by the treatment he had received, resigned from the company.

6. In the version orchestrated by Rimsky-Korsakov.
7. The only dancer, apart from Pierina Legnani, ever to be given the title.
8. Kshessinska later made it up with Diaghilev and danced in the company's first season in London in 1911.
9. Vladimir Teliakovsky, *Vospominaniia*, Leningrad, Moscow, 1965, p. 63.
10. Robert Brussel, 'Gabriel Astruc: mars 1864–juillet 1938' in *Revue Musicale* September–November 1938, no. 186, p. 113: 'par le véritable idéal du journalisme: répandre rapidement, avec clarté, précision et vérité les idées nouvelles capables de créer un mouvement d'opinion.'

11. The principal guarantors according to Lynn Garafola, *Diaghilev's Ballets Russes*, New York, 1989, p. 173.
12. Called the '*Répétition générale publique*' or Public Dress Rehearsal, often a grander occasion than the official first night, which in this case was on 19 May.
13. Richard Buckle, *Diaghilev*, London, 1979, p. 141.
14. Tamara Karsavina, *Theatre Street*, London, 1948, pp. 197–8.
15. Michel Fokine, *Memoirs of a Ballet Master*, London, 1961, p. 148.
16. It consists of a Prelude (op. 28, no. 7) played as an overture, a Nocturne (op. 32, no. 2) danced by the company, followed by a Waltz (op. 70, no. 1) danced by a *première danseuse*, Mazurka (op. 33, no. 2) danced by the prima ballerina, another Mazurka

(op. 67, no. 3) for the *premier danseur*, a repeat of the Prelude danced by another *première danseuse*, a Waltz (op. 64, no. 2) as a *pas de deux*, and the final Grand Waltz (op. 18, no. 1) for the full company.
17. Both Pavlova and Rubinstein left Diaghilev after 1910 to start their own companies.
18. Alexandre Benois, *Rech'*, 8 July 1909.
19. Polish by birth, her maiden name was Godebska. She married a succession of rich husbands, first Thadée Natanson, founder and editor of *La Revue Blanche*, then Alfred Edwards, the owner of *Le Matin*. She then married the Spanish painter José-Maria Sert, who would design the sets for *La Légende de Joseph*.

20. Jacques-Emile Blanche, *Portraits of a Lifetime*, London, 1937, p. 262.
21. Quoted in Cyril W. Beaumont, *Michel Fokine and His Ballets*, London, 1945, p. 62.
22. Igor Stravinsky, *Chronicle of My Life*, London, 1936, p. 61.
23. Louis Vuillemin in *Comoedia illustré*, 30 May 1912, p. 2: 'M. Nijinsky compte parmi les artistes les plus sensibles, les plus intelligents, et aussi les plus musiciens. Etranges d'abord, le geste, l'attitude des nymphes – ou du Faune – opèrent à la façon d'un charme. Ils épousent, ils reflètent, si j'ose ainsi dire, chacune des inflexions, des courbes, des envolées, des réticences, de la musique.'
24. Igor Stravinsky, op. cit. p. 81.

25. Tamara Karsavina op. cit. p. 236.
26. Although he had already commissioned the French composers Ravel, Debussy and Reynaldo Hahn, after 1914, Diaghilev began to commission many more Western artists, dancers and composers.
27. A sobriquet invented by Alexandre Benois.

Valentin Serov:
Schéhérazade: **Design for the front cloth** 1910
Cat.129

Diaghilev's Unruly Dance Family

On 22 July 1910, at the end of Diaghilev's second Paris ballet Season, Lydia Lopokova, his first 'baby ballerina', wrote to Alexander Krupensky, the head of the St Petersburg office of the Imperial Theatres:

> Much respected Alexander Dmitrievich!
> Your benevolence towards me provides the reason to narrate what has happened to me: thanks to my success in Berlin and Paris, different agents began to approach me, inviting me to various cities and various countries; the propositions were very tempting, but I refused them all, remembering that, after all I have attained, I should be grateful to the School and to you.... And now, imagine what has been done to me. Surrounded and prevailed upon on all sides, I signed a contract for New York. The next day I changed my mind; I cried; God knows what I would give for this not to have happened … but the agents are like Cerberuses to my soul, and the consequences of not fulfilling the contract would be horrible to me … I beg of you to give me a leave of absence.[1]

Although Lopokova got her leave, she never returned to the Mary-insky. Nor did she return to the Ballets Russes, except when the Company followed her to America more than five years later.

Lopokova was not the first dancer to break away from the Diaghilev family, nor was she unique in striking out on her own. From the end of its very first Season, the Company witnessed a long line of 'defections' and dismissals that over the years included practically all its stellar figures as well as numerous lesser lights. Although some returned to Russia, many more chose to remain in the West, even in the years before 1917. For this second group, which included not only Lopokova, but also Anna Pavlova, Ida Rubinstein and the Kosloff brothers, the West was the fabled land of opportunity. Gold and international stardom were there for the taking, and the chance to remake oneself as an artist. For the ambitious, the pastures of the West were not only greener than those at home; they were also greener than those offered by the Ballets Russes.

For Ida Rubinstein, who abandoned the Ballets Russes at the same time as Lopokova, the lure was neither money nor stardom. Independently wealthy and already a celebrity, she left the Company because of what she perceived as Diaghilev's refusal to acknowledge her ambitions as an artist. Unlike the vast majority of his dancers, Rubinstein lacked professional ballet training. She had studied at the Imperial Theatre Schools of Moscow and St Petersburg, but in their

drama rather than dance departments: her professional training was that of an actress enriched, beginning in 1907, by private tuition with choreographer Michel Fokine. As a student, she had appeared in a number of plays, including *A Winter's Tale*, *Macbeth*, *Mary Stuart* and *Richard III*, all presented that year as examination performances.[2]

Her ambitions, however, extended far beyond those of a conventional actress. Already, in 1904, she had persuaded Georgii Ozarovsky, a director of the Alexandrinsky Theatre with whom she was studying privately, to stage Sophocles' *Antigone* for her. For this production, a forerunner of the more than thirty ballets, plays and mime-dramas that she would bring to the stage by 1939, she not only played the title role but also enlisted the collaboration of Léon Bakst and choreography from Fokine in a partnership that anticipated Diaghilev's 'method' and called on two of his most celebrated artists.

Léon Bakst:
Portrait of Ida Rubinstein 1913
Cat.167

Valentin Serov:
Sketch of Ida Rubinstein as Cleopatra *c.*1910
Cat.116

Although the play was banned by the Imperial censor shortly before its première, the Dance of the Seven Veils became the vehicle for Rubinstein's début as an art dancer on both the concert and music-hall stage.

As the list of Rubinstein's own projects makes clear, antiquity interested her as much as orientalist subject matter. Her usefulness to Diaghilev, however, lay exclusively in her identity as an exotic. In the title role of *Cléopâtre* and as Zobéide in *Schéhérazade*, the only parts he allowed her to play, she was an idol of perverse and deadly sexuality, a voluptuous dominatrix in the veils and semi-undress of orientalist fantasy. Her foil was Vaslav Nijinsky, transformed from a *danseur* of conventional masculinity into a pantherine creature destroyed by the thrilling – and misogynist – combination of female power and sexuality.

Rubinstein left the Company because, as Prince Peter Lieven claims she told Diaghilev, she was 'bored by … caresses, embraces, and stabbing herself'.[3] Well aware (at this time, at least) of her limitations as a dancer, she knew equally well that Diaghilev's interest in unconventional roles embraced neither female heroes (many of whom she would impersonate in the years to come) nor male heroes *en travestie* (several of whom she would also impersonate). The chance to play one such male role in *Le Martyre de Saint Sébastien*, a mime-drama in verse written for her by Gabriele d'Annunzio and the first of a half-dozen collaborations with the Italian poet, prompted her to leave the Ballets Russes (although she subsequently appeared with the Company in Monte Carlo and at a post-war Paris gala). Her departure marked the beginning of a long career in France as an actress and a dancer, chiefly in works that she also commissioned and produced. In 1928, moreover, she launched her own ballet company, Les Ballets de Madame Ida Rubinstein, which drew on many Diaghilev veterans,

while introducing dancers and choreographers who would come to the fore in the 1930s.

Although it is easy to ascribe Rubinstein's difficulties with Diaghilev to her limitations as a classical dancer, Anna Pavlova's abandonment of the Ballets Russes suggests that those difficulties at least partly arose from an unwillingness on his part to accommodate the needs of any of his female dancers, regardless of technical accomplishment. The flower of her generation at the Maryinsky, a legendary Giselle, and Fokine's earliest muse, Pavlova was theoretically the star of Diaghilev's first ballet season. At the Maryinsky she had already figured in most of the choreographer's offerings: *Les Sylphides* (or *Chopiniana*, as it was called in Russia), *Le Pavillon d'Armide* and *Cléopâtre* (or *Egyptian Nights*, as it was initially called). And she came to Paris, unlike the vast majority of Diaghilev's dancers, with touring experience and the beginnings of an international reputation.

Arriving in Paris after the Season was well under way, she discovered to her chagrin that her absence was hardly missed. Others had eclipsed her – Tamara Karsavina, who had danced most of her roles,

Anna Pavlova in *Giselle* 1903
State Museum of Theatre and Music, St Petersburg

and Nijinsky, the *Wunderkind* of the season, who had dazzled the public and walked away with most of the publicity. As it happened, Diaghilev had fallen in love with Nijinsky, and with characteristic energy, set about remaking the Company in his image. At a Paris Opéra gala in June 1909, the last-minute replacement of Pavlova dancing the title role in *Giselle* with Nijinsky dancing a prominent part in *Les Sylphides* and *Le Festin*, a suite of divertissements, served as notice of the subordinate position that Diaghilev intended her to occupy in his future enterprise. Not even the promise of *The Firebird* and *Giselle*, both of which Diaghilev produced the following year, could induce her to return to the fold.

Pavlova had no intention of playing second fiddle to Nijinsky (or any male dancer, for that matter), and she certainly did not see herself as the dominatrix that numerous Diaghilev scenarios called for. Moreover, she had parleyed her success in Paris into lucrative and prestigious engagements at New York's Metropolitan Opera House and London's Palace Theatre. In London, especially, she was a triumph. Her seasons lengthened from weeks to months, the beginning of a twenty-year love affair with the British public. It was in London, in the autumn of 1911, that she briefly rejoined the Ballets Russes. This time she had the upper hand: Diaghilev needed ballerinas for his productions of *Giselle* and *Swan Lake*. Pavlova made several appearances that Season, dancing not only *Giselle* (although the first-night performances went to the loyal Karsavina) but also *Les Sylphides*, *Cléopâtre*, *Le Pavillon d'Armide* and Fokine's *Carnaval* – all to acclaim, although critics liked neither the music nor the old-fashioned choreography of *Giselle*. After this Season, she took leave of Diaghilev for good.

The Company that Pavlova now launched was in many ways the antithesis of the Ballets Russes, even if it ended, like the Diaghilev enterprise, with its founder's death. Female- rather than male-centred, serving the needs of its star rather than embodying the visions of its director, the Pavlova Ballet Russe remained faithful to Fokine's earliest principles and to selected aspects of Maryinsky tradition and repertoire. Like Diaghilev, she favoured one-act ballets, although in her case the category embraced old as well as new works – Petipa's *Halt of the Cavalry*, *The Awakening of Flora*, the 'Grand Pas Hongrois' from *Raymonda*, Lev Ivanov's *Magic Flute*, the Legat brothers' *Fairy Doll*. She offered versions of *Coppélia*, *Don Quixote*, *La Fille Mal Gardée* and numerous revivals of *Giselle*, the last in 1930, the year before she died. Apart from Diaghilev's production of *The Sleeping Beauty* in 1921, which made a lasting impression on British audiences, it was Pavlova's offerings from the Maryinsky repertoire that revealed the treasures of Russian classicism to the West.

Although the Pavlova Company largely eschewed the modern-

Giselle: Vaslav Nijinsky as Albrecht, 1909
Victoria and Albert Museum, London

ism of its Diaghilev counterpart, Pavlova herself was a new kind of ballerina. Even apart from the expressiveness that differentiated her stylistically from the period's old-school ballerinas, she was unique in choosing to remain independent of established organisations. After 1910, she retained only the most tenuous links with the institution that had formed her. As one of the privileged few to enjoy the rank and prestige of a Maryinsky ballerina, she had much to lose by going her own way. She also had much to gain: money, international fame, the opportunity to dance as often as she liked and in an environment free of bureaucratic routine and intrigue.

As the Maryinsky's *prima ballerina assoluta*, Mathilde Kshessinska had even less to gain than Pavlova from throwing in her lot with Diaghilev. A dazzling technician, superb mime and compelling onstage personality, Kshessinska danced most of the Maryinsky's greatest classical roles – Aspicia in *The Daughter of Pharaoh*, Aurora in *The Sleeping Beauty*, Odette/Odile in *Swan Lake*, Lise in *La Fille mal gardée*, Nikiya in *La Bayadère*, the title role in *Esmeralda*. Her talents

Mathilde Kshessinska at home *c*.1911
Central State Archive of Cinema and Photo Documents, St Petersburg

appearances in *Coppélia* and *La Korrigane* did not go unnoticed, nor the *Coppélia* she danced at the Opéra the following year; but compared to the publicity that attended *Boris Godunov* and the extraordinary interest aroused by Diaghilev's first ballet Season, they were events of distinctly minor importance.[5] Clearly, his stock had risen since being fired from the Maryinsky eight years before. If Kshessinska could not upstage or rival him at his own game, she had better join him.

Thus, in 1911, she accepted with alacrity his invitation to dance *Swan Lake* in London, even if she had to share the ballet with Karsavina, already a favourite with British audiences. In London, Kshessinska was as unknown as she had been in Paris. But with the single-minded ambition that kept her enthroned at the top of the Maryinsky hierarchy, she set out to dazzle the British capital with furs, diamonds, parties and an entourage at the Savoy. In *Le Pavillon d'Armide* she wore her famous sapphires, while in *Swan Lake* she had the Russian violinist Mischa Elman play the adagio solo in the lakeside scene, as well as the Kadletz music for the variation she had insisted on interpolating. She also danced in *Carnaval*, where her success was considerably greater than in *Swan Lake* or the Third-Act *pas de deux* from *The Sleeping Beauty* that she chose for her début. For critics enamoured of the fluidity and expressiveness of Fokine's 'new ballet', the virtuosity of Petipa's 'old ballet' and the academic style of its most brilliant exponent seemed cold and wanting in beauty.[6] Diaghilev himself was sufficiently impressed with Kshessinska's performance in *Swan Lake* that he invited her to repeat it in Monte Carlo the following spring, again with Nijinsky as her partner.[7] And when he revived the ballet in the 1920s, he had her coach some of the Company's younger dancers.

Diaghilev never 'broke' with Kshessinska, as he did with so many of his artistic colleagues, because she was never central to his vision of the Company: he used her for what she was when it suited his purpose – exactly as she used him. By contrast, his relationship with Fokine, who supplied the vast majority of the Company's new works up to 1914, ended in a bitterness that neither of the parties ever forgave or forgot. After the First World War, the two never spoke, never wrote, or otherwise communicated, despite revivals of the choreographer's works and their presence on the Ballets Russes programmes until the Company's demise. Probably no episode in Diaghilev's career shows his ruthlessness as an artistic director in so naked a light as his relationship with Fokine.

Unlike Alexandre Benois and Léon Bakst, whose friendship with Diaghilev dated from the 1890s, Fokine was a latecomer to Diaghilev's circle. Indeed, it was Benois, the librettist of *Le Pavillon d'Armide*, rather than 'Sergei Pavlovich', as Fokine still called

extended beyond the stage. She had a choice collection of lovers that included Tsar Nicholas II (before he ascended the throne), his cousin, Grand Duke Sergei, and another cousin, Grand Duke André (by whom she had a son), liaisons that made her rich and a power behind the scenes. Crossing her could be dangerous. When Prince Sergei Volkonsky dared to fine her for refusing to wear the costume assigned for her role in *Camargo*, Nicholas himself ordered the fine rescinded, an act that prompted Volkonsky to resign as director of the Imperial Theatres.[4] No wonder Diaghilev, taken on by Volkonsky as a special assistant, treated her warily.

Although a star at home, Kshessinska was unknown abroad, as the Imperial Ballet never toured. However, in 1908, with Diaghilev's production of *Boris Godunov* in the offing at the Paris Opéra, she decided to add some guest performances there to her laurels. Her

Carnaval: Michel Fokine as the Harlequin 1910
Bibliothèque Nationale, Paris

Diaghilev in 1908, who first informed the choreographer of plans for a ballet Season in Paris the following year.[8] At this point, Diaghilev obviously needed Fokine; his work was not only familiar but, in its innovative approach to ballet dramaturgy and form, also attuned to the artistic ideas of the Diaghilev circle. Moreover, his ballets were extraordinarily successful. Critics raved about them, and impresarios vied to engage both the stars who danced them and the celebrity choreographer who made them. Vast sums were offered and, in many cases accepted, although Fokine himself remained loyal to Diaghilev. Every Season now brought at least three new commissions, in addition to assignments at the Maryinsky, where Fokine's choreographic worth was enhanced by his success abroad.

In 1911, with the formation of his own Company, Diaghilev (as his *régisseur*, Sergei Grigoriev, later wrote) 'shelved' Fokine as a dancer, so as to 'obviate any rivalry between him and Nijinsky'.

To sweeten the pill, Diaghilev offered the choreographer a two-year contract at a 'very high salary' and agreed to Fokine's demand for the title of 'Choreographic Director'.[9] Within months, this position would also be in jeopardy and again because of Nijinsky, the first of the choreographers groomed by Diaghilev to give form to his ideas at a critical moment of artistic change. In 1912, when Diaghilev first opened the door to Modernism, the price of such change was Fokine.

Diaghilev did not actually dismiss Fokine, but in lavishing most of his attention on Nijinsky's *L'Après-midi d'un faune* to the detriment of Fokine's works, especially *Daphnis and Chloë* (which, like *Faune*, had a distinguished score and a Grecian setting and was thus a potential rival to Nijinsky's ballet), he virtually forced him to resign. In doing so, Diaghilev made it clear to Fokine that he considered his choreography uninteresting and passé. He also made it clear, by deed if not by word, that he brooked no criticism of his sexual politics, even when these threw the Company into havoc and undermined the well-being of the vast majority of its dancers.

Nijinsky's tenure as choreographer was brief. In the autumn of 1913, while touring with the Company in South America, he married Romola de Pulzsky. Diaghilev, who had remained in Europe, dismissed him: his rage was fully the equal of his former love. Then, with an effrontery that virtually defies belief, he telephoned Fokine, and after a conversation that went on for five hours (!), persuaded the choreographer to return to the Company. By all accounts, the 1914 Season was peaceful behind the scenes, even if only *Le Coq d'Or* was an unqualified success. Nijinsky's ballets were dropped, and Fokine stepped into most of the dancer's roles. For *La Légende de Joseph*, however, Diaghilev engaged a handsome young dancer from the Bolshoi Theatre. His name, suitably gallicised, was Léonide Massine. Diaghilev was much taken with him; Massine, for his part, was talented and intellectually curious, attributes that appealed to Diaghilev's passion for mentorship. He took the youngster's education in hand and promoted him to his inner circle. Within little more than a year Massine had created his first ballet.

There is no record of Diaghilev formally 'breaking' with Fokine in 1914. At the conclusion of the Season the choreographer returned to Russia where he remained for the duration of the war. In 1915, with an American tour in the offing, Grigoriev, on Diaghilev's instructions, spoke to Fokine about rejoining the Company. Fokine declined, saying that he could not leave Russia in wartime. This may well have been the truth, although it is also possible that he had learned of Massine's early choreographic efforts and, fearing a repeat of the humiliating Nijinsky episode, refused to become entangled in another of Diaghilev's artistic triangles. Certainly, after leaving Russia in 1918, he made no effort to

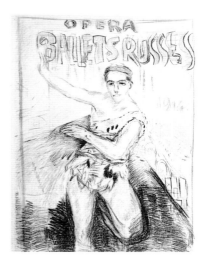

Pierre Bonnard:
La Légende de Joseph:
**Study for the poster
featuring
Léonide Massine**
*c.*1914
Cat.145

for extended periods, as in that of Fokine. Moreover, even when 'defectors' like Pavlova and Rubinstein rejected key elements of Diaghilev's aesthetic, they incorporated others that identified their enterprises with the larger movement brought into existence by the Ballets Russes. Finally, none, including Fokine, viewed their association with the Ballets Russes as anything less than a badge of honour. For better or for worse, they were Diaghilev artists.

contact Diaghilev, as so many émigrés did, nor did their paths cross in Paris in 1921, when Fokine restaged *Daphnis and Chloë* at the Opéra. By then, he had settled in New York and would visit Europe only occasionally during the following decade.

   Although some of Fokine's ballets failed to survive the First World War, many more did. Indeed, in the mid-1920s, there was a revival of interest in his work, especially in England, and several of his most popular ballets returned to repertoire. At no time, however, did Diaghilev ever consult Fokine, or invite him to coach, freshen up or refurbish his ballets, even when the addition of new designs (as in the case of *The Firebird*) entailed changes in staging. And he certainly never asked Fokine for permission to re-do large chunks of his creations, including the *Polovtsian Dances*, which Bronislava Nijinska extensively revised in 1923.[10] Although Fokine's works remained a foundation of the later Ballets Russes repertoire, the choreographer himself was banished from the Company.

   For all the bitterness that attended his estrangement from Diaghilev, the Ballets Russes changed Fokine's life, as it did for practically everyone who passed through the Company's ranks. However well known Pavlova, Fokine and Rubinstein may have been in Russia, it was their association with Diaghilev that made them stars of the international marketplace and thus able to pursue celebrity careers in the West. For dancers of lesser stature, too, the Ballets Russes proved a turnstile to careers on three continents, the beginnings of a diaspora that would change the face of ballet throughout the world.

   As remarkable as Diaghilev's ability to ferret out talent was his penchant for alienating the artists who served him. Still many returned to him, sometimes only briefly, as in the case of Pavlova, sometimes

1. Lydia Lopokova, Letter to A.D. Krupensky, 22 July 1910, fond 497, op. 5, ed. khr. 1866, Central State Historical Archive, St Petersburg.
2. For the curriculum, teaching personnel, and Rubinstein's grades at the Moscow Theatre School, as well as her transfer to its St Petersburg counterpart, see 'Vedomosti ob ispytaniakh uchashchikhsia Dramaticheskikh Kursov 1901–1908' (Official Bulletin of the School Examinations in the Drama Department 1901–1908), TsGALI, fond 682 (Moscow Theatre School), op. 1, ed. khr. 192. In a letter to Akim Volynsky inviting him to attend the examination performances, Rubinstein noted that she appeared 'in one act of each play' (TsGALI, fond 95 [Volynsky], op. 1, ed. khr. 761, 1. 49–50).
3. Prince Peter Lieven, *The Birth of Ballets-Russes*, trans. L. Zarine, London, 1936, p. 119.
4. This incident is described in Prince Serge Wolkonsky, *My Reminiscences* (trans. A.E. Chamot), London, 1925, II, pp. 98–110.

5. In 1908, *Figaro* published a front-page article about the ballerina by Robert Brussel ('La Vie de Paris: Mathilde Kchesinska', *Figaro*, 22 May 1908, p. 1), in addition to listing her performances (among the Opéra's daily offerings) in the theatre column. According to the same column, 'the Opéra's entire *corps de ballet*, from the *premiers sujets* to the *rats*' attended the last rehearsal before her début and gave her an 'ovation that lasted several minutes' ('Courrier des Théâtres', *Figaro*, 23 May 1908, p. 4), while after her last performance, she sent flowers and sweets to 'all her colleagues in the ballet who had danced with her' ('Courrier des Théâtres', *Figaro*, 12 June 1908, p. 6). In 1909, Olga Preobrajenska, the Maryinsky's other senior ballerina and Kshessinska's main rival for the affections of the St Petersburg audience, danced two guest performances of *Javotte* at the Opéra ('Courrier des Théâtres', *Figaro*, 20 May 1909, p. 6). Kshessinska herself had apparently intended to postpone her return to Paris until the following year (that is, 1910), when, as *Figaro* announced, 'she will come … with the approval of the Imperial Court and accompanied by all her colleagues, the two hundred *danseuses* of the Maryinsky Theatre' ('Courrier des Théâtres', *Figaro*, 20 April 1909, p. 7). This undertaking never materialised.

6. For Kshessinska's press coverage and critical responses to *Swan Lake*, see Nesta Macdonald, *Diaghilev Observed by Critics in England and the United States 1911–1929*, New York, 1975, pp. 55–63.
7. Cyril W. Beaumont, *The Ballet Called Swan Lake*, London, 1952; rpt. New York, 1982, p. 151.
8. Michel Fokine, Letter to Alexandre Benois, 28 June 1908. In M. Fokine, *Protiv Techeniia: Vospominaniia baletmeistera, stat'i, pis'ma*, ed. and introd. Yuri Slonimskii, Leningrad, 1962, pp. 480–1.
9. S.L. Grigoriev, *The Diaghilev Ballet 1909–1929*, trans. and ed. Vera Bowen, London, 1953, pp. 43, 45.
10. In April 1923, according to programmes for the company's Monte Carlo season, the ballet's *'deux premières danses'* were by Nijinska and the *'grand ensemble final'* by Fokine. In March 1924, when the ballet was performed in Monte Carlo as part of the opera *Prince Igor*, the 'first dance' was by Nijinska and the 'final ensemble' by Fokine; it was given in this form the following spring (on ballet as well as opera programmes) as well as in April–May 1926.

The Diaghilev Seasons and the Early Russian Avant-Garde

On 24 May 1914 the ballet *Le Coq d'Or*, staged by Michel Fokine to the music of Rimsky-Korsakov, opened at the Paris Opéra. For the first time the masters of the World of Art group, with whom, till now, Diaghilev had invariably worked, had not been commissioned to design the setting and costumes; they were the work of Natalia Goncharova [cat. 155A–B, 156, 157], a young Moscow artist representing the newest tendency in painting, a movement which would become known as the Russian avant-garde.

She was invited on the initiative of Benois, who had seen and admired her work at her exhibition in 1913. From the end of the 1900s and into the beginning of the next decade the artist had been attracted by Russian icons and the *lubok* (popular woodcut). At her exhibition she showed works that reflected the spirit of both. All of them were permeated by an interest in 'primitive cultures', an expressive tendency towards antiquity and the Orient. In Benois's own words, 'Goncharova's "concentration of colour" makes one dream of whole cathedrals that might be ornamented by such radiant painting.'[1] Some of the canvases revealed in the artist not only the potential monumentalist but the stage designer. If the colours of her *Evangelists* literally 'shone' with intensity from the darkness, in *Peacock in Bright Sunlight* they blazed with a fierce fire.

Diaghilev, who had not attended this exhibition, set off for Moscow, to see the artist's work in her studio. He was impressed both by her paintings and by the sketches for *Le Coq d'Or*, made in the winter of 1913-14.[2] He recognised at once that there was something in Goncharova's evolution during this period which matched his own artistic aims. The artists and musicians of the Diaghilev enterprise were attracted no less than Goncharova, though in a different manner, by the primeval power of 'primitive cultures'. This attraction is apparent in Roerich's décor, both for the *Polovtsian Dances* from Borodin's opera *Prince Igor* [cat. 112] and for Stravinsky's *Rite of Spring* [cat. 162A–C]; it is revealed even more clearly in the Stravinsky score itself, in the dances of the crowds in *Petrushka*, in the mass-movements of *The Rite of Spring*, where it seemed as though the lust for freedom of the earth itself had been awakened.

There is 'primitivism', too, in Rimsky-Korsakov's *Coq d'Or*, the music of which was used in the Seasons even before the 1914 production.[3] The figure of Tsar Dodon, amongst others, is characterised by the simplified outlines of the *lubok*; the composer based his 'love aria' on the theme of a well-known *chastushka*, a popular piece of humorous doggerel, about a little songbird; its 'stupid insistence' on two or three intervals carries musical naïveté to the extreme. Fokine adopted the same idiom in his choreography. He too was inspired, he said, by all the things that Goncharova loved so much; the *lubok*, the little hand-made toys, the conventions of the icon, the traditions of the embroidered wall-hanging. '*But most of all he listened to the music. From it he derived the primitive, doll-like, crudely-painted tinsel kingdom of Dodon*'[4] [author's italics].

Another link between Goncharova and the artists of the *Saisons russes* was their shared enthusiasm for the theme of 'the East'. The Diaghilev Company wanted to show to the 'effete West' a unified Russian-Oriental element, vivid and immediate in movement and feeling. The *corps de ballet* of St Petersburg's Maryinsky Theatre thrilled French audiences with their appearances as Polovtsians, or the odalisques of an Eastern harem, while Bakst specialised in creating

Natalia Goncharova:
Le Coq d'Or: **Costume design for a Russian Peasant** 1914
Victoria and Albert Museum, London

Alexandre Golovine:
The Firebird: **Costume design** 1909–10
Cat.125B

costumes for voluptuous slaves and eunuchs, or for Cleopatra and her retinue of women. The *Polovtsian Dances, Cléopâtre* and *Schéhérazade* were performed every Season with unvarying success; Ida Rubinstein, dancing in the two last-named ballets, never ceased to amaze the Parisians with her uniquely oriental appearance.

The Diaghilev company even made use of oriental imagery in works on Russian themes. The Firebird in the Stravinsky-Fokine ballet had flown from Eastern gardens, and Tamara Karsavina danced the role in flowing oriental trousers. Petrushka, in the ballet of that name by Stravinsky, became the victim of a Moor. The East in Russian tales was alternately alluring and cruel, just as it was in the productions based on oriental themes. Rimsky-Korsakov's *Le Coq d'Or* was close, in some respects, to that same tradition, although the Firebird who, in the Fokine-Stravinsky ballet, was a combination of bird and woman, presented here a divided image, half golden-plumed bird, half oriental maiden – the Queen of Shemakha.[5] Even in Pushkin, from whom Rimsky-Korsakov had taken his subject, and in the opera itself, the

oriental queen and the astrologer enter into a cunning conspiracy of East against West, leading to the destruction of Tsar Dodon and his sons.

Goncharova, with her great reverence for the East, was in her element. And Larionov, her assistant on the production, encouraged her. It has been assumed, till now, that his help was of a purely technical nature: 'It was touching to see how Goncharova and Larionov between them personally painted all the properties. Every single object on stage was a work of art',[6] we read in Fokine's recollections of May 1914, when *Le Coq d'Or* was in rehearsal at the Paris Opéra. But recently it has become clear that Larionov's role was not confined to the painting of properties. Among the several gouaches of his which have survived there are two superb costume sketches, *The Queen of Shemakha* and *Shemakhan Slave-Girl with Shaitan* (both in the State Tretyakov Gallery, Moscow). These paintings reveal how strongly he was drawn to the Eastern imagery of *Le Coq d'Or*. The figure of the Queen in green oriental trousers, reminiscent of his drawings for the little book *Pomada*, is especially good. But the *Shemakhan Slave-Girl with Shaitan* (the devil of the East), is an extremely expressive piece of work. It is not impossible that the two artists collaborated on the nuptial procession of the Queen in which, apart from the camels envisaged by Goncharova, there were plans for all kinds of oriental marvels. Larionov's 'East' was playful and spiced with humour; Goncharova's was intensely serious. However, co-operation – or possibly competition – with Larionov could not fail to stimulate her imagination and give her conception of 'Oriental Russia' a sharper edge.

It would be quite incorrect to conclude, however, that Goncharova, in her *Coq d'Or*, was merely joining the circle of Diaghilev's artists with all their well-tried intonations. Both eye-witness accounts and recent research testify to the fact that this contact with the latest trends in Russian painting or, in other words, with the tendencies of the 'early avant-garde', turned a page in the history of the Diaghilev ballets.

It is important to remember which of the Seasons' programmes included the new production. On 24 May 1914, *Le Coq d'Or* shared the evening with the ballet *Petrushka*; on 26 and 28 May, with the opera-ballet *Le Rossignol*. In both of these productions the composer was Stravinsky, the designer Benois. It is especially interesting to compare the work of Goncharova for *Le Coq d'Or* with that of Benois for *Petrushka*. The productions do indeed have something in common. Both Russian characters, Petrushka and Tsar Dodon, are subjected to the machinations of the East, although, of course, the two artists employ very different images to convey their impressions, both of the East and of Russia.

Alexandre Benois:
Le Rossignol: **Costume Design for Sword Dancer** 1914
Cat.143C

Petrushka: Alexander Orlov as the Moor 1911
Victoria and Albert Museum, London

Benois was a great admirer of Goncharova's work and was her 'godfather' during the Seasons. On the whole he approved of her *Coq d'Or*: 'The spectacle was absolutely amazing' and the audiences were 'fascinated' by it. 'Goncharova has conquered Paris with her brightly multi-coloured settings and costumes,' he wrote. 'At the première I shared a box with Misia Edwards [also known as Misia Sert and Misia Natanson], where all the top-ranking "amis des Russes" were gathered. I still remember the "Ah!" with which the entire box greeted each new effect – the appearance of Dodon's "silver horse on wheels", for instance, in the last Act's procession.'[7]

Nevertheless, Benois did not entirely approve. And the form of his disapproval reveals the incompatibility of approach which divided this World of Art painter from Goncharova, twentieth-century primitivist. 'I didn't like the fact that, in spite of my convictions, she adhered to the tradition which insisted that a Russian tale could only be presented in this garish Asiatic style, *when I would have preferred the semi-European quality of the eighteenth century lubok*'[8] [author's italics].

Benois had in mind the humorous *lubok* of that period with all its theatricality; he delighted in both the doll-like character of the figures and its terrifying reversal, whose ghostly Hofmannesque quality had attracted several other World of Art painters. 'I was particularly sad about the last Act – my own favourite. Goncharova's procession was amusing and quite effective, but where was that mood of terror, which becomes more and more intense from the moment the sun disappears behind a black cloud? The artist had even forgotten the cloud!'[9]

Benois, in *Petrushka*, had been able to abstract effects of a dramatic grotesquerie from these little prints. At some moments the benumbed, doll-like quality of his heroes contrasted with their humanity, even their lyricism (as in the figure of Petrushka); at others it exposed their wooden insensitivity (in the characters of the Moor and the Ballerina); while behind the insensitivity lay the half-concealed sense of terror which Benois sought to instill, now by means of the gloomy background of Petrushka's room [cat. 142B], now by the

Natalia Goncharova:
Self-Portrait 1907
Cat. 71

Natalia Goncharova:
Le Coq d'Or: **Set design for Finale** 1914
Cat.157

ominous portrait of the puppet-master hanging on one of its walls.

Goncharova, however, was preoccupied with other varieties of *lubok*, particularly those of the Old Believers. These were, as a rule, not engraved but drawn, which gave them an especially lively, colourful appearance. They contained neither social satire nor grotesque portrayals of living characters, but expressive representations of hell and devils, which at that time Goncharova found extraordinarily attractive. What was even more important, they showed her an image of paradise – a blossoming garden in the branches of whose trees sang the sweet-voiced Sirin and Alkonost. These were the dreams of the common people. It will be remembered how, in Rimsky-Korsakov's opera *Sadko*, the oriental guest tells the citizens of Novgorod about a magical Phoenix from the southern seas, 'a bird with the face of a maiden . . . who sings her joyous songs so sweetly that he who hears that bird forgets all else'. Was the composer not thinking, again, of this bird when he wrote, for the second act of *Le Coq d'Or*, the piercingly sweet aria of the Queen of Shemakha, entirely consisting of interwoven chromatic patterns?

Goncharova's Queen is the delightful dream of Dodon. Wearied by war, the Tsar is driven to such dreams. In the middle scene of the first act Goncharova shows us his couch, from which grows a tall, tree-like flower – their visible image. His dreams are embodied, too, in the oriental maiden, a new Phoenix or Sirin, singing amidst the huge flowers.[10] The ravine in the second act, to which Dodon is transported in his dreams, and where the captivating Queen appears to him, is canopied over by the same enormous flowers. The magical maiden herself even sings about them, remembering the oriental gardens whence, like the Firebird, she has flown. 'Do the roses and lilies still shine there on the burning bushes?' she inquires of a star rising in the East. The whole of Dodon's kingdom, sunk in mindless indolence, follows him into this dream of paradise and beauty. The dream of Dodon as an old man is his last; when it fades he is dying, his kingdom collapsing about him. Goncharova's East and her Russia are not separate; they coexist side by side. Her 'East' is no longer cruel and cunning, as it was in Bakst's *Schéhérazade* or in *Le Coq d'Or* from Pushkin to Rimsky-Korsakov. With her it was only one facet, so to speak, of national self-awareness, a dream of simple, unearthly happiness quite incompatible with hidebound traditionalism.

The fundamental difference, however, between Goncharova and the masters of the preceding phase, including Benois with all his World of Art affiliations, lies in her completely new approach to primitive art. To icons, provincial sign-boards and *lubki*. The World of Art painters experienced these styles of a bygone age as historically and irrevocably past, hence their understandable 'alienation'. Benois

admired the crowd of simple Russian folk around the little puppet theatre from a great distance, like something unreal, in certain respects just as doll-like as the figures of the Ballerina or Petrushka.

The new artists did not experience this sense of alienation. While the World of Art generation, admiring the popular prints, dreamed of establishing a small museum dedicated to such artefacts,[11] the Goncharova-Larionov group, at the 1913 group exhibition, *Target*, showed *lubki* side by side with their own canvases. For them the world of these old prints was more than museum material which had once had reality; it was a timeless phenomenon, not historically limited but rooted in the national consciousness. The masters of the avant-garde experienced what was expressed by these primitives as something alive, convincing. Goncharova's procession in the last act of *Le Coq d'Or* with its camels and Dodon's silver horse may have been 'amusing', but beneath her fascination for the old prints lay the desire to look into 'the mysterious eyes of life . . . to show in its simplest form what is concealed in the soul and struggles to escape'. It was Benois who drew this to the attention of Russian artists at the time, not as the representative of the World of Art, but as a perceptive art critic.[12]

Goncharova's most important feature as a master of the new movement was a purification, a kind of emancipation in her use of colour which made her contemporaries compare her in this respect to Matisse.[13] But her colours had acquired, in addition, a symbolic content. The 'garish Asiatic style' of Dodon's towers was not an historically faithful reproduction of another age, but the image of a happy world which could liberate the soul. The red and yellow tones of the towers have been poeticised over the centuries in the popular mind; red, for Russians, remains the colour of goodness and beauty, as does the golden-yellow of the sun.

A more radical quality, peculiar to the Goncharova colour both in the sketches and the settings of 1914, was precisely that effect on the *spatial perception* of the viewer which characterised the new trend in painting. In Benois's *Petrushka* the eye travelled without let or hindrance into the realistic depths of the town-scape; behind the crowd rose the walls of the little fair-ground booths, and behind them, outlined against the sky, the Admiralty spire [see cat. 142A]. In *Le Coq d'Or*, Dodon's towers are positioned in a naïve, four-square manner, parallel to the proscenium arch; thanks to their accentuated colours, however, both the towers themselves and the flowers painted on them appear capable of 'growing in size' or 'advancing on the audience' [see cat. 157]. This is especially so in the case of the crimson flowers on the dream-tree, growing from Dodon's couch.

Here the question arises of the dates of numerous sketches made by Goncharova which have found their way into the collections of the world.[14] The majority of them were made in the 1920s and 1930s, 'in the wake', as it were, of the 1914 production. In his review of the Diaghilev exhibition of 1939, Benois wrote about the 'original version' of a Goncharova sketch for *Le Coq d'Or* (that is, the 1913-14 version), '*which she replaced by a more striking and interesting composition*' [author's italics].[15] Goncharova invariably dated these new sketches '1914', referring not to the date of their completion but to the year of her legendary Paris première, that 'fortunate hour' which brought her international fame. At the same time, the later sketches enable us to trace the course of her artistic evolution after she had broken with the traditions of the Russian avant-garde.

During the years 1913-15 the newest movement in Russian art was at a crucial stage. Some representatives of the avant-garde, Malevich, Tatlin and several others, were immersed in their own radical style of painting, which they carried to its logical abstract conclusion. Others, belonging to the Knave of Diamonds group, such as Konchalovsky, Lentulov and Mashkov, no longer followed the avant-garde lead. Either they chose a more tranquil course or they moved out of its orbit in some other way. Goncharova belongs in the second category. If in 1910 her canvases, with their expressive energy and bold brushwork, had been compared with the works of the German Expressionists or with those of Picasso's African period, in the second half of that same decade the energy of her brushwork and colour was diminishing, while in the 1920s and 1930s this master of the avant-garde was turning into a subtle, stylising illustrator, almost in the manner of Stelletsky. Even Benois, a loyal World of Art associate, with whom she collaborated in 1922 on the designs for *Aurora's Wedding*, would have been happy to put his name to her costume sketch for the Shah of Shakhriar, now in the Lobanov-Rostovsky collection.

First to disappear, in the later versions of the sketches for *Le Coq d'Or*, was precisely that spatial perception of colour. Its use became somewhat flat, ornamental, achieving a decorative beauty and resonance but losing its former dynamic. With increasing frequency the artist would call these works not 'sketches for the décor' of this or that act of the ballet, but 'Unrealised project for a front-cloth for *Le Coq d'Or*', which combined the most successful decorative elements of the latter work with those of her other productions on Russian themes.[16]

None of this was in evidence in the 'original versions' of 1913-14, nor in the magnificent sketch of the third act (finale) in Moscow's Bakhrushin Museum [cat. 157]. One longs to believe that this is how the stage of the Paris Opéra looked during those performances of *Le Coq d'Or* at the end of May 1914, when the colours of the set must have literally filled the space, drawing the audience into their dream.

The spectacle was received as 'a revelation of a joyous world filled with colour, glittering with red and gold'.[17] In commissioning Goncharova, Diaghilev and Fokine were not disappointed in their expectations of 'something colourfully beautiful, profoundly national and at the same time, magical'.[18]

The period of collaboration between the Diaghilev enterprise and the masters of the new European twentieth-century art began with *Le Coq d'Or*. By 1915, Larionov, working alongside Goncharova, was beginning to make his name, no longer as her assistant but in his own right. Those Russian artists of the 'early avant-garde' would be joined by such world figures as Picasso, Matisse, Braque, Derain and others, who were to pave the way ahead for the theatre of Diaghilev.

Translated from the Russian by Mary Hobson

1. A. Benois, 'Dnevnik khudozhnika', in *Rech'*, 21 October 1913.
2. 'I have just returned from Moscow,' Diaghilev said, in an interview given at the end of January 1914, 'where I have been looking at Goncharova's sketches for *Le Coq d'Or*, and I am very happy with them.' In Zilberstein and Samkov, *Sergei Diagilev i Russkoe iskusstvo: Stat'i, otkrytye pis'ma, interv'iu, perepiska, sovremenniki o Diagileve*, 2 vols, Moscow, 1982, vol. I, p. 236.
3. The overture and wedding march from *Le Coq d'Or* were heard in concert arrangements during the Seasons, and the march was included in the score of the ballet *Le Festin*, in which the performers filed across the stage to it.
4. M. Fokine, *Protiv techeniia: Vospominaniia baletmeistera. Stat'i, Pis'ma*, Leningrad-Moscow, 1962, pp. 319-20.
5. In 1914 the cockerel was made of papier-mâché, but in 1937, for a revival of the ballet on the stage of London's Covent Garden, Fokine introduced the role of the Golden Cockerel, superbly danced by Tatiana Riabushinskaia. Ibid p. 237.

6. Ibid p. 317.
7. A. Benois, *Moi vospominaniia*, Moscow, 1980, books IV-V, p. 537.
8. Ibid p. 538.
9. Ibid.
10. In Moscow's Bakhrushin Museum there is a gouache by Goncharova of Sirin, sitting in the branches – with large, bird-like feet and the face of an oriental beauty from a Persian miniature. This gouache dates from those same years, 1913-14, during which Goncharova was working on the sketches for *Le Coq d'Or*.
11. A. Benois, 'Khudozhestvennye pis'ma. Vystavka, "soiuza molodezhi"', *Rech'*, 21 December 1912.
12. A. Benois, 'Khudozhestvennye pis'ma. Ikony i novoe russkoe iskusstvo', *Rech'*, 5 April 1913; 'Diary of an Artist', 21 October 1913.
13. Louis Vauxcelles, 'A propos du *Coq d'Or*', *Gil Blas*, Paris, 26 May 1914.
14. Such as the colour gouaches on the theme of *Le Coq d'Or* in the Tretyakov Gallery, the Victoria and Albert Museum, the Lobanov-Rostovsky collection and numerous others.

15. A. Benois, 'The Diaghilev Exhibition', in *Sergei Diagilev i russkoe iskusstvo*, ed. Zilberstein and Samkov, vol. II, p. 278. The sketch for the first act of *Le Coq d'Or* in the Lobanov-Rostovsky collection is just such an 'interesting and striking composition'. It cannot be related to the revival of the production, since it depicts rows of the chorus at each side of the stage which were no longer present in the 1937 version. It is evidently 'in memory' of the 1914 production, very probably made at the beginning of the 1920s.
16. Such as the sketch 'Project for a curtain-cloth', for instance, in the Museum of San Antonio, USA.
17. From Militsa Pozharskaia, *Russkie sezony v Parizhe: eskizy dekoratsii i kostiumov, 1908-1929*, Moscow, 1988, p. 28.
18. M. Fokine, *Protiv techeniia*, op. cit. p. 317.

Sergei Diaghilev and his Times

COMPILED BY ANN KODICEK AND TOMOKO SATO

DIAGHILEV	RUSSIA	EUROPE

Diaghilev's family, 1870s:
far left, standing: his father
far left, sitting: stepmother
centre, sitting: grandfather
Diaghilev Foundation, Perm

1870 — Association of Travelling Art Exhibitions founded in St Petersburg. — Franco-Prussian War; siege of Paris. Monet, Pissarro, Tissot and Alma-Tadema arrive in London.

1871 — — Commune of Paris, following German occupation of the city. Courbet imprisoned. Sisley arrives in London.

1872 — 31 March: Sergei Pavlovich Diaghilev born Selishchenko, Novgorod Province. His mother dies a few days later. — 31 March: Misia Sert born St Petersburg. Mathilde Kshessinska born. Alexander Scriabin born. — Monet paints *Impression: Sunrise*, which gives rise to term Impressionism when exhibited in 1874.

1873 — — Alliance of Emperors of Russia, Germany and Austria-Hungary. Fyodor Chaliapin born. — Germans evacuate France except Alsace and part of Lorraine; Third Republic constituted in France. Courbet escapes to Switzerland.

1874 — Sergei's father, Pavel Pavlovich Diaghilev, marries Elena Valerianovna Panaeva. The family moves to St Petersburg. — Savva Mamontov founds his art colony at Abramtsevo: he attracts outstanding visual and musical artists of the day, later publicised in *World of Art* magazine and exhibitions. — First Impressionist Exhibition at Nadar's, Paris.

1875 — — — Uprising in Bosnia-Herzegovina, suppressed by Turks.

1876 — — — Moreau's *Salomé (The Apparition)* exhibited in Paris Salon. Mallarmé's poem 'L'Après-midi d'un faune' published. Wagner's Festival Theatre opened at Bayreuth. Whistler starts painting the Peacock Room in London.

1877 — — Russo-Turkish War: Russia renews its pressure on Turkey through Pan-Slavism. — Queen Victoria proclaimed Empress of India.

1878 — — Congress of Berlin: extensive changes to boundaries of Balkan nations; European powers restrict Russia's gains in recent wars with Turkey. — Attempt to assassinate Wilhelm I of Germany fails. Paris *Exposition Universelle*. Van Gogh preaches among the miners of the Borinage, Belgium. Whistler-Ruskin trial, following the opening exhibition of the Grosvenor Gallery, London (1877), which includes Whistler's *Nocturne – The Falling Rocket*.

Diaghilev's stepmother,
Elena Panaeva-Diaghileva, 1880s
Diaghilev Foundation, Perm

ace Embankment,
Petersburg
ly 1900s
tral State Archive
inema and Photo Documents,
Petersburg

1880		Michel Fokine born.	Foundation of the French Socialist Party. Zola's *Le Naturalisme au salon* published.
1881		Tsar Alexander II approves progressive political reform providing for some form of representative assembly. 1 March: Alexander II assassinated; his successor Alexander III abandons reforms. Wide-ranging emergency powers given to authorities. Pogroms encouraged by government to divert peasant unrest. Fyodor Dostoevsky dies. Modest Mussorgsky dies. Mikhail Larionov born. Natalia Goncharova born.	Pablo Picasso born.
1882	The Diaghilev family removes to Perm. Summers spent at Sergei's grandfather's estate at nearby Bikbarda.	Mamontov's Private Russian Opera opens Moscow with première of Rimsky-Korsakov's *Snegurochka* (*The Snow Maiden*). Igor Stravinsky born.	Triple Alliance formed between Germany, Austria-Hungary and Italy. In the interests of improving public taste, the Société des Arts Décoratifs and the Union Centrale des Beaux-Arts amalgamate to form the Union Centrale des Arts Décoratifs, Paris.
1883			Marx dies in London. Wagner dies. Manet dies. Engels's *Die Entwicklung des Sozialismus von der Utopia zur Wissenschaft* published. Les XX formed in Brussels by Octave Maus and twenty Belgian artists.
1884			First Salon des Indépendants held in Paris. Retrospective Manet exhibition at the Ecole des Beaux-Arts, Paris. Huysmans's *A Rebours* published. Fabian Society founded in London.

Diaghilev's grandfather,
Pavel Dmitrievich Diaghilev
Diaghilev Foundation, Perm

1885	Tamara Karsavina born. Ida Rubinstein born.	Symbolist journal *Revue wagnérienne* founded in Paris. Naturalist periodical *Die Gesellschaft* founded in Munich. Nietzsche completes *Also sprach Zarathustra*. Whistler gives 'Ten o'clock' lecture in London.
1886		Eighth (last) Impressionist Exhibition. Retrospective Whistler exhibition at the Petit Palais, Paris. Van Gogh arrives in Paris. Gauguin paints at Pont-Aven. Symbolist manifesto by Jean Moréas appears in *Le Figaro*. The New English Art Club founded in London.
1887		Golden Jubilee of Queen Victoria. Van Gogh organises an exhibition of Japanese prints at the café Le Tambourin, Paris.
1888	Vaslav Nijinsky born.	Wilhelm II becomes Emperor of Germany. Construction of the Eiffel Tower begins. The Nabis formed in Paris. Van Gogh stays with Gauguin in Arles.

1889		Society for Self Improvement started by Alexandre Benois and fellow students of the May School, St Petersburg.	Second International Working Men's Association formed in Paris. Paris *Exposition Universelle*. Jean Cocteau born. Symbolist journals *La Revue blanche* and *La Plume* founded in Paris; Ricketts's and Shannon's *The Dial* in London. First French Symbolist Exhibition: Gauguin and the Pont Aven School. London Impressionist Exhibition held at the Goupil Gallery. Eastman's Kodak camera comes into production using photographic film.
1890	Sergei Diaghilev begins studies at the Law Faculty of St Petersburg University. Diaghilev joins Society for Self Improvement.	Mikhail Vrubel joins Mamontov's circle at Abramtsevo: active in ceramic workshops founded same year. First St Petersburg performances of: Borodin's *Prince Igor*, and Tchaikovsky's *Queen of Spades* and *The Sleeping Beauty*.	Bismarck dismissed by Wilhelm II. Van Gogh commits suicide at Auvers.
1891		Harvest fails in 22 provinces; widespread famine. Construction begins on Trans-Siberian Railway. St Petersburg *Northern Herald [Severny Vestnik]* starts to publish work by young Symbolist writers, including Dmitry Merezhkovsky, Fedor Sologub, Zinaida Gippius, Konstantin Balmont: these writers later contribute to *World of Art*.	Pan-German League founded in Prague. Moreau appointed Professor at the Ecole des Beaux-Arts, Paris. Gauguin goes to Tahiti. Wilde's *The Picture of Dorian Gray* published.
1892		Sergei Witte appointed Finance Minister. Russia enters era of unprecedented industrialisation, to detriment of peasants: industry financed by wholesale grain export. Tretyakov brothers donate art collections and their building to city of Moscow.	Pan-Slav conference held in Cracow. Anarchist demonstrations in Paris. Salon de la Rose + Croix opened in Paris. Munich Secession formed.
1893	Diaghilev comes of age: inherits from his mother; begins modest collection of art and furniture.	Pavel and Sergei Tretyakov present their art collection to the City of Moscow. Princess Mariya Tenisheva sets up art colony at Talashkino (modelled on Abramtsevo). Vladimir Ulyanov (Lenin) joins group of Marxist intellectuals in St Petersburg. Tchaikovsky's 6th Symphony (*Pathétique*) has first performance, St Petersburg; two weeks later, Tchaikovsky dies.	Wilde's *Salomé* written in French, published in Paris. *The Studio* magazine founded in London.
1894		Tsar Alexander III dies; accession of Nicholas II. Nicholas II marries Alexandra of Hesse (granddaughter of Queen Victoria). Russo-French Alliance. First Congress of Russian Artists held in Moscow. St Petersburg Academy relaxes educational régime. Formerly dissident painters of the Wanderer group admitted to teaching staff. Valery Bryusov publishes three collections of poems.	Debussy's *L'Après-midi d'un faune*, inspired by Mallarmé's poem (1876), first performed in Paris. Beardsley's art magazine *The Yellow Book* founded in London. Lumière invents cinematograph.
1895	Diaghilev graduates from University. First European tour.	Léonide Massine born. Russian artists of Diaghilev's circle studying/working abroad: in Paris, Léon Bakst (since 1893), Anna Golubkina, Alexandre Benois, Evgeny Lanceray, Konstantin Somov, Anna Ostroumova (from 1896) and Alexandre Golovine (1897, 1899); in Munich, Igor Grabar, Ivan Bilibin, Mstislav Dobuzhinsky and Vassily Kandinsky.	S. Bing's shop L'Art Nouveau opened in Paris. First major exhibition of Cézanne's work in Paris. Periodical *Pan* appears in Berlin. Oscar Wilde trial and imprisonment.

1896

May: Coronation of Tsar Nicholas II; he visits London and Paris.
Mamontov's Private Opera mounts Humperdinck's *Hansel and Gretel* (designed by Vrubel); Chaliapin makes Moscow début in Mamontov production of *A Life for the Tsar* (*Ivan Susanin*). All-Russian Exhibition of Industry and Art held at Nizhny Novgorod: important designs by Konstantin Korovine; Vrubel's panels rejected – Mamontov constructs special pavilion to house them. Première of Chekhov's *The Seagull*, unsuccessful.

Paul Verlaine dies. William Morris dies. Munich reviews *Jugend* and *Simplizissimus* founded. *The Savoy* magazine founded in London. Salon de l'Art Nouveau, Paris. Stained glass by Louis Comfort Tiffany first promoted from USA. Marconi demonstrates wireless telegraphy.

1897

March–May: Diaghilev's Exhibition of *English (Scottish) and German Watercolours*, Baron Stieglitz Museum, St Petersburg. First significant representation of art from Britain. Features Whistler, Paterson and the Glasgow Boys, as well as Lenbach, Menzel, Böcklin and Bartels. October: At the Society for Encouragement of the Arts, an *Exhibition of Scandinavian Art*, the first introduction of Scandinavian art to Russia, featuring Anders Zorn. Following Diaghilev's lead, the collectors Mamontov, Tenisheva and Sergei Shchukin purchase works by Thaulow, Munthe, Zorn and Werenskiold.

Rimsky-Korsakov's opera *Sadko* has its première at Mamontov's Private Opera: (sets by Korovine, Maliutin and Vrubel); in a revival of Rimsky-Korsakov's *Pskovitianka* (*The Maid of Pskov*), Chaliapin sings the role of Ivan the Terrible. Sergei Shchukin meets Paul Durand-Ruel in Paris and begins his collection of avant-garde art.

Diamond Jubilee of Queen Victoria. Formation, in Vienna, of Secession Group.

1898

January: Diaghilev's *Exhibition of Russian and Finnish Artists* at the Stieglitz Museum shows Vrubel for the first time, together with Lanceray and Somov. This controversial choice is tempered by works of more traditional artists, including Levitan, Apollinari Vasnetsov, Serov, Purvit and Ryabushkin. November: Diaghilev founds the magazine of the World of Art group; the first issue features Beardsley, Whistler, Degas and Moreau.

In St Petersburg, the Alexander III Russian Museum opens to public. *The Seagull* performed at Hermitage Theatre.

Moreau dies. Burne-Jones dies. Felicien Rops dies. Beardsley dies. First exhibition of Vienna Secession, with the poster designed by Klimt.

1899

February: First World of Art exhibition opens at Stieglitz Museum, St Petersburg. It consists of 322 works by 41 artists from France, Germany, Italy, Switzerland, England and Scandinavia. Includes works by Monet, Degas, Moreau, Rivière, Whistler and Böcklin from the West; Repin, Benois, Bakst from Russia; crafts from Abramtsevo, glass by Lalique and Tiffany. Diaghilev begins work at the Imperial Theatres.

Mamontov arrested and imprisoned on charges of fraud. *Uncle Vanya* premièred at Moscow Arts Theatre, a new theatre founded that year by Konstantin Stanislavsky.

Boer War begins. International Women's Congress held in London. Berlin Secession formed.

1900

First World of Art exhibition to feature Russian art only, held in St Petersburg.
Diaghilev produces the Jubilee Edition of Imperial Theatres *Yearbook*.

150th Jubilee of the Russian Theatre founded by Fyodor Volkov in Yaroslavl. April: Large Russian Section at Paris *Exposition Universelle* (Crafts Pavilion designed by Korovine and Golovine, in Neo-Russian style). Pictures featured in *World of Art*. Philosopher Vladimir Soloviev dies. Lenin goes into exile.

British Labour Party founded. King Umberto of Italy assassinated. Paris *Exposition Universelle* opens. Ruskin dies. Wilde dies in Paris. Nietzsche dies.

1901 Diaghilev resigns from the Imperial Theatres. Most ambitious World of Art exhibition held at the Imperial Academy of Arts, largely arranged by Valentin Serov.

Léon Bakst and Diaghilev
at a World of Art exhibition
early 1900s
Diaghilev Foundation, Perm

Symbolist Almanac *Northern Flowers [Severnye Tsvety]* begins publication: contributions from Balmont, Bely, Blok and Bryusev, all of whom also contribute to *World of Art*. Sergei Rachmaninov gives first full performance of 2nd Piano Concerto. First exhibition of the Thirty-Six Society, led by Vrubel and Serov, opens in Moscow. Chaliapin makes Western début at La Scala, Milan.

Queen Victoria dies; accession of King Edward VII. Kandinsky forms the Phalanx group in Munich.

1902 March: Fourth World of Art exhibition opens in St Petersburg, travels to Moscow. Diaghilev publishes a monograph on eighteenth-century Russian portrait painter Dmitry Levitsky.

April: Sipyagin (Minister of the Interior) assassinated by Social Revolutionary member. Maxim Gorky's *Lower Depths* premièred at Moscow Arts Theatre. Exhibition opens in Moscow of Architecture and Design of the new *style moderne*, including Mackintosh, Olbrich, Ivan Fomin, Korovine, Polenova. Merezhkovsky's novel *Leonardo da Vinci* published.

Fourteenth exhibition of Vienna Secession: Klimt's *Beethoven Frieze* and Klinger's Beethoven statue displayed. International Exhibition of Modern Decorative Arts opens in Turin. André Gide's *L'Immoraliste* published.

1903 Easter: Three-day pogrom at Kishinev. Widespread Black Sea strikes. July: Social Democrat Party emerges; immediate split Bolsheviks/Mensheviks. *Contemporary Art*, an exhibition comprising objects and interiors in *style moderne*, Russian neo-historical and neo-baroque styles, shown in St Petersburg by the World of Art artists and their associates operating independently of Diaghilev: exhibitors include Grabar, Benois, Lanceray, Bakst, Golovine, Korovine and Shcherbatov, with objects contributed by Somov, Vrubel and von Meck; the exhibition travels to Moscow. St Petersburg première of *Götterdämmerung*: designs by Benois and Korovine reviewed by *World of Art*. Symbolist journal *Novyi Put'* started by orthodox Symbolist writers formerly on editorial board of *World of Art*: it runs until 1904.

King of Serbia assassinated. First Salon d'Automne held at the Grand Palais in Paris.

1904 The *World of Art* magazine closes: last two volumes illustrate paintings by French Post-Impressionists and Russian ecclesiastical embroidery. Grand Duke Nikolai Mikhailovich starts work on a catalogue raisonné of the Russian portrait, with Diaghilev and Benois.

January: Outbreak of Russo-Japanese War, following Japanese attack on Port Arthur; disaster for Russia. July: Assassination of Plehve (Interior Minister) by Social Revolutionaries. Magazine *The Scales [Vesy]* launched. Moscow Arts Theatre premières *The Cherry Orchard*. Chekhov dies. New Society of Artists holds first exhibition, St Petersburg. Scarlet Rose *[Alaia roza]* Exhibition starts up Blue Rose Group. Isadora Duncan first performs in St Petersburg.

Anglo-French Entente Cordiale. General strike in Italy. Freud's *Psychopathology of Everyday Life* published.

1905 March: Diaghilev's *Historical Exhibition of Russian Portraits* mounted at St Petersburg's Tauride Palace, which has an Imperial opening and closes in September.

Tauride Palace
St Petersburg
Courtesy Victor Kennett

January: Russia torn by civil disturbances, leading to the 1905 Revolution. February: Grand Duke Sergei, Tsar Nicholas II's uncle, assassinated by Social Revolutionaries. First ever Soviet evolves from strike committee. May: Russian Baltic fleet virtually annihilated by Japan. June: Crew of battle-ship *Potemkin* mutinies in Odessa. Street fighting. July: Russo-German treaty signed by Tsar Nicholas II and Kaiser Wilhelm but not ratified by their governments. August: Government decree provides for consultative assembly at whim of Tsar. Universities granted autonomy. September: New wave of strikes. Soviets formed in most towns. Country grinds to near-halt. Autumn: The monarchist, nationalist, anti-Semitic Union of the Russian People is formed. Countless pogroms in south and south-west, carried out by counter-revolutionary 'Black Hundred'. Tsar's October Manifesto provides for fundamental civil liberties and Duma with limited powers. Universal Suffrage (all classes). November: Rasputin first appears at Imperial Court. December: General Strike in Moscow turns into an armed uprising, lasting twelve days; brutal suppression; troops make punitive forays all over Russia. Emergence of satirical magazines *Zritel'*, *Adskaya Pochta*, *Zhupel'* (artists include Dobuzhinsky, Chekhonin, Bilibin, Anisfeld, Lanceray, Zamirailo). Rimsky-Korsakov involved in riot at St Petersburg Conservatoire. Dancers of the Maryinsky Theatre go on strike. Sergei Legat commits suicide.

First Fauve exhibition at the Salon d'Automne, Paris. Die Brücke group formed in Dresden. Strauss's opera *Salomé* written after Wilde's French play, first performed in Dresden. Einstein's *General Theory of Relativity* published.

1906 February: Last World of Art exhibition at the Catherine Hall, St Petersburg (includes Larionov); reviews in *Golden Fleece*.
October: Diaghilev organises *Exhibition of Russian Art* at Paris Salon d'Automne: the first comprehensive retrospective of Russian art, the first to be mounted by an independent selector, and the first to feature contemporary art by non-academicians.

April: First Duma dissolved. July: Petr Stolypin appointed Chairman of Council Ministers. January: First foreign tour of Moscow Arts Theatre (Berlin). *Golden Fleece [Zolotoe runo]* magazine founded.

Fauves' triumph at the Salon des Indépendants and the Salon d'Automne. Cézanne dies. Picasso visits Paris and later settles there. Adolph Loos opens the Free School of Architecture in Vienna.

1907 May: Diaghilev's first *Saisons russes* (concerts). First appearance in Paris of soloists Chaliapin and Litvine, and composer-conductors Rachmaninov and Rimsky-Korsakov.

February: Second Duma convenes, again proves unworkable, dissolved June. Triple Entente of Russia, France and Britain. Tsar Nicholas II convenes Hague Peace Conference. Joseph Dugashvili (Stalin) organises bank robbery in Tblisi. Lenin leaves Russia until 1917. November: Third Duma convenes under Stolypin; survives until 1912. First exhibition of Blue Rose group, Moscow. Pavlov starts work on conditioned reflexes. Vaslav Nijinsky graduates from Imperial Theatre School of Dancing, St Petersburg.

Retrospective Cézanne exhibition in Paris. Picasso finishes *Les Demoiselles d'Avignon* and meets Braque.

1908	May: Diaghilev exports Bolshoi Company's Imperial production of *Boris Godunov* to Paris Opéra.	First performance of Scriabin's *Poème d'Extase*. First *Golden Fleece* Salon includes Larionov, Goncharova and selected Fauves. Rimsky-Korsakov dies. Sculptor Archipenko settles in Paris.	Pan-Slav Congress held in Prague. German Social Democratic Party rally in Nuremberg. Matisse founds his academy with Purrmann in Paris and publishes *Notes d'un Peintre*.
1909	May: Diaghilev's first Opera and Ballet Season at the Théâtre du Châtelet, Paris. Repertoire: *Les Sylphides, Polovtsian Dances (Prince Igor), Le Pavillon d'Armide, Cléopâtre, Le Festin, Ivan the Terrible, Ruslan and Lyudmila*.	Second *Golden Fleece* Salon of French/Russian Art, includes Matisse. First Moscow performance of Rimsky-Korsakov's *Zolotoi Petushok* (designed by Bilibin). *Apollon* magazine starts publication in St Petersburg. Third *Golden Fleece* Salon features Larionov and Goncharova. *The Scales* and *Golden Fleece* magazines cease publication.	Marinetti's *Futurist Manifesto* appears in *Le Figaro*.
1910	June: Diaghilev's second Paris Season at the Paris Opéra. Repertoire: *The Firebird, Les Sylphides, Schéhérazade, Carnaval, Giselle, Les Orientales*.	Tsar Nicholas II meets Wilhelm II at Potsdam. Mikhail Vrubel dies after long mental illness. Leo Tolstoy dies. Second phase of World of Art exhibitions, run independently by artists, instituted St Petersburg, to last till 1924. Chagall settles in Paris. First Knave of Diamonds [*Bubnovy valet*] exhibition opens in Moscow, including Kandinsky, Jawlensky, Larionov, Goncharova, David and Vladimir Burliuk and Kasimir Malevich, all showing a new interest in folk and primitive art.	Death of King Edward VII; accession of King George V. *Der Sturm* magazine founded in Berlin. Roger Fry organises *Manet and the Post-Impressionists* exhibition at the Grafton Gallery, London.
1911	Founding of Diaghilev's Ballets Russes Company. June: Ballets Russes give first performances at the Théâtre du Châtelet, Paris, of Stravinsky's *Petrushka, Le Spectre de la Rose, Sadko, Narcisse*. Ida Rubinstein leaves Diaghilev's Company. Ballets Russes seasons in Rome, Monte Carlo, Paris, Royal Opera House, London (Coronation Gala).	Rasputin banished from St Petersburg. September: Stolypin assassinated Kiev, during Imperial Gala Performance of Rimsky-Korsakov's *Tsar Saltan*. First performance of Scriabin's *Prometheus*, Moscow. Autumn: Goncharova and Larionov break from Knave of Diamonds group and now associate with Donkey's Tail/Rayonnism. October–November: Matisse visits Moscow and St Petersburg. Valentin Serov dies.	First group exhibition of Cubists in Paris. Kandinsky and Franz Marc found Der Blaue Reiter in Munich. Sickert forms the Camden Town Group in London.
1912	Fokine resigns from Diaghilev's Company. Ballets Russes seasons at the Théâtre du Châtelet, Paris, Royal Opera House, Covent Garden. Also at Berlin, Vienna, Budapest. Repertoire: *Daphnis and Chloë, Thamar, Le Dieu Bleu, L'Après-midi d'un faune*. Nijinsky's *Faune* creates theatrical scandal in Paris.	April: 170 striking miners killed at British-owned Lena goldfield, Siberia; wave of strikes to outbreak of the First World War. First issue of Workers' Paper *Pravda*. Liberal films by Goncharov and Protazanov are banned. Futurists, led by Mayakovsky, attack the bourgeois class and the Symbolists in a miscellany entitled *A Slap in the Face of Public Taste [Poshchechina obshchestvennomu vkusu]*.	Balkan Wars begin. China becomes a Republic. Italian Futurist exhibition in Paris. First exhibition of the Section d'Or artists. Léon Bakst has one-man exhibition at Fine Art Society, London.

Programme for
Royal Opera Covent Garden's
Season of Russian Ballet
1912
Cat.149E

1913	May: Ballets Russes at the new Théâtre des Champs-Elysées, Paris. Also in London, Royal Opera House and Drury Lane. First South American Tour under direction of Baron Gunsburg. Repertoire: *The Rite of Spring, Jeux, La Tragédie de Salomé, Boris Godunov, La Nuit de Mai*. Seasons, Monte Carlo, Paris, London. Bakst leaves the Company. Diaghilev dismisses Nijinsky following Nijinsky's marriage.	Romanov Tercentenary: Imperial Amnesty for political prisoners. August: Goncharova's one-man show, Moscow: her work is admired by Benois, subsequently seen by Diaghilev. Performance in St Petersburg of Matyushin's opera *Victory over the Sun [Pobeda nad solntsem]* to texts of the Futurist poets Khlebnikov and Kruchenykh, with first Suprematist sets by Kasimir Malevich.	Apollinaire's *Cubist Aesthetic Considerations* published. Proust's *A la recherche du temps perdu* published.
1914	Diaghilev invites Goncharova to design *Le Coq d'Or*, following her exhibition. Ballets Russes seasons in Paris and London. Repertoire: *Le Coq d'Or, La Légende de Joseph, Papillons, Midas, Le Rossignol*.	January–July: almost 3,500 strikes. July: Bolshevik General Strike, St Petersburg, ended by Russians entering war. Duma convoked for one session only. Turkey enters war on Austro-German side: Russia's Baltic and Black Sea ports blockaded. St Petersburg renamed Petrograd. Fokine returns to Russia. Kandinsky returns to Russia. Kshessinska, Karsavina and other dancers begin to consider escape to Western Europe.	Austrian Archduke Francis Ferdinand assassinated. Outbreak of the First World War. Werkbund Exhibition in Berlin. Wyndham Lewis's Vorticist magazine *Blast* founded in London.
1915	July: Larionov and Goncharova leave Russia to join Diaghilev in Switzerland, then settle in Paris. Diaghilev in Italy and Switzerland. Charity Gala, Paris. First tour of USA.	May–September: Russian troops forced to retreat. Scriabin dies. Last Futurist Painting Exhibition: Malevich first shows Suprematist paintings.	Marcel Duchamp visits New York.
1916		Rasputin assassinated.	Battle of Verdun: both French and German armies suffer considerable loss. Accession of the new Austro-Hungarian Emperor Charles Josef. Dadaists' Cabaret Voltaire opens in Zurich.
1917		March: Following 'February Revolution', Tsar Nicholas II is forced to abdicate; fifteen months later, he and his family are executed. Provisional government replaced by coalition government led by Oleg Kerensky. October–November: Kerensky's government overthrown by Bolsheviks; new Soviet government established, with Lenin as its head. December: Peace Conference at Brest-Litovsk between the Central Powers and the Russian Bolsheviks (led by Trotsky).	Peace Congress of the Socialist International held in Stockholm. Galerie Dada opens in Zurich. Dutch journal *De Stijl* launched.

Diaghilev's Company
leaving Chicago, 1916
State Museum of Theatre and Music
St Petersburg

1918		Lenin orders an armistice with Germany. Moscow becomes Soviet Russia's capital.	Treaty of Brest-Litovsk signed. Surrender of Austrians and Germans. Abdication of Emperor Charles Josef of Austria-Hungary.
1929	Diaghilev dies in Venice: buried on Isola San Michele.		

Catalogue

Within each section, entries for individual works are arranged chronologically, grouped under the same artist, publisher or topic. Artists' dates are given at first mention only.

Sizes of two-dimensional objects are given height before width. For sculpture, height only is given. Measurements of irregularly shaped exhibits are those of their greatest dimension. Unless otherwise stated, all paintings and drawings are on paper.

Konstantin Somov:
**Portrait of
Léon Bakst and Alexandre Benois**
1896
Cat.28

Diaghilev's Early Years

Sergei Diaghilev was born at Selishchenko in Novgorod Province, a south-western region of Russia, to Pavel Pavlovich Diaghilev, professional army officer, and Evgenia Nikolaevna, née Evreinova, who died in giving birth to Sergei, on 31 March 1872. In 1874 Pavel Diaghilev married Elena Valerianovna Panaeva. She bore him two more sons and the family removed to Perm. The Diaghilevs' estate, Bikbarda, was also situated near Perm and, from time to time, the family resided at St Petersburg. Wherever they lived, music was a central part of their existence.

After graduation from Perm Gymnasium, Diaghilev enrolled in 1890 at St Petersburg University Law Faculty. At the same time he studied composition under Rimsky-Korsakov (1844-1908) and took singing lessons from the Italian tenor Antonio Cotogni. Diaghilev spent much of his time in the company of his cousin, Dmitry Filosofov, with whom he first stayed in St Petersburg. The two would travel abroad together, and Diaghilev would spend his summers at the Filosofovs' estate, Bogdanovskoe. Through Dmitry Filosofov, Sergei Diaghilev joined the Society for Self Improvement, a group consisting of old friends from the May High School, who met regularly to discuss culture at the house of Alexandre Benois [see p. 126]. Founder members of this circle included Benois, Filosofov, Konstantin Somov [see p. 130], and Walter Nouvel. Diaghilev joined them in 1890, the same year as Léon Bakst [see p. 125]. Although the circle was disbanded in 1891, the group continued to meet to discuss matters of mutual cultural interest.

Ilya **REPIN**
1844-1930

Repin is, without doubt, Russia's best known artist. Taught by the founder-member of the Wanderer school of realists, Ivan Kramskoy, he later studied in Paris but remained committed to Russian themes. A fine portrait painter, Repin elevated genre painting to a monumental form capable of forceful social comment. He himself joined the Wanderer movement in 1871 but disappointed his admirers by returning in 1893 to St Petersburg's Imperial Academy of Arts as Professor. Repin was a fine teacher; his pupils became the leading artists of the next generation, including a number, such as Konstantin Somov and, especially, Valentin Serov [see pp. 129-30], who were closely linked with Diaghilev and the World of Art group [see p. 125].

1 ⊹ Portrait of the composer Mikhail Glinka 1887

Oil on canvas, 98 × 117 cm
State Tretyakov Gallery, Moscow

Glinka (1804-57) is generally considered to be the father of the Russian national school of music and one of the founders of the Romantic movement. After initial training as a pianist under John Field in St Petersburg, he resolved at the age of thirty to write a Russian opera, for which he studied in Berlin. In 1836, he produced *A Life for the Tsar*, which was set in 1613 and concerned the foundation of the Romanov dynasty following the Polish invasion and interregnum. His next opera, *Ruslan and Lyudmila*, was based on a fairy-tale poem by Pushkin and laid the foundations for a truly Russian national style. Both operas were much admired by Diaghilev and his family, and the First Act of *Ruslan and Lyudmila* was produced by Diaghilev in Paris in 1909.

2 ⊹ Portrait of the composer Alexander Glazunov 1890

Watercolour and pencil, 29 × 39.1 cm
State Museum of Theatre and Music, St Petersburg

A pupil of Rimsky-Korsakov, Glazunov (1865-1936) was a youthful prodigy who wrote his first symphony at the age of sixteen. A brilliant orchestrator and sound melodist, he wrote three ballets, all choreographed by Marius Petipa, which further developed the innovations of Tchaikovsky's *Sleeping Beauty* [see Production Notes].

Cat. 2

The World of Art Movement

Diaghilev at first inclined more towards music than art. When, however, his hoped-for career as a composer and musician proved unrealisable, he began to train himself as a connoisseur of art. He was much helped in this by Alexandre Benois and Dmitry Filosofov. After travelling abroad, Diaghilev became more actively involved with the former members of the Society for Self Improvement, for whom, in 1898, he started the magazine *World of Art (Mir iskusstva)*. By covering all the arts internationally, the magazine set out to break new ground in Russia. It was modern in content and presentation. Its parameters were to an extent suggested by such Western magazines as *The Studio*.

At the same time, Diaghilev began to organise a series of art exhibitions in St Petersburg. The first four, held between 1897 and 1900, featured primarily contemporary Western European art. From 1900, however, annual World of Art exhibitions were of contemporary Russian painting, sculpture and applied arts. The works were by artists from St Petersburg's World of Art group and selected artists from Moscow's Thirty-Six group, an exhibiting society founded by Apollinari Vasnetsov, Vinogradov, Pasternak, Perepletchikov, Doseikin and others.

Léon **BAKST**
1866 – 1924

Born Lev Samoilovich Rozenberg, the artist adopted his grandmother's maiden name in 1889, becoming Léon Bakst while he was still working as a caricaturist. He studied art at the Imperial Academy of Art as an external student from 1883 until 1887, took watercolour lessons from Albert Benois from 1893 to 1896, and studied in Paris under Jean-Léon Gérôme and at the Académie Julian. Bakst joined the Society for Self Improvement in 1890 and, with the launch of *World of Art* magazine, became active on the production side. He designed the group's insignia, an eagle motif, and spent long hours retouching photographs for reproduction in the magazine. He was a prolific designer of frontispieces, endpapers and vignettes for a number of books and periodicals. In 1903, he assisted in mounting an exhibition of Japanese prints in St Petersburg and subsequently was prominent as a designer for many of Diaghilev's productions, starting with the large exhibitions of 1905 and 1906 and continuing with the early ballets.

3 ✣ **Portrait of Alexandre Benois** 1898

Mixed media on canvas, 64.5 × 100.3 cm
State Russian Museum, St Petersburg
Illustrated p.17

4 ✣ **Designs for** *World of Art* **magazine**

A   **Design for illuminated heading**
1901
Pen and ink, 23.2 × 19.8 cm
State Tretyakov Gallery, Moscow

B   **Design for illuminated heading**
1902
Pen and ink, 7.8 × 22.3 cm
State Tretyakov Gallery, Moscow

Cat. 4B

5 ✣ **Designs for the book** *Tsar Dodon* **by A. Remizov**

A   **Vignette** *c*.1905
Pen and ink, heightened with white, 10 × 6.5 cm
Benois Family Museum, St Petersburg

B   **Vignette** *c*.1905
Pen and ink, heightened with white, 14.1 × 22.3 cm
Benois Family Museum, St Petersburg

From the days of the Society for Self Improvement, members of the World of Art group had access to magazines from the West, many of which were suppressed in Russia; they took an interest in the work of Western artists regarded as morally dubious even in their own countries. Among these were drawings by Aubrey Beardsley. The group also admired Japanese prints (which several of the artists collected). It is highly likely that Bakst saw Beardsley's erotic drawings during the period 1898 to 1906, when cat. 5A–B was executed.

6 ✣ **Portrait of Diaghilev with his Nanny** 1904-6
Oil on canvas, 161 × 116 cm
State Russian Museum, St Petersburg
Illustrated p.14

Alexandre **BENOIS**

1870-1960

Descended from several generations of architects and composers, Benois was the youngest son of a large family originating on his father's side from France and Germany and on his mother's side from Venice. A founder member of the Society for Self Improvement, he subsequently proved a moving force in Diaghilev's later ventures, World of Art and the early Ballets Russes. Slightly older than the rest of the group, Benois would receive his colleagues at his parental home, where a cosmopolitan, bookish atmosphere proclaimed a Western cultural outlook. His last post in Russia before emigrating to Paris was as Curator of French and English painting at the Hermitage Museum (1918-26).

Articulate and well read, Benois was a prolific writer [see cat. 8 and cat. 17 A–C] as well as a painter. In 1893, he wrote the chapter on Russian art for Richard Muther's *Geschichte der Malerei im XIX Jahrhundert*. Like the rest of the group, he was largely self taught, having left the Imperial Academy of Arts within a year of enrolling. He also travelled, worked and studied in Western Europe, at first mainly in Germany. During the late 1880s, he attended Whistler's classes at the Académie Carmen in Paris.

He entered the legal faculty of St Petersburg University in the same year as Diaghilev. His memoirs are informative about the aims and activities of himself and his World of Art colleagues. They clearly identify Sergei Diaghilev as the only person who could have brought the group's aspirations to life.

7 ✣ Illustration for 'The Bronze Horseman' by Alexander Pushkin

1903

Ink, heightened with white, 30.2 × 42.5 cm
State Tretyakov Gallery, Moscow

The bronze sculpture by Etienne Falconnet of Peter the Great on horseback was completed in 1782. Largely through Pushkin's poem 'The Bronze Horseman', it is now the best known symbol of St Petersburg, representing, as it does, the might of autocracy, challenged in Pushkin's poem by the little man. Cat.7 represents Benois's earliest venture into book illustration. The whole set of illustrations appeared in the first issue of *World of Art* magazine in 1904 [cat. 12D], engraved in wood by Anna Ostroumova-Lebedeva [see p.129].

Cat.7

8 ✣ *Tsarskoe Selo in the Reign of Empress Elizabeth* 1910

Book, 34 × 27 × 7 cm
Victoria and Albert Museum (National Art Library), London

Ivan **BILIBIN**

1876-1942

Bilibin studied with Azbé in Munich, with Repin and at Princess Tenisheva's art workshops on her estate at Talashkino, near Smolensk. In 1899, he came into contact with the World of Art group, when he was commissioned by Bakst to do a series of illustrations for the magazine. He soon developed a deep interest in Russian indigenous art and spent long periods studying it at source on location in the regions of Arkhangelsk, Vologda and Olonets. His particular interest was wooden church architecture. In 1904, his article 'Popular Art of the Russian North', which described the most important discoveries of his journeys, was published in the *World of Art* magazine, where his drawings and photographs were reproduced. Bilibin also illustrated fairy tales. Artists whose graphic work interested him included Albrecht Dürer, Aubrey Beardsley and Walter Crane.

Apart from decorative pages for books and magazines, Bilibin contributed drawings to the new satirical magazines which emerged following the revolution of 1905. His involvement with the World of Art group later led him into the field of theatre design. After a period of emigration, Bilibin returned to Soviet Russia in 1936. He died of starvation during the siege of Leningrad in 1942.

9 ✣ Illustrations for the fairy tale 'Falcon's Feather'

A **Cathedral Square** 1900

Watercolour, gouache and ink, 13.2 × 19.8 cm
State Tretyakov Gallery, Moscow

B **House in the Palace Grounds** 1900

Watercolour, gouache and ink, 22 × 29.5 cm
State Tretyakov Gallery, Moscow

10 ✣ Fairy tale motif 1902

Watercolour and pencil, 34.8 × 24.9 cm
State Tretyakov Gallery, Moscow

Sergei **CHEKHONIN**

1878-1936

Chekhonin was active in the second phase of the World of Art group (from 1910) after the closure of the magazine. He was one of the group who did much to promote the cause of graphic art in Russia and to raise standards of book production.

11 ✣ Sketch for title-page for *Old Foundations* by S.A. An-skii (Sergei Rappoport) 1910-11

Pencil, pen and ink, 23 × 17.2 cm
State Museum Reserve, Peterhof

Edited by Sergei **DIAGHILEV**

12 ✣ *World of Art (Mir iskusstva)*

A **First issue** 1898–9
Magazine, 33 × 27 × 3.5 cm
National Library of Russia, St Petersburg
Illustrated p. 42

B **1902, vol.VII, no. 2**
Magazine, 33 × 27 × 3.5 cm
National Library of Russia, St Petersburg
Illustrated p. 27

C **1903, vol.IX, no. 3**
Magazine, 33 × 27 × 3.5 cm
National Library of Russia, St Petersburg

Detail from Cat.12C

D **1904, vol. XI, no. 1**
Magazine, 33 × 27 × 3.5 cm
National Library of Russia, St Petersburg

Although Benois, Filosofov and others provided encouragement, Diaghilev started *World of Art* magazine alone. His new-found confidence in the field of fine art was expressed in his somewhat bombastic editorial essay, 'Difficult Questions' (vol.1, nos 1–4, 1899). The magazine itself was a quality production, combining new, often risqué material from the West. Each issue contained an art chronicle, giving a comprehensive digest of current European exhibitions and magazine news. Diaghilev made significant original contributions to the magazine in the fields of opera criticism and art-historical research (vols I and II, 1902). The last volume (XII, 1904) was edited by Benois.

Mstislav **DOBUZHINSKY**
1875–1957
Dobuzhinsky trained at Azbé's studio in Munich, where he met Igor Grabar, then Munich correspondent for *World of Art*. On his first meeting with Diaghilev, he felt he was not quite ready to offer his services to the magazine. Supported by Grabar, he gradually gained strength in his drawing and printmaking and was able to contribute highly personal views of St Petersburg and other cities, including his native Vilnius in Lithuania.

13 ✣ **Views of St Petersburg**

A **Evening** 1903
Watercolour and gouache, 27.5 × 36.5 cm
State Tretyakov Gallery, Moscow

B **Courtyard** 1903
Gouache, 45 × 54 cm
State Tretyakov Gallery, Moscow

C **Old House** 1905
Pencil and gouache, 25.6 × 30.9 cm
State Tretyakov Gallery, Moscow

D **Trinity Cathedral, St Petersburg**
1905
Gouache, 18.5 × 28 cm
State Tretyakov Gallery, Moscow
Illustrated p. 22

Elizaveta **KRUGLIKOVA**
1865–1941
Kruglikova began to execute silhouettes at the time she joined the World of Art group, in the post-1910 phase.

14 ✣ **Silhouette portraits of the World of Art group and associates**

A **Narbut, Makovsky, Lanceray, Lukomsky, Kruglikova and Rachmaninov** *c*.1910–20
Black paper cut-out on white paper, 13.6 × 26.6 cm
State Tretyakov Gallery, Moscow

B **Benois, Yaremich, Somov and Dobuzhinsky** *c*.1910–20
Black paper cut-out on white paper, 14.5 × 24.5 cm
State Tretyakov Gallery, Moscow

Evgeny **LANCERAY**
1875–1946

Lanceray was the nephew of Alexandre Benois through the marriage of Benois's eldest sister, Ekaterina, to Lanceray's father, also named Evgeny Lanceray, a sculptor who died of consumption in 1886. The young widow returned to her parents with her son Evgeny, then aged eleven, and her daughter Zinaida (later Serebryakova). Since Benois and his nephew Evgeny were close in age, they worked collaboratively for a number of years, until Benois married and began to spend much of his time in Paris. In 1903, they exhibited a dining room together at the exhibition of interior design, *Contemporary Art*, and both worked prolifically on *World of Art* magazine, where Lanceray proved himself an imaginative graphic artist of outstanding technical precision. Lanceray exhibited with the World of Art group at every exhibition, from 1900 to 1906, and he designed the poster for Diaghilev's *Historical Exhibition of Russian Portraits* of 1905. When Benois became involved with the Ballets Russes, Lanceray was already committed to Socialism. Lanceray never worked for the ballet, nor did he emigrate, but became a respected artist and professor of the Soviet Union. Between 1916 and 1934, he lived and taught in Dagestan and Georgia, returning to Russia in 1934, to settle in Moscow.

15 ❖ *A Private Hunting Party*
Illuminated heading for *The History of the Tsarist and Imperial Hunt in Old Russia in the late Seventeenth and the Eighteenth Centuries* **by Nikolai Kutepov** 1902
Watercolour, ink and pencil, 18.9 × 30.5 cm
State Tretyakov Gallery, Moscow

In common with Benois and Serov, Lanceray was interested at this period in recreating scenes of pageantry from the seventeenth and eighteenth centuries in Russia.

16 ❖ **Views of St Petersburg**

A **Peter I's Boat House** 1906
Gouache, watercolour and ink, 19.3 × 35.2 cm
State Tretyakov Gallery, Moscow

B **Vasilevsky Island, St Petersburg** 1901
Watercolour heightened with white, 25.3 × 32 cm
State Tretyakov Gallery, Moscow

C **Old St Petersburg** early 1900s
Watercolour and pencil heightened with white, 20.5 × 30 cm
State Tretyakov Gallery, Moscow

17 ❖ **Illustrations to** *Tsarskoe Selo in the Reign of Empress Elizabeth* **by Alexandre Benois**

A **Capture of the Swedish Cape** 1908
Watercolour, gouache, ink and pencil, 23 × 25.5 cm
State Tretyakov Gallery, Moscow

B **Road to Tsarskoe Selo at the Time of Empress Anna** 1908
Watercolour, gouache, ink and pencil, 18.1 × 30.5 cm
State Tretyakov Gallery, Moscow

C **Empress Elizabeth Inspects Building Work at Tsarskoe Selo** 1908
Watercolour, gouache, ink and pencil, 10.4 × 32 cm
State Tretyakov Gallery, Moscow

Isaak **LEVITAN**
1860–1900

The landscapes of Levitan are as much a breakthrough in realistic art as were the genre compositions of Ilya Repin [see p. 124]. He exhibited with the Wanderers [see p. 124] from 1884, becoming a member in 1891. Diaghilev and his colleagues much admired the sensitive, poetic quality of quintessential Russia captured in his views of the Russian countryside and his works were represented in the World of Art exhibitions, also the *Exhibition of Russian and Finnish Artists* of 1898. Levitan, in turn, was an associate of the group from 1899 to 1906 and corresponded regularly with Diaghilev. In 1900, following Levitan's death, a special issue of *World of Art* (nos 15–16) written largely by Diaghilev, served as a retrospective homage.

18 ❖ **Autumn** *c.*1896
Watercolour and pencil, 31.5 × 44 cm
State Tretyakov Gallery, Moscow

19 ❖ **Copse by a Lake (Autumn)** *c.*1898
Oil on paper, 11.1 × 15.1 cm
Ashmolean Museum, Oxford
Illustrated p. 25

Cat. 18

Filipp **MALIAVINE**
1869 - 1940

Maliavine was interested in Russian folk art and in peasant scenes, which he rendered in vivid, decorative form. After starting as an icon painter, Maliavine then became a portrait painter of surprising sophistication. He was represented in the World of Art exhibitions and in the 1906 Salon d'Automne. In 1922, Maliavine emigrated to France. He died in Nice.

20 ❖ **Girl with a Flowered Shawl** *c.*1898

Pencil and chalk, 38.5 × 28.5 cm
Ashmolean Museum, Oxford

Anna **OSTROUMOVA-LEBEDEVA**
1871 - 1955

Ostroumova was a student of Ilya Repin in St Petersburg and later of James McNeill Whistler in Paris, where she made friends with Konstantin Somov and Alexandre Benois. She travelled widely in Europe. On her return to St Petersburg, her delicate, expressive engravings soon came to the attention of Sergei Diaghilev, who featured them in *World of Art* magazine. After marrying the chemist Sergei Lebedev in 1905, Ostroumova remained in St Petersburg, which she continued to celebrate into the Soviet era.

21 ❖ **Views of St Petersburg**

A **White Nights** early 1900s

Watercolour, 8.4 × 13.4 cm
State Tretyakov Gallery, Moscow
Illustrated p.18

B **Stock Exchange** early 1900s

Watercolour, 9 × 13.7 cm
State Tretyakov Gallery, Moscow

C **Tuchkov Bridge** early 1900s

Watercolour, 8.2 × 13.7 cm
State Tretyakov Gallery, Moscow

D **Admiralty and Senate** early 1900s

Watercolour, 10 × 15.8 cm
State Tretyakov Gallery, Moscow

Elena **POLENOVA**
1850 - 1898

Polenova was a painter, graphic artist, illustrator, crafts worker and major influence on the revival of interest in Russian applied and folk arts. Her father was an archaeologist, her brother the landscape painter Vasily Polenov. She studied under Chistyakov and Kramskoy before becoming fascinated with folk art and artefacts, which she collected for the Abramtsevo Museum. She learned and illustrated folk tales and worked closely on decorative interiors with Alexandre Golovine [see p.133]. After her death, a handsome issue of *World of Art* (vol.II, 1899) was devoted to her work. It included illustrations of the works below. The embroidery workshop which she had set up at Abramtsevo was adopted by Mariya Yakunchikova [see p.132].

22 ❖ **Illustrations to the fairy tale** *Young Filipko*

A **Baba Yaga lures Filipko** 1897-8

Watercolour, 31 × 22 cm
State Tretyakov Gallery, Moscow

Cat. 22A

B **Filipko at Baba Yaga's** 1897-8

Watercolour, 31 × 22 cm
State Tretyakov Gallery, Moscow

Ilya **REPIN**

Repin was closely linked with the art circles both of Abramtsevo and Talashkino on the estates of Savva Mamontov [see Biographical Notes] and Princess Mariya Tenisheva respectively. Both patrons collected his work. In 1895, he became Director of Tenisheva's art school.

23 ❖ **Portrait of Savva Mamontov** 1880

Oil on canvas, 73 × 64 cm
A.A.Bakhrushin State Central Theatre Museum, Moscow

Andrei **RYABUSHKIN**
1861 - 1904

A history and genre painter whose chief theme was village life in the seventeenth century, Ryabushkin belonged to the second generation of the Wanderers, along with Valentin Serov [see below] and Mikhail Nesterov. His original approach in the evocation of an historical period was admired by the World of Art group. Diaghilev exhibited his work at the 1906 Salon d'Automne.

24 ❖ **Old Moscow** early 1900s

Watercolour, pen and ink on paper, 33.5 × 25.7 cm
State Tretyakov Gallery, Moscow

Valentin **SEROV**
1865 - 1911

Son of the composer Alexander Serov, the young Valentin was adopted by Mamontov [see Biographical Notes] at an early age, after the boy had lost his father. Trained by Ilya Repin, who was also an early father figure, Serov proved the most talented of his students. Technically adept, a remarkable draughtsman with subtle painterly skills, Serov was able to adapt academic disciplines to achieve new triumphs in the use of light and colour. He was a versatile artist, but is known above all as a consummate painter of portraits.

Based primarily in Moscow, Serov was never a member of the World of Art group, but was the group's closest Moscow associate, exhibiting with artists of the circle and spending much time with them on his visits to the capital, generally staying with Diaghilev. He was admired not only for his talents but for his forthright and rather crude manner, in which he refused to resort to sycophancy, even towards the Tsar, whose wife he offended during an Imperial portrait sitting. He resigned his post at the Imperial Academy in protest at the events of the revolution of January 1905. He continued his influential career, however, at the Moscow College, where he taught from 1897 to 1909. After 1905, Serov was active both in the field of political art and as a designer for Diaghilev's theatrical enterprises.

25 ⊹ **Portrait of Rimsky-Korsakov** 1898
Oil on canvas, 94 × 111 cm
State Tretyakov Gallery, Moscow

26 ⊹ **Portrait of Tsar Nicholas II** 1900
Oil on canvas, 71 × 58.8 cm
State Tretyakov Gallery, Moscow
Illustrated p. 32

Pavel **SHCHERBOV**
1866 – 1938
Shcherbov was a World of Art associate who exhibited with the group between 1902 and 1903. He executed a number of frank but not unaffectionate caricatures of Diaghilev and his circle, engaged in their various endeavours.

27 ⊹ **Milking the Cow:**
Caricature of Diaghilev and
Princess Tenisheva early 1900s
Pen and ink, 25.7 × 41.7 cm
State Tretyakov Gallery, Moscow
Illustrated p. 42

Konstantin **SOMOV**
1869 – 1939
Somov had the longest art training of any World of Art member, both in St Petersburg and Paris. None the less, he did not complete his Academy training, since he was expelled for his involvement in a student strike. His Paris training was at the Académie Colarossi and, occasionally, at Whistler's Académie Carmen. His work was much admired by colleagues, but never accepted by the older generation. In 1923, at the time of an exhibition in the USA, he emigrated from Russia, soon moving to Paris, where he remained until his death. A founder member of the World of Art group, he left the circle in its early stages, after a disagreement with Diaghilev and Filosofov. He exhibited with other members of the group at the interior design exhibition, *Contemporary Art*, in 1903, and had a one-man show in the same year. Although his work is supremely theatrical, Somov never designed for the theatre.

28 ⊹ **Portrait of Léon Bakst**
and Alexandre Benois 1896
Watercolour and gouache, 37.3 × 22.2 cm
State Tretyakov Gallery, Moscow
Illustrated p. 123

29 ⊹ **Summer: Ladies on**
a Bench 1896
Watercolour and coloured pencil on card,
25.6 × 34.7 cm
State Tretyakov Gallery, Moscow

30 ⊹ **Twilight in the Old Park** 1897
Watercolour and gouache, 46 × 64 cm
State Tretyakov Gallery, Moscow

31 ⊹ **Park at Versailles** 1897
Gouache and pencil, 17 × 25.7 cm
State Tretyakov Gallery, Moscow

32 ⊹ *Exhibition of Russian*
and Finnish Artists:
sketch for a poster 1897
Gouache, 102.5 × 70.8 cm
State Tretyakov Gallery, Moscow

33 ⊹ **'Sultana':**
drawing for a snuff box 1899
Gouache, ink and gold paint, 13.2 × 27 cm
State Tretyakov Gallery, Moscow
Illustrated p. 29

34 ⊹ **Design for** *World of Art*:
illuminated heading early 1900s
Watercolour, white and gold paint, 10.2 × 24.8 cm
State Tretyakov Gallery, Moscow

35 ⊹ **Design for** *World of Art*:
frontispiece 1900
Pen and ink on paper, 34 × 26 cm
State Tretyakov Gallery, Moscow

36 ⊹ **Design for the magazine**
Art Treasures of Russia:
cover 1901
Watercolour, pen and ink, 29 × 22.2 cm
State Tretyakov Gallery, Moscow

37 ⊹ **Self-portrait** 1902
Pencil, 26.8 × 13.8 cm
State Tretyakov Gallery, Moscow

38 ⸙ **Sleeping Woman in Blue Dress** 1903
Watercolour and gouache, 18.9 × 18.5 cm
State Tretyakov Gallery, Moscow

39 ⸙ **Lady in Pink** 1903
Watercolour and gouache, 42.4 × 31 cm
State Tretyakov Gallery, Moscow
Illustrated p. 21

40 ⸙ **Illustrations to the book**
Das Lesebuch der Marquise 1905
Benois Family Museum, St Petersburg

A   Printed proof, 22.3 × 14.9 cm

B   Printed proof, 7.7 × 12.2 cm

C   Printed proof, 23.8 × 15.7 cm

D   Printed proof, 22.6 × 14.8 cm

E   Printed proof, 25.1 × 18.8 cm

F   Printed proof, 25.4 × 19 cm

G   Printed proof, 13.5 × 15 cm

41 ⸙ *Le Livre de la Marquise* 1918
Book, illustrated by Konstantin Somov,
25.8 × 19.4 cm
National Library of Russia, St Petersburg

42 ⸙ **Portrait of Evgeny Lanceray** 1907
Pencil and crayon, heightened with white,
26.5 × 51.2 cm
State Tretyakov Gallery, Moscow

Pavel **TRUBETSKOI**
1866 – 1938
Prince Pavel (Paolo) Trubetskoi was born and
trained as a sculptor in Milan, where he also died.
His work is characterised by a dynamic touch and
fluent, tactile surfaces. For a period, Trubetskoi
taught at Moscow Academy and he exhibited with
the World of Art group 1899-1903. Also in 1899, he
first began to exhibit regularly with the Wanderers.
His sculpture was represented by Diaghilev at the
1906 Salon d'Automne [see p.135].

43 ⸙ **Moscow Coachman** 1898
Bronze, height 24 cm
State Tretyakov Gallery, Moscow

44 ⸙ **Mariya Sergeevna Botkina
and Daughter** 1900
Bronze, height 39 cm
State Tretyakov Gallery, Moscow

Mikhail **VRUBEL**
1856 – 1910
Probably the most highly acclaimed of all Russian
artists, Vrubel was a master in all fine art media as
well as theatre and furniture design. Closely involved with the Abramtsevo potteries, his ceramic
tiles and sculpture were much exhibited both in
Russia and abroad. In 1900, he won a medal at the
Paris *Exposition Universelle*. He also painted scenery
for Mamontov's Private Opera Company (1889) and
restored the frescoes of the Cathedrals of St Cyril
(1884 - 5) and St Vladimir (1887) in Kiev. He was the
most inspired of the Russian Symbolists, and came
nearest in his work to Abstract Expressionism.

His imaginary work has a visionary quality and
a recurrent theme is the demon of the poems of
Lermontov. Always obsessive, Vrubel went mad in
1902. In 1906, he lost his sight, dying four years later
in an asylum.

45 ⸙ **Portrait of the Artist's Wife
(Singer Nadezhda Zabela-Vrubel)**
1898
Oil on canvas, 124 × 75.7 cm
State Tretyakov Gallery, Moscow

46 ⸙ **'Roberto Monachini' Group** 1898
Coloured plaster, height 96 cm
State Tretyakov Gallery, Moscow

47 ⸙ **Volga** 1898 - 9
Majolica fireplace, polychrome ceramics,
226 × 275 cm
State Tretyakov Gallery, Moscow

A *tour-de-force* of ceramic craftsmanship, cat. 47 was
one of a whole series exhibited by Vrubel, both at the
Paris *Exposition Universelle* of 1900 and at the World
of Art exhibition of 1901. Prominent in exhibition
photographs in *World of Art* magazine in 1900 and
1901, his fireplaces also appeared there illustrating
two special articles during 1903.

Mikhail Vrubel's *Volga* as exhibited at
the World of Art exhibition of 1901
Reproduced in *World of Art* magazine
British Library, London

48 ❖ **Pan** 1899
Oil on canvas, 124 × 106.3 cm
State Tretyakov Gallery, Moscow
Illustrated p. 44

49 ❖ **Swan Princess** 1900
Oil on canvas, 142.5 × 93.5 cm
State Tretyakov Gallery, Moscow
Illustrated p. 45

THE WORLD OF ART PAINTERS

50 ❖ **Set of postcards from St Evgenia's Fund**
Benois Family Museum, St Petersburg

These Charity postcards, showing selected works by artists associated with the World of Art group, were used as advertisements for the group's selling exhibitions.

Alexandre **BENOIS**

A **The Summer Gardens at the Time of Peter the Great** 1904
Postcard from lithograph, 9 × 14 cm

B **The Fontanka at the Time of Catherine the Great** 1904
Postcard from lithograph, 9 × 14 cm

C **Paul I Reviewing Troops in Front of the Winter Palace** 1904
Postcard from lithograph, 9 × 14 cm

D **The Empress Elizaveta Petrovna Takes a Walk in the Splendid Streets of St Petersburg** 1904
Postcard from lithograph, 9 × 14 cm

E **Oranienbaum** 1904
Postcard from lithograph, 9 × 14 cm

Mstislav **DOBUZHINSKY**

F **Vaults of Hanging Garden at Tsarskoe Selo** 1904
Postcard from lithograph, 9 × 14 cm

G **Fontanka, Palace of Peter I** 1904
Postcard from lithograph, 9 × 14 cm

H **Izmailovsky Regiment, St Petersburg** 1913
Postcard from lithograph, 9 × 14 cm

Evgeny **LANCERAY**

I **Building of the Twelfth College** 1904
Postcard from lithograph, 9 × 14 cm

Anna **OSTROUMOVA-LEBEDEVA**

J **The Columns of Kazan Cathedral** 1904
Woodcut, 9 × 14 cm

K **By the Stock Exchange** 1910
Woodcut, 9 × 14 cm

L **The Admiralty Under Snow** 1910
Woodcut, 9 × 14 cm

Mariya **YAKUNCHIKOVA-WEBER**
1870 – 1902

An associate of the Abramtsevo group, the painter, graphic artist and embroiderer Yakunchikova was a pupil of various artists of the neo-national school, especially Elena Polenova [see p. 129]. Born at Wiesbaden, she grew up in Moscow in a family with many artistic connections. She studied privately from 1883, and as an external student of Moscow College from 1885. From 1886 to 1889 she took evening classes with Polenova, through whom she became involved in the revival of vernacular handicrafts. She travelled to France in 1888, where she studied at the Académie Julian and the studios of Bouguereau and Fleury, and to Germany in 1889, after which she worked mainly in Western Europe.

In 1898, Diaghilev commissioned from Yakunchikova a design for the cover of *World of Art* magazine, which came out in issues 13–24 in 1899. She exhibited with the World of Art group from 1899 and also with the Thirty-Six group.

51 ❖ **The Pond** 1890s
Gouache, 31 × 23.8 cm
State Tretyakov Gallery, Moscow

Cat. 51

52 ❖ **Tree in Sunlight** 1899
Gouache, 62.5 × 46 cm
State Tretyakov Gallery, Moscow

Arbiter of Russian Taste

Prince Sergei Volkonsky became the youngest ever Director of the Imperial Theatres when he took over the post from his uncle Ivan Vsevolozhsky [see p.134] in 1899. Volkonsky had briefly been connected with the World of Art group and had written for the magazine. On his appointment, Volkonsky swiftly annexed his old friends from the circle, with Diaghilev and Filosofov at the head, giving them jobs at the theatres. Diaghilev was entrusted with the task of compiling and editing the *Yearbook* for 1898-9 and 1899-1900: an annual digest of the previous season's activities in all six of the public theatres in Moscow and St Petersburg, which were run by the Imperial Court. The year 1900 was the 150th anniversary of the founding of the public theatre in Russia. Diaghilev used the occasion to produce a lavish two-volume Jubilee edition for the second Season [cat. 55]. It was a superb publication containing important essays and illustrations.

The success of the *Yearbook* led Diaghilev to embark on an endeavour which failed: the creation of a new production of the ballet *Sylvia* [see cat. 54], to the music of Delibes, which he planned for the 1901-2 Season at the Maryinsky Theatre. Had the project worked, it would have been Diaghilev's first World of Art theatre production. However, problems with production staff put an end to this project and even led to Diaghilev's resignation from his Imperial post. His first theatre enterprise was thus postponed until 1908-9, when Diaghilev was to export the Imperial Opera and Ballet to Paris.

Léon **BAKST**

53 ❖ **Portrait of Isadora Duncan** 1907-8

Brush and Indian ink over traces of pencil, 48.9 × 33.3 cm
Ashmolean Museum, Oxford
Illustrated p. 76

Alexandre **BENOIS**

54 ❖ **Set design for the projected production of** *Sylvia* 1902

Watercolour and pencil on board, 33.5 × 51 cm
State Museum of Theatre and Music, St Petersburg
Illustrated p.34

Sylvia was the last ballet composed by Léo Delibes. It was considered by Diaghilev's circle to be a milestone in the history of ballet music, the precursor of historic ballets such as *The Sleeping Beauty* [see Production Notes] and *The Nutcracker*, composed by Tchaikovsky.

Edited by Sergei **DIAGHILEV**

55 ❖ **Yearbook of the Imperial Theatres** 1899-1900

Book (2 volumes), 28 × 23.5 × 5.5 cm
National Library of Russia, St Petersburg

Alexandre **GOLOVINE**

1863-1930

Golovine was an artist and designer of versatility and a fine portrait painter. He was interested both in traditional Russian folk art and in international culture. He designed for the Imperial Theatres and for Mamontov's Private Opera Company, and his designs were frequently acclaimed in *World of Art* magazine. Tenuously associated with the World of Art group, Golovine participated in *Contemporary Art*, the interior design exhibition by World of Art members organised by Prince Shervashidze in 1903. He subsequently designed the sets for *Boris Godunov*, Diaghilev's first opera production in Paris [see Production Notes]; and for the first production of *The Firebird* by Diaghilev's Ballets Russes [see Production Notes].

56 ❖ **Set design for the opera** *The House of Ice*: **Winter Palace** 1901

Gouache, 34 × 57 cm
State Tretyakov Gallery, Moscow
Illustrated p. 59

Golovine designed this production, to the music of Koreschenko, for the Bolshoi Opera Company in Moscow. It was hailed as a triumph in a review by Diaghilev in the first issue of *World of Art* magazine in 1901.

Konstantin **KOROVINE**

1861-1939

Associated with Moscow and with the Abramtsevo workshops, Korovine worked as designer both for the Imperial Theatres and for Mamontov's Private Opera Company. He exhibited a series of important panels in the Russian Pavilion at the Paris *Exposition Universelle* in 1900. Acclaimed in his own right as a painter of Russian themes in 'Impressionist' style, and in the pages of *World of Art*, with Golovine [see above] as a designer, Korovine designed the costumes for Diaghilev's Paris productions of *Ruslan and Lyudmila* (1909), *Le Festin* (1909) [see Production Notes] and *Les Orientales* (1910). Like Golovine, Korovine was prevented from further collaboration with Diaghilev by the ill-will of Vladimir Teliakovsky, who succeeded Prince Volkonsky as Director of the Imperial Theatres.

57 ❖ Set design for *Don Quixote* 1900

Watercolour and gouache, 29.4×45.3cm
State Tretyakov Gallery, Moscow

Benois's review of the production of this ballet in
World of Art (1902, no. 2) declares Korovine's designs
far superior to the production itself, which was
choreographed to music by Tchaikovsky and
Glazunov. First produced in Moscow, it represented
the début of the choreographer Alexander Gorsky.

Ivan **VSEVOLOZHSKY**

1835-1909

The Russian diplomat Vsevolozhsky was Director
of the Imperial Theatres from 1881 to 1899. He was
also a gifted theatre director and the designer of
some twenty-five ballets. Vsevolozhsky played an
important role in the revival of ballet in Russia.
He wrote the libretto for Tchaikovsky's ballet *The
Sleeping Beauty* [see Production Notes], which was
first performed at the Maryinsky Theatre in 1890.
He had a great influence on the choreographer
Marius Petipa, suggesting to him the new and
successful 1895 staging of *Swan Lake* [see Production Notes]; and he engaged the Italian dancers
Zucchi, Brianza and Cecchetti [see Biographical
Notes]. By originating the so-called production
council, bringing librettist, choreographer, composer and designer together, Vsevolozhsky played
an important role in achieving the unity of style in
Russian ballet which was subsequently brought to
such perfection by Diaghilev's Ballets Russes. An
interesting article about him appears in Diaghilev's
Imperial Theatres *Yearbook* of 1899-1900 [cat. 55],
with examples of his designs. He epitomises the last
triumphant stage of the Imperial Ballets as a court
institution. Shortly after Diaghilev joined the
Imperial Theatres, Vsevolozhsky retired to make
way for his nephew Prince Sergei Volkonsky.

From a design by Ivan **VSEVOLOZHSKY**

58 ❖ *The Sleeping Beauty*:
Cloak for the Queen 1890

Velvet, silk, gold thread
State Museum of Theatre and Music,
St Petersburg

DIAGHILEV AS HISTORIAN OF RUSSIAN ART 1902-5

World of Art and its protagonists were
strongly pro-eighteenth century. The 1700s in
Russian history correspond to the Renaissance in
Western European culture. In their art and writing,
many World of Art artists were concerned with capturing the mood of an historical period. Alexandre
Benois was absorbed mainly with architecture.
Diaghilev became interested in painting. During the
eighteenth century, painters in Russia, emerging
from the era of icons as the only pictorial art form,
began to execute portraits, mainly of Imperial and
aristocratic personages. A fascination for the history
of the Russian nobility led Diaghilev to research
seriously both portrait artists and their sitters. He
began planning a series of books on Russian artists
of the eighteenth century. The first volume of this
[cat. 59] was a monograph on the portrait painter
Dmitry Levitsky (1735-1822). It proved as great
a success as the Imperial Theatres *Yearbook* [cat. 55].
Nicely produced, with full and choice illustrations,
the book's texts covered not only the painter's life
but also aspects of his technique that broke new
ground in the academic history of Russian art.
The acclaimed volume was awarded the Gold
Medal of the Academy of Sciences.

In 1902, the year that the Levitsky monograph was completed, Diaghilev began to research
for an *Historical Exhibition of Russian Portraits*.
The exhibition was to be an overview of the Russian
portrait over the past 150 years, from its earliest
manifestations up until 1905, and was to be the first
exhibition of its kind. Apart from the sheer size of
the exhibition (2,226 works), another unique factor
was its presentation, which raised the importance
of the artist to the same level as the sitter. Diaghilev
continued to apply his principles of sparse hanging
and of tasteful juxtaposition of works begun in his
exhibitions of the World of Art period. A large number of the works selected for this exhibition were
ultimately not hung.

The exhibition took place at the disused
Tauride Palace, St Petersburg's first neo-classical
building, commissioned by Catherine the Great
from the architect Starov as a reward to her ex-lover
Prince Grigory Potemkin for his victories during
the late 1770s against the Turks in Taurida, in the
Crimea. The palace had fallen into disrepair after
the prince's death and had been put to no use prior
to this occasion. Diaghilev restored it and the
exhibition was a triumph.

Sergei **DIAGHILEV**

59 ❖ *Russian Painting in
the Eighteenth Century*
(vol. 1): 'Dmitry Levitsky' 1902

Book, 33.5×27.3×5cm
Victoria and Albert Museum (National Art
Library), London

Grand Duke **NIKOLAI MIKHAILOVICH**

1859-1919

60 ❖ *Russian Portraiture of the XVIII
and XIX centuries* (vol. III)
Catalogue of *The Russian Portrait*

1907

Book, 37.8×28.5×2cm
Sotheby's, London

Diaghilev's interest in the Russian portrait led him
to serious research into the portraits that existed in
Russia's private and museum collections. He resolved not only to exhibit but to catalogue them:
an endeavour in which he was assisted and funded
by Grand Duke Nikolai Mikhailovich, grandson of
Tsar Nicholas I and great-uncle of Nicholas II.

Promoter of Russian Art

THE EXHIBITION OF RUSSIAN ART AT THE GRAND PALAIS, PARIS, 1906

In the early 1900s, Diaghilev had noticed that exhibitions in the West did not cover the whole spectrum of Russian art. In particular, they did not promote the more interesting aspects of contemporary painting and sculpture. Above all, Diaghilev saw the need to show the West what was uniquely Russian about Russian art.

At the end of 1905, following the closure of the successful *Historical Exhibition of Russian Portraits*, Diaghilev began working towards a retrospective exhibition of Russian art that would display its entire history, from icons to the then present day, with the emphasis on enduring Russian traits in art and on unique features of the work of Russian artists individually and of Russian art in general.

Through his diplomatic contacts in Paris, Diaghilev managed to secure the Paris Salon d'Automne for October 1906. His exhibition, which consisted of 750 works of fine and decorative art, filled twelve halls of the Grand Palais. The Russians shared the building with the Fauves, whose influence could already be seen in the work of some of the Russian exhibitors.

All Diaghilev's exhibitions from 1897 onwards were mounted in a manner unique for their time. In October 1906, as before, the arrangement and design of the exhibition elicited admiring comments from visitors. The exhibitions were always expressly designed, an idea that very possibly stemmed from the exhibitions of James McNeill Whistler at the Fine Art Society in London and elsewhere. Willing and inspired exponents of this were Léon Bakst and Alexandre Benois. In 1906, they were helped in mounting the exhibition by the painters Pavel Kuznetsov [see p. 140], Mikhail Larionov [see p. 136] and Sergei Sudeikin [see p. 152], whose works were represented in this display. Although the Salon d'Automne catalogue does not give details of dates, dimensions or media, it contains some black-and-white reproductions from which it has been possible to reassemble certain exhibits. Other works have been selected for their probable similarity to those in the original exhibition.

Alexandre BENOIS

61 ❖ **Ceres's Pool, Versailles** 1897
Watercolour and charcoal heightened with white, 25.8 × 35.7 cm
State Tretyakov Gallery, Moscow

62 ❖ **Near the Palace of Mon Plaisir** 1900
Gouache and charcoal, 31 × 41.7 cm
State Tretyakov Gallery, Moscow

63 ❖ **Interior of the Palace of Mon Plaisir: Dining Hall** 1900
Watercolour heightened with white, 43.2 × 31.5 cm
State Tretyakov Gallery, Moscow

64 ❖ **Japanese Hall at Oranienbaum** 1901
Watercolour and pencil, 27.9 × 42.8 cm
State Tretyakov Gallery, Moscow

Cat. 62

65 ❖ **Park at Versailles** 1901
Watercolour, gouache and charcoal, 26.8 × 40.5 cm
State Tretyakov Gallery, Moscow

66 ❖ **Italian Comedy: The Love Letter** 1905
Watercolour and gouache, 49.6 × 67.4 cm
State Tretyakov Gallery, Moscow
Illustrated p. 20

67 ❖ **Orangery** 1906
Watercolour and gouache, 67 × 70 cm
State Tretyakov Gallery, Moscow

Cat. 63

Mstislav **DOBUZHINSKY**

68 ⊹ **The Hairdresser's Window** 1906
Gouache, chalk and charcoal, 29.7 × 21.7 cm
State Tretyakov Gallery, Moscow
Illustrated p. 23

69 ⊹ **Old Wharf in London** 1906
Black chalk and body colour, 28.2 × 38 cm
Ashmolean Museum, Oxford

Anna **GOLUBKINA**
1864 – 1927
Golubkina studied architecture before settling down
to the creation of sculpture. Her forte was considered to be portraiture but she also made decorative pieces. An interest in formal experimentation
gave rise to interesting art nouveau sculpture.

70 ⊹ **Vase: 'Mist'** 1899
Marble, 52.5 × 32.5 × 31 cm
State Tretyakov Gallery, Moscow

Natalia **GONCHAROVA**
1881 – 1962
Goncharova first studied sculpture in Moscow
under Trubetskoi and Volnikin, then painting under
Korovine. In 1900, the year she became a painter, she
met Mikhail Larionov, who became her life partner.
She met Diaghilev in 1905. By 1909 she was active
as a theatre designer. She participated in the 1906
exhibition at the Salon d'Automne and her first
Diaghilev theatre commission was the opera-ballet
Le Coq d'Or [see Production Notes].

71 ⊹ **Self-portrait** 1907
Oil on canvas, 77 × 58.2 cm
State Tretyakov Gallery, Moscow
Illustrated p. 110

Mikhail **LARIONOV**
1881 – 1964
Larionov was one of the first protagonists of the
Russian avant-garde. In 1906, when still a student,
he was noticed by Diaghilev, who exhibited his
works that year on two occasions: first in St Petersburg's Catherine Hall and then at the Paris Salon
d'Automne. Larionov was closely associated with
the Ballets Russes from 1915 to 1929. Diaghilev's
collaboration with Larionov and Goncharova [see
above] represents the beginning of his renowned
association with the international avant-garde in art.

72 ⊹ **Through the Net** 1903
Oil on canvas, 58 × 69 cm
State Tretyakov Gallery, Moscow

Cat.72

73 ⊹ **Red Horse: Landscape** 1909 –10
Oil on canvas, 70 × 90 cm
State Tretyakov Gallery, Moscow

Isaak **LEVITAN**

74 ⊹ **Grey Day: Marsh
Study** 1898
Oil on cardboard, 16.5 × 24.7 cm
State Tretyakov Gallery, Moscow

75 ⊹ **Haystacks** 1899
Oil on canvas, 59.8 × 74.6 cm
State Tretyakov Gallery, Moscow
Illustrated p. 24

Nikolai **MILIOTI**
1874-1962
Milioti was a leader of the Blue Rose group of the Russian Symbolist movement. His first association with Diaghilev was his inclusion in the Salon d'Automne exhibition. Possibly he was recommended by Pavel Kuznetsov, a leading protagonist of the Symbolist movement and an important exhibitor and designer of this exhibition.

76 ❖ **Lovers** 1905
Oil on card, 50.5 × 40 cm
State Tretyakov Gallery, Moscow

Ilya **REPIN**

Repin's 'democratic' political stand won him the support of the liberal critic Vladimir Stasov, who was inimical to the 'decadent' aesthetic of the World of Art movement. Apart from tendentious works containing unequivocal social comment, Repin also enjoyed history paintings. Since this approach was anathema to members of the World of Art group, the limited representation of Repin's work in the Salon d'Automne exhibition shows minimal regard for a major living artist.

77 ❖ **Sketch for** *Zaporozhian Cossacks*
c.1880
Oil on canvas, 67 × 87 cm
State Tretyakov Gallery, Moscow
Illustrated p.33

The final version of cat. 77, a large oil canvas (State Russian Museum 1891), is an example of Repin's genius for producing works of intense drama containing a perfect blend of theatricality and compositional balance. Its high standard of technical finish and compelling content later made this painting Stalin's favourite and the prototype for Socialist Realism.

Edited by Nikolai **RYABUSHINSKY**
1876-1912
A textile tycoon and writer, Ryabushinsky founded the magazine *The Golden Fleece (Zolotoe runo / La Toison d'Or)* in 1906. Published in Moscow, it ran until 1909-10. The magazine promoted the Blue Rose Symbolist group, and covered the fine and applied arts in Russia and Western Europe, much as *World of Art* had done before its closure in 1904. It was printed in parallel text in Russian and French.

78 ❖ *Golden Fleece*
(Zolotoe runo / La Toison d'Or),
vol. II 1906
Magazine, 35 × 31 × 6 cm
David Elliott, Oxford

Cat. 78 is of interest primarily for its many reproductions of contemporary works shown in the World of Art exhibition in St Petersburg in 1906. Many works by the same artists were shown later at the 1906 Salon d'Automne in Paris.

Konstantin **SOMOV**

79 ❖ **Confidences** 1897
Oil on canvas, 53 × 72.2 cm
State Tretyakov Gallery, Moscow

80 ❖ **Baigneuses** 1899
Oil on card, 75 × 104.2 cm
State Tretyakov Gallery, Moscow

81 ❖ **Ile d'Amour** 1900
Oil on canvas, 62.3 × 81.7 cm
State Tretyakov Gallery, Moscow
Illustrated p. 28

82 ❖ **Lovers** 1905
Coloured porcelain, height 14 cm
State Tretyakov Gallery, Moscow

83 ❖ **Lady with a Mask** 1905
Coloured porcelain, height 22.5 cm
State Tretyakov Gallery, Moscow

Mikhail **VRUBEL**

84 ❖ **Sea King: relief** 1899-1900
Coloured ceramic, height 52 cm
State Tretyakov Gallery, Moscow

Cat. 84 and the sculptures below [cat. 85-7] are part of a series personifying Russian rivers. The inspiration for the series came from two operas by Rimsky-Korsakov: *Sadko* [see Production Notes] and *Snegurochka* (*The Snow Maiden*).

Cat. 84

85 ❖ **Mizgir** 1899-1900
Majolica, height 47 cm
State Tretyakov Gallery, Moscow

86 ❖ **Volkhova** 1899-1900
Majolica, height 42 cm
State Tretyakov Gallery, Moscow

87 ❖ **Tsar Berendei** 1899-1903
Terracotta, height 49 cm
State Tretyakov Gallery, Moscow

Konstantin **YUON**
1875-1958
Yuon's association with Diaghilev was sporadic. He exhibited with World of Art between 1902 and 1903, at the 1906 Salon d'Automne, and designed some of the costumes in 1908 for Diaghilev's Paris production of Mussorgsky's opera *Boris Godunov* [see Production Notes]. A Russophile, he became famous in the Soviet period for his jolly Russian folk scenes.

88 ❖ **Trinity Church** 1903
Oil on canvas, 53 × 107 cm
State Tretyakov Gallery, Moscow

The First Russian Seasons (Saisons russes) 1907-1909

The opening of the 1906 exhibition in Paris was followed by a concert of Russian music. Attended by a large audience, it was favourably reviewed in the French press, and Diaghilev was soon planning an entire Season of concerts for the following year.

The 1907 Season of Russian concerts took place at the Paris Opéra and comprised five events during May and June. Consisting of operatic and symphonic works by Glinka (1804-57), Rimsky-Korsakov (1844-1908), Borodin (1822-87), Glazunov (1865-1936), Rachmaninov (1873-1943) and Tchaikovsky (1840-93), the music Season again exemplified Diaghilev's policy of showing aspects of Russian culture little known in Western Europe.

Paris audiences had heard of 'The Five' (or '*Moguchaia kuchka* [Mighty Handful]') and appreciated their compositions, which represented an important breakthrough in Russian music, consisting of a distillation of the nationalist features of such composers as Glinka and Dargomijsky (1813-69). 'The Five' were Balakirev (1837-1910), Cui (1835-1918), Borodin, Mussorgsky (1839-81) and Rimsky-Korsakov, who shared with the painters of the World of Art group a certain dilettante reputation, since no member of either group had undergone a full professional training. All five composers pursued music in addition to a career in the armed forces or the legal, medical or academic professions.

Many of their works were never finished, or were completed as a joint effort by two or more of the group; the collaborative bent was another feature shared with members of the World of Art group. Finally, their work was championed and published by the wealthy timber merchant Mitrofan Belyaev, an amateur viola player who held musical evenings at his home and funded public concert seasons, thus fulfilling a role analogous to those of Diaghilev and Mamontov [see Biographical Notes]. Like Diaghilev's *World of Art* magazine, the libretti of these works published by Belyaev contained much that was inspired by the poetry of Alexander Pushkin (1799-1837). In opera, Pushkin was the basis of a cult of nationalism which was further expressed through the use of folk themes both in the music and in the accompanying sets and costumes. The strong influence of folk culture allies 'The Five' with Mamontov, whose Private Opera Company performed many of their works.

Pyotr Ilyich Tchaikovsky was the first conservatoire-trained Russian composer, representing a crucial development in the tradition begun by Glinka. Particularly in the field of symphonic music, he was able to realise projects beyond the scope of 'The Five'. Yet he was the composer least appreciated at this period by the French and was regarded abroad as heavy and sentimental. Diaghilev presented Tchaikovsky's second symphony in Paris against the advice of his promoters.

Several of the works performed were conducted by their composers (Rachmaninov, Rimsky-Korsakov) and important Russian vocal soloists appeared. One of the stars of the 1907 Season was Fyodor Chaliapin [see Biographical Notes]. This was not his first appearance in the West, but he had not performed before in Paris. Previous appearances had been at La Scala in Milan and at the Metropolitan Opera House in New York.

Chaliapin also starred in the opera Season which Diaghilev staged in Paris in 1908, again at the Opéra. It consisted of seven performances of Modest Mussorgsky's *Boris Godunov* [see Production Notes], being performed for the first time in the West, in a new production adapted by Diaghilev and Rimsky-Korsakov. Western spectators were impressed by the dramatic integrity of the productions: a superb totality of music, sets, costumes, musical performance and acting made for a spellbinding and quintessentially 'Russian' production. The sheer numbers of performers involved in the production created an overwhelming impression. In addition to the soloists, the entire chorus and orchestra of Moscow's Bolshoi Theatre appeared at the Paris Opéra for each performance: a feat that was not repeated in subsequent Seasons.

The success of the 1908 Season justified plans for further *Saisons russes* during 1909. A combination of circumstances ensured that Diaghilev's contribution to these comprised both opera and ballet.

Although the ballets shown in Paris were all from the most recent repertory of the Maryinsky Theatre, they were choreographed by Michel Fokine [see Biographical Notes]. In this form, they represented a breakthrough in ballet worldwide, consisting of the newest dance techniques, combined with character acting. Most of these ballets had been devised for the Imperial Ballets, with specially commissioned designs, and set to expressly arranged music, making for a harmonious and compelling ensemble.

Another Fokine innovation, which closely paralleled the dramatic techniques deployed in opera by Chaliapin, was the introduction of mime as a vital, rather than a conventionally gestural, element of ballet. Dancers in the new Fokine productions were required to create dramatic roles as much as to perform virtuoso steps.

Since the Paris Opéra was not available at this time, and moreover, ballet was not considered suitable for its stage, another theatre was found for Diaghilev by his Paris impresario, Gabriel Astruc. This was the old Théâtre du Châtelet, which was renovated for the occasion. Even the spectators in the auditorium were seen as part of the choreography. The front row of the dress circle, filled with a hand-picked selection of beautiful young women, was nicknamed the '*corbeille*' or basket, a name still used for this part of the auditorium at the Châtelet Theatre.

The ballet repertory for the first Season consisted of the *Polovtsian Dances* from *Prince Igor*, *Le Pavillon d'Armide*, *Cléopâtre*, *Les Sylphides* and a divertissement entitled *Le Festin*. The soloists were Adolph Bolm, Michel Fokine, Vaslav Nijinsky, Tamara Karsavina and Anna Pavlova: all from the Imperial Theatres. The actress Ida Rubinstein triumphed as a mime soloist. Her sensual presence in the title role of *Cléopâtre* took Paris by storm. [For further information on the repertory, soloists and performers, see Biographical and Production Notes.]

Diaghilev's patrons during the early concert and ballet Seasons included the businessman Baron Gunsburg, the musician Misia Sert and a pleiad of aristocrats, both Russian and French, headed by Grand Duke Vladimir, who had also helped with the 1906 Salon exhibition. His death in early 1909 reduced the support that could be expected from Russian Imperial circles. Western sponsors included the Countess Greffulhe, the Princesse de Polignac, Lady Ottoline Morrell and many others. Associated with the Season of concerts were the composers Fauré (1845-1924), Saint-Saëns (1835-1921), Vincent D'Indy (1851-1931), Debussy (1862-1918), Dukas (1865-1935), Rimsky-Korsakov and Glazunov, and the critics Calvocoressi, Pierre Lalo and Robert Brussel. The French composers and critics were profoundly affected by the Russian music they heard.

Boris **ANISFELD**

1879 - 1973

Anisfeld (Ber Anisfeldt) was born in Bessarabia and began his artistic career working on satirical magazines, graduating later to portraits. His first theatrical engagement was at the Maryinsky Theatre and his association with Diaghilev began with the opera *Sadko* [see Production Notes]. In 1918, Anisfeld left Russia, travelling first to Japan and then to the USA, where he spent the rest of his life as a designer for the Metropolitan and Chicago opera houses.

89 ✣ *Sadko:* **Costume designs, Scene 6: 'The Kingdom under the Sea' (ballet insert)** 1911

A **Volkhova**
Pencil, watercolour and gouache mounted on card, 46 × 28.6 cm
State Museum of Theatre and Music, St Petersburg

B **The Sea Queen**
Watercolour, gouache and pencil, 45.5 × 19.9 cm
State Museum of Theatre and Music, St Petersburg

C **The Golden Fish**
Watercolour, gouache and bronze paint, 45.8 × 25.9 cm
State Museum of Theatre and Music, St Petersburg
Illustrated p. 68

D **The Sea Queen**
Watercolour, gouache and pencil, 45 × 24 cm
State Museum of Theatre and Music, St Petersburg

Léon **BAKST**

90 ✣ *Boris Godunov:* **Set design for Act III** *c.*1913
Watercolour, charcoal and pastel, 97.8 × 101.6 cm
Robert L. B. Tobin,
courtesy of the McNay Art Museum,
San Antonio, Texas
Illustrated p. 66

91 ✣ *Boris Godunov:* **Costume design for Marina** *c.*1913
Pencil, watercolour and gold paint, 26.7 × 21 cm
Robert L. B. Tobin,
courtesy of the McNay Art Museum,
San Antonio, Texas

Cat. 91

Alexandre **BENOIS**

Initially, Benois played a principal part in setting up Diaghilev's Paris enterprises. Much involved with the mounting of the Salon exhibition of 1906, he was equally prominent in staging *Boris Godunov* in 1908 and designed the sets for Scene 4.

92 ✣ *Boris Godunov:* **Set design for Scene 4: 'Fountain Scene'** 1908
Watercolour and gouache on card, 45 × 53.5 cm
State Tretyakov Gallery, Moscow

Ivan **BILIBIN**

93 ✣ *Boris Godunov:* **Costume design for Boyar's Wife** 1908
Pen and ink and watercolour, 27.5 × 18.5 cm
State Museum Reserve, Peterhof
Illustrated p. 57

Alexandre **GOLOVINE**

Golovine designed most of the sets for Diaghilev's 1908 production of *Boris Godunov*. In 1910 he designed the sets and all but three of the costumes for *The Firebird*. He never became fully involved with Diaghilev's enterprises and belonged to the Teliakovsky camp, a faction of the Imperial Theatres which was inimical to Diaghilev.

94 ✣ *The Maid of Pskov* (*Pskovitianka*): **Set designs for the Bolshoi Theatre production** 1901

A **Prologue: Dawn**
Watercolour and gouache, 54 × 95 cm
State Tretyakov Gallery, Moscow

B **City Council of Pskov Kremlin**
Watercolour and gouache, 54 × 95 cm
State Tretyakov Gallery, Moscow
Illustrated p. 70

C **On the Street of Pskov**
Watercolour and gouache, 54 × 95 cm
State Tretyakov Gallery, Moscow

D **Palace of Prince Tokmakov**
Watercolour and gouache, 54×95 cm
State Tretyakov Gallery, Moscow

E **Garden of Prince Tokmakov**
Watercolour and gouache, 54×95 cm
State Tretyakov Gallery, Moscow

95 ❖ *Boris Godunov:*
Set designs 1908

A Watercolour, gouache and bronze paint on
cardboard, 66.5×82 cm
A.A.Bakhrushin State Central Theatre Museum,
Moscow

B Gouache on canvas, 61.5×81.5 cm
State Museum Reserve, Peterhof
Illustrated p.58

Konstantin **KOROVINE**

Also an important designer of the Imperial Theatres,
Korovine's association with Diaghilev's enterprises
was limited. In the private theatre, he worked
harmoniously with Mamontov [see Biographical
Notes]. Korovine was a close friend and professional
ally of Chaliapin [see Biographical Notes].

96 ❖ *Sadko:* **Set design**
for St Petersburg production 1906
Pen and ink, gouache and bronze paint, 46.8×66 cm
A.A.Bakhrushin State Central Theatre Museum,
Moscow

Pavel **KUZNETSOV**
1878-1968
A leading painter and theatre designer of the early
Soviet period, Kuznetsov exhibited with the World
of Art group from 1902. Associated with the Scarlet
Rose and Blue Rose groups of Symbolist painters,
he trained both in Saratov with Viktor Borisov-
Musatov and in Moscow with Leonid Pasternak
[see below]. Influenced by Cézanne and Cubism,
Kuznetsov was inspired by the cultures of Central
Asia, where he travelled and worked. In 1906, a
number of his works were shown in Diaghilev's
Salon d'Automne show. Although he designed for
the theatre, Kuznetsov had no direct association
with Diaghilev's theatrical enterprises. Many of his
works, however, are based on theatrical and musical
themes and he was one of countless admirers of the
singer Chaliapin [see Biographical Notes].

97 ❖ **Portrait of Chaliapin** 1902
Oil on canvas, 74.5×61.5 cm
A.A.Bakhrushin State Central Theatre
Museum, Moscow

Leonid **PASTERNAK**
1862-1945
Pasternak's attitude to the World of Art group and
to Diaghilev was ambivalent. In his memoirs, he
reduced their innovative achievements to 'monocles,
smooth hairstyles and visiting cards'. None the less,
he exhibited with them on two occasions and was
excited by some of their work, both for its technique
and for its avoidance of narrative. Morally, however,
he could never fully accept what he saw as their he-
donistic aestheticism, devoid of apparent principles.
His own work consisted largely of portraits of his
family and close associates, compositions involving
family groups and, in 1898, the illustrations for
Tolstoy's novel *Resurrection*.

98 ❖ **Concert by Wanda Landowska:**
Diaghilev and Company Seated
1907
Pastel on canvas
State Tretyakov Gallery, Moscow

Born in Warsaw and resident for many years in Paris,
where she started her own music school, Landowska
(1879-1959) was a virtuoso keyboard player who
pioneered the revival of live performance on the
harpsichord of music from the seventeenth and

eighteenth centuries. At the time, there was considerable opposition to the reintroduction of the
harpsichord, an instrument which had been super-
seded by the piano. Diaghilev's appearance at a
Landowska concert of such an early date shows him
typically at the forefront of new thinking in the arts.

Nikolai **ROERICH**
1874-1947
Roerich was a versatile man: a painter, graphic artist
and theatre designer, as well as a scholar, archaeologist and mystic. He travelled the world studying
prehistoric culture, especially in the Himalayas.
Mainly associated in Russia with Princess Tenisheva
[see cat. 23 and 27], Roerich worked for long years
at her estate at Talashkino, near Smolensk. When
she emigrated to France, he was placed in charge of
the archaeological work in the Smolensk area. As a
painter, he exhibited with the World of Art group
in 1903 and was represented at the 1906 Salon
d'Automne. His main association with Diaghilev,
however, came with his designs for the 'primitive'
ballets: the *Polovtsian Dances* [cat. 112, 113A-C]
from *Prince Igor* (1909) and *The Rite of Spring* (1913)
[cat. 161A-D, 162A-C, 163; see also Production
Notes] which admirably expressed his pre-
occupation with the earliest history of Russia.
Roerich died in the USA.

99 ❖ *The Maid of Pskov*
[*Pskovitianka*]: **Set design** 1908-9
Pastel on coloured paper, 27.5×36.6 cm
A.A.Bakhrushin State Central Theatre Museum,
Moscow

Valentin **SEROV**

Apart from his unique talent as a painter, Serov produced some striking designs for the theatre. He had a natural interest in staging operas by his father, the composer and critic Alexander Serov (1820–71) who had achieved a reputation during his lifetime for his folk operas which, between 1865 and 1870, were the most frequently performed Russian works in the Maryinsky repertoire. His opera *Judith* was perhaps the most popular of all, with the role of Holofernes rendered unforgettable by Chaliapin [see Biographical Notes].

100 ❖ **Portrait of Chaliapin** 1905
> Pastel and charcoal on canvas, 235 × 133 cm
> State Tretyakov Gallery, Moscow
> *Illustrated p.71*

Pavel **TRUBETSKOI**

101 ❖ **Portrait of Chaliapin** *c.*1899–1900
> Bronze, 46 × 34 × 30 cm
> A.A. Bakhrushin State Central Theatre Museum, Moscow

Léon **BAKST**

102 ❖ *Le Festin:* **Costume design for Vaslav Nijinsky** 1909
> Pencil, watercolour, gold and silver paint, 33.5 × 21.5 cm
> Private collection
> *Illustrated p.90*

103 ❖ *Cléopâtre:* **Costume designs** 1910

A   **Jewish Dancer**
> Pencil, watercolour and gold paint, 31.5 × 23 cm
> Private collection

B   **Slave Boy**
> Pencil and gouache, 43.5 × 28 cm
> B. Stavroski Collection, Prague, courtesy of Julian Barran Ltd, London

104 ❖ *Cléopâtre:* **Set design** 1909
> Watercolour, 51 × 77 cm
> Musée des Arts Décoratifs, Paris

Cat.103A

Cat.104

Alexandre **BENOIS**

105 ❖ *Les Sylphides:* **Set model** *c.*1907
Pencil and watercolour on paper mounted on card,
consisting of 7 parts: backcloth and 3 pairs of wing
flaps
36.8 × 50.8 × 2.54 cm (unassembled)
Theatre Museum, London

106 ❖ *Le Pavillon d'Armide:*
Costume designs 1907

A Marquis (Pavel Gerdt)
Pencil and watercolour, 38.4 × 27 cm
State Museum of Theatre and Music,
St Petersburg

B Marquis (Pavel Gerdt) in Scene 2
Watercolour, 22 × 28.5 cm
Fine Arts Museums of San Francisco,
Achenbach Foundation for Graphic Arts,
Gift of Mrs Alma de Bretteville Spreckels

C Armida's Slave (Vaslav Nijinsky)
Pencil, watercolour and silver paint, 35.6 × 27.2 cm
State Museum of Theatre and Music,
St Petersburg

Cat.106C

D Armida's Slave (Vaslav Nijinsky)
Pencil, watercolour and bronze paint, 38.7 × 27 cm
State Museum of Theatre and Music,
St Petersburg

E Armida's Slave (Vaslav Nijinsky)
Watercolour and pencil, 37.5 × 26.5 cm
Victoria and Albert Museum, London
Illustrated p.60

**F Courtiers at
King Hydrao's Court**
Pencil, brush and ink and watercolour on paper,
52.7 × 42.5 cm
Theatre Museum, London

107 ❖ *Le Pavillon d'Armide:*
Set designs 1907

**A Backcloth (tapestry):
Rinaldo and Armida**
Watercolour and gouache on card, 59.3 × 68 cm
State Tretyakov Gallery, Moscow
Illustrated p.55

B Sketch for backcloth (tapestry)
Pencil, watercolour and gouache on paper laid on
card, 44 × 40.5 cm
A.A. Bakhrushin State Central Theatre Museum,
Moscow

C Set for Scene 1, with figures
Pencil, pen and ink and watercolour on paper,
78.7 × 88.9 cm
Theatre Museum, London

**D Set for Scene 2:
'The Garden'**
Pencil, watercolour and gouache, 22.5 × 30 cm
Private collection, New York,
courtesy of Julian Barran Ltd, London
Illustrated p.54

**E Set for Scene 2:
'Armida's Garden (Dream Scene)'**
Watercolour, 22 × 28.5 cm
Fine Arts Museums of San Francisco,
Achenbach Foundation for Graphic Arts,
Gift of Mrs Alma de Bretteville Spreckels

From designs by Alexandre **BENOIS**

108 ❖ *Le Pavillon d'Armide:*
Costumes 1907

A Armida's Friend
Silk, tulle and velvet
State Museum of Theatre and Music,
St Petersburg

B Knight
Cotton, silk and metal lamé
State Museum of Theatre and Music,
St Petersburg

Cat.108B

C Male costume
Cotton and silk
State Museum of Theatre and Music,
St Petersburg

D Piper
Linen and lamé
State Museum of Theatre and Music,
St Petersburg

E Courtier
Pink overjacket, tunic, green and purple sash,
pink tights, gold belt and headdress
Theatre Museum, London

Boris **FRODMAN-KLUZEL**
 Dates unknown
A Russian sculptor of Swedish extraction working
in St Petersburg, Frodman-Kluzel exhibited at
the Paris Salon from 1927. Apart from theatrical
portraits [see cat. 109-10], he executed a wide range
of commissions, including the modelling of hard
stone animals for Karl Fabergé's Sandringham series
(1906-7) commissioned by King Edward VII.

109 ❖ *Prince Igor:*
 Adolph Bolm as
 Polovtsian Warrior Chief *c.*1909
 Bronze, height 58.5 cm
 Theatre Museum, London
 Illustrated p. 81

110 ❖ **Portrait of Michel Fokine** *c.*1910
 Bronze, height 32 cm
 Philip Dyer, Deal

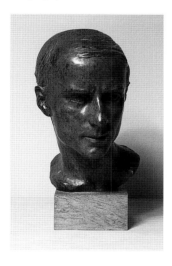

Vaslav **NIJINSKY**
 1888 - 1950 [see Biographical Notes]

111 ❖ *Prince Igor:* **Drawing of**
 a Polovtsian Maiden 1911
 Pencil on Savoy Hotel menu card,
 20.3 × 15.2 cm
 Theatre Museum, London

Nikolai **ROERICH**

112 ❖ *Prince Igor:* **Set design for**
 the 'Polovtsian Camp' *c.*1908
 Tempera and body colour on canvas, 58.5 × 84.5 cm
 Victoria and Albert Museum, London

From designs by Nikolai **ROERICH**

113 ❖ *Prince Igor:* **Costumes** 1909

 A **Polovtsian Warrior**
 (Michel Fokine)
 Satin
 State Museum of Theatre and Music
 St Petersburg
 Illustrated p. 62

 B **Polovtsian Dancer: Boy**
 Wrapover coat with trousers, belt and headdress
 Theatre Museum, London

 C **Polovtsian Dancer: Maiden**
 Silk caftan, purple, green, yellow and white
 Theatre Museum, London

Valentin **SEROV**

Although not directly connected with the Ballets
Russes, Serov followed its progress with interest,
making designs for Diaghilev's productions [cat.
115, 129] and portraits of the protagonists [cat. 114,
116]. An obsessive interest in Ida Rubinstein
prompted him to do several studies of her in the
beguiling role of Cleopatra [cat. 116] as well as
at least one life drawing.

114 ❖ **Portrait of**
 Vaslav Nijinsky *c.*1910
 Pencil, 24.3 × 21.3 cm
 State Museum of Theatre and Music,
 St Petersburg

115 ❖ *Saisons russes*:
 Poster with the Portrait
 of Anna Pavlova in *Les Sylphides*
 1909
 Lithograph, 187 × 158 cm
 State Museum of Theatre and Music,
 St Petersburg
 Illustrated p. 60

116 ❖ **Sketch of Ida Rubinstein**
 as Cleopatra *c.*1910
 Pencil (page from a sketchbook), 26.5 × 42.3 cm
 State Tretyakov Gallery, Moscow
 Illustrated p. 102

Cat. 116 was a preliminary drawing for a large oil
portrait (State Russian Museum, St Petersburg)
of Ida Rubinstein [see Biographical Notes] as
a reclining nude. The Russian art historian Gleb
Pospelov believes that the portraits were themselves
studies for a poster design planned, but never
executed, for the ballet *Cléopâtre* [see Production
Notes].

Pavel **TRUBETSKOI**

117 ❖ **Portrait of**
 Anna Pavlova, seated 1920s-1930s
 Bronze, height 31.8 cm
 Fine Arts Museums of San Francisco,
 Achenbach Foundation for Graphic Arts,
 Gift of Mrs Alma de Bretteville Spreckels

Ballets Russes: The First Phase
1910-1914

Cat. 118B

In 1910, a number of artists from the Maryinsky and Bolshoi Companies, who had participated in Diaghilev's theatrical enterprise the previous year, elected to leave the Imperial Theatres and join Diaghilev. These included Sergei Grigoriev, Adolph Bolm, Bronislava Nijinska, Vaslav Nijinsky and Tamara Karsavina. None of them realised that their decision was irrevocable. [For further information on Bolm, Nijinsky and Karsavina, see Biographical Notes]

For the first time, Diaghilev was able to form his own touring dance troupe, rather than representing Russia through the Imperial Theatres, which had become hostile to his enterprises. The Ballets Russes became a Company in 1911. A decade later, the Company was to have its business base in Monaco and it was at the Théâtre de Monte-Carlo that Diaghilev's spring premières took place [cat. 149A], as a kind of dress rehearsal for the main performances in Paris.

In 1909, Diaghilev had discovered the talented young composer Igor Stravinsky [see Biographical Notes], thus adding a musician to his team of artists, literati, choreographers and financiers who planned his programmes for the *Saisons russes*. Between 1910 and 1912, these consisted of ballets only.

Productions seen in Paris for the first time in 1910 were: *Schéhérazade*, *Carnaval*, *Les Orientales* and *The Firebird*. *Giselle* was also performed, initially with Anna Pavlova in the title role. Plans to tour the ballets of the 1910 Season to London were cancelled owing to the death of King Edward VII.

The new ballets performed in 1911 were *Le Spectre de la Rose* and *Petrushka*, which were a triumph, first in Paris and subsequently in London, where the Seasons formed part of the Coronation Gala for King George V at Covent Garden's Royal Opera House [cat. 149B]. The Gala included a performance of *Swan Lake*, using Korovine's sets from Moscow's Bolshoi Ballet production of 1901 [cat. 158] and starring Mathilde Kshessinska, *prima ballerina assoluta* of the Imperial Ballets.

In 1912, Diaghilev presented the first new ballet choreographed by Nijinsky: *L'Après-midi d'un faune* caused the first theatrical scandal in Paris since *Hernani* (1830). Although lasting only fourteen minutes, the sensation occasioned by this ballet quite eclipsed the impact of the other ballets of the 1912 Season, which, as before, was choreographed by Michel Fokine. On the face of it, the scandal was caused by the Faun's unequivocally onanistic gesture which closes the ballet. In reality, the shock value of the ballet was far more comprehensive. It represented Diaghilev's first break with classical tradition. With its emphasis on static, frieze-like poses and the primacy of mime over dance, Nijinsky's new ballet represented the first experiment in what was to become modern dance. Musically, the ballet, which was choreographed to a symphonic prelude by Claude Debussy, represented Diaghilev's first step towards the international modern movement.

If the scandal of 1912 was caused by Nijinsky's choreography, that of 1913, again aroused by a Nijinsky ballet, was occasioned by Stravinsky's music. In the new Théâtre des Champs-Elysées, the first performance of *The Rite of Spring* evoked a riot that eluded control. For Diaghilev and his artists, this effect was quite unexpected. The ballet was based on an idea of Stravinsky's which arose from a vision of a primitive fertility ritual. An admirable visual echo to the music was expressed in the elemental designs of Nikolai Roerich [cat. 161A–D, 162A–C]. The production had taken an unprecedented number of rehearsals, as the dancers found the asymmetrical rhythms of the music difficult. However, Diaghilev and Stravinsky, who saw the work as a natural progression from the same composer's instantly successful ballets of the two previous years, *The Firebird* (1910) and *Petrushka* (1911), were thrown by the reaction of the public. Paris proved to be unready for the impact of the ballet's first night, although subsequent performances, including the London première, proved uneventful. The first work in Stravinsky's mature style, *The Rite of Spring* represented Diaghilev's alliance with the avant-garde, a stance which he was to maintain until the end of his career. [For further information on Diaghilev's productions, see Production Notes.]

Léon **BAKST**

118 ✦ *Carnaval:*
Costume designs 1910

A **Columbine (Tamara Karsavina)**
Watercolour, 29.5 × 22.7 cm
Victoria and Albert Museum, London

B **Estrella (Ludmilla Schollar)**
Watercolour and pencil heightened with white,
mounted on card, 32.5 × 25.8 cm
State Museum of Theatre and Music,
St Petersburg

C **Florestan (Michel Fokine)**
Watercolour and pencil heightened with white,
mounted on card, 27.8 × 21.2 cm
State Museum of Theatre and Music,
St Petersburg

119 ✦ *Schéhérazade:* **Costume designs**
1910

A **Golden Negro (Vaslav Nijinsky)**
Watercolour, 35.5 × 22 cm
Musée d'Art Moderne et Contemporain
de Strasbourg
Illustrated p.98

B **Chief Eunuch (Enrico Cecchetti)**
Watercolour, 35.5 × 22 cm
Musée d'Art Moderne et Contemporain
de Strasbourg

C **Shah Zeman**
Graphite, watercolour and gold paint,
31.8 × 24.9 cm
Fine Arts Museums of San Francisco,
Achenbach Foundation for Graphic Arts,
Gift of Mrs Alma de Bretteville Spreckels

D **Odalisque**
Pencil, watercolour and gold paint, 21.5 × 35 cm
Private collection
Illustrated p.95

From designs by Léon **BAKST**

120 ✦ *Carnaval:*
**Costume for Harlequin
(Michel Fokine)** 1910
Silk and knitted cotton
State Museum of Theatre and Music,
St Petersburg

121 ✦ *Schéhérazade:*
**Costume for
an Adolescent** 1910
Jacket and trousers
Theatre Museum, London

From a design by Alexandre **BENOIS**

122 ✦ *Giselle:*
**Costume for Albrecht
(Vaslav Nijinsky) in Act** II 1908–9
Tunic and breeches
Theatre Museum, London

Jacques-Emile **BLANCHE**
1861–1942
This artist was dubbed by Diaghilev the 'Godfather
of the Ballets Russes'. In his memoirs, Blanche tells
of his social and professional acquaintance with
Karsavina, Nijinsky, Rubinstein and other members
and associates of the Ballets Russes, many of whom
sat to Blanche for their portraits.

123 ✦ **Study for Portrait of
Igor Stravinsky** 1913
Oil on canvas, 60 × 60 cm
Musée des Beaux-Arts, Rouen

Henri **GAUDIER-BRZESKA**
1891–1915
In 1911, Gaudier-Brzeska was in London and produced his series of sculptures of dancers, which he
considered an important part of his development.
His career was cut short when he was killed in the
First World War.

124 ✦ *The Firebird:*
**Tamara Karsavina and
Adolph Bolm** 1912
Bronze, height 61 cm
Mercury Gallery, London
Illustrated p.92

Alexandre **GOLOVINE**

In a later assessment of the achievements of the
Ballets Russes, Alexandre Benois criticises
Golovine's designs for *The Firebird*, finding the
subtle mosaic-like quality of the sets superficial
and insufficiently figurative. The costumes he
dubbed 'ethnographic'.

125 ❖ *The Firebird:*
Costume designs 1909-10

A **Male costume**
Watercolour and pencil, 35.5 × 22 cm
State Museum of Theatre and Music,
St Petersburg

B **Female costume**
Watercolour and pencil, 36.5 × 24.3 cm
State Museum of Theatre and Music,
St Petersburg
Illustrated p.108

C **Male costume**
Watercolour, pencil heightened with white,
32.7 × 24.8 cm
State Museum of Theatre and Music,
St Petersburg

126 ❖ *The Firebird:*
Set design for Scene 2:
'Spiritual Kingdom of Koshchei'
1909
Watercolour, gouache and bronze paint,
82.5 × 102 cm
State Tretyakov Gallery, Moscow

Cat. 125c

Laura **KNIGHT**
1877 - 1970
From the first London Seasons, Laura Knight was
anxious to work backstage. Since Diaghilev did not
allow outsiders to disturb the performers, she was
refused permission, although the management reserved seats for her in the stalls. In 1919, however,
during the Coliseum Seasons, she was finally
granted permission to work backstage and never
missed a performance. Lydia Lopokova [see p.101]
later suggested that she observe the Company at
Cecchetti's classes [see Biographical Notes],
and Knight later spoke of the great influence
they had on her work.

127 ❖ **Portrait of**
Enrico Cecchetti *c*.1921-3
Pencil, 24 × 30 cm
Cecchetti Society, London,
Gift of Laura Wilson

Randolph **SCHWABE**
1885 - 1948
A theatre designer, printmaker and illustrator,
Schwabe collaborated on several ballet albums with
the balletomane and publisher Cyril William Beaumont. He trained at the Royal College of Art, the
Académie Julian and the Slade School of Art, joined
the New English Art Club in 1917 and was a War
Artist 1914-18. He also taught at Wimbledon School
of Art and was Professor of Drawing at the Royal
College. In 1930, Schwabe succeeded Henry Tonks
as Principal of the Slade School of Art.

128 ❖ **Enrico Cecchetti** *c*.1921-3
Poster, 49 × 39 cm
Cecchetti Society, London
This poster was displayed at all centres of the
Cecchetti Society to remind students of
Cecchetti's method, which was governed
by strict principles of discipline.

Valentin **SEROV**

Serov was fascinated by Diaghilev's Ballets Russes,
executing a curtain design [cat. 129] as well as posters
[cat. 115] and portraits of the artistes [cat. 114, 116].

129 ❖ *Schéhérazade:*
Design for the front cloth
(1st sketch) 1910
Tempera on card, 56 × 72 cm
State Russian Museum, St Petersburg
Illustrated p.99

Léon **BAKST**

130 ❖ *Le Spectre de la Rose:*
Design for
stage properties *c.1911*
Pencil, watercolour, gouache and gold paint,
53.3 × 38.1 cm
Theatre Museum, London

131 ❖ *Narcisse:*
Costume designs 1911

A **Boeotian**
Crayon and gouache, 40 × 26.5 cm
Bibliothèque Nationale, Paris

B **Boeotian**
Pencil and watercolour, 40 × 27.5 cm
State Museum of Theatre and Music,
St Petersburg

C **Boeotian**
Pencil, watercolour and silver paint,
44.3 × 32.8 cm
Theatre Museum, London

D **Boeotian**
Pencil and watercolour, 39 × 26.8 cm
State Museum of Theatre and Music,
St Petersburg

E **Bacchante (Vera Fokina)**
Pencil and watercolour, 40.5 × 27.5 cm
State Museum of Theatre and Music,
St Petersburg

F **First Bacchante**
Pencil and watercolour, 39.5 × 26 cm
State Museum of Theatre and Music,
St Petersburg

G **Bacchante**
Charcoal, crayon and gouache, 67.5 × 48 cm
Musée National d'Art Moderne,
Centre Georges Pompidou, Paris
Illustrated p.155

H **Boeotian Woman**
Pencil and watercolour, 40 × 26.7 cm
State Museum of Theatre and Music,
St Petersburg

I **Devil**
Pencil, watercolour and highlight on cardboard,
26.5 × 39.8 cm
A. A. Bakhrushin State Central Theatre Museum,
Moscow

J **Costume design**
Pencil and watercolour, 39.5 × 27 cm
State Museum of Theatre and Music,
St Petersburg

132 ❖ *Le Dieu Bleu:*
Costume designs 1911–12

A **Young Rajah**
Pencil, watercolour and gouache, 53.3 × 38.1 cm
Theatre Museum, London
Illustrated p.158

B **Temple Dancer**
Pencil, watercolour and highlight, 43 × 28 cm
Musée National d'Art Moderne,
Centre Georges Pompidou, Paris

C **Pilgrim**
Pencil, watercolour, gouache and silver paint,
43 × 27.5 cm
Private collection
Illustrated p.159

133 ❖ *Le Dieu Bleu:*
Set design 1911
Charcoal, watercolour and gouache, 55.8 × 78 cm
Musée National d'Art Moderne,
Centre Georges Pompidou, Paris
Illustrated p.91

134 ❖ *Thamar:* **Set design** 1912
Watercolour and gouache, 74 × 86 cm
Musée des Arts Décoratifs, Paris

Cat.131C

Cat.132B

135 ❖ *Daphnis and Chloë:*
Costume designs 1912

A Likénion

Pencil and watercolour, 26.5 × 12.5 cm
Theatre Museum, London

B Warrior

Graphite, watercolour and silver paint,
26.9 × 16.2 cm
Fine Arts Museums of San Francisco,
Achenbach Foundation for Graphic Arts,
Gift of Mrs Alma de Bretteville Spreckels

C Shepherdess

Watercolour and silver paint, 26.5 × 21 cm
Private collection, London
lent by Julian Barran Ltd, London

136 ❖ *Daphnis and Chloë* 1912

A Set for Scene I

Watercolour, 70 × 103 cm
Musée des Arts Décoratifs, Paris
Illustrated p.78

B Chloë Abandoned

Watercolour, 26.5 × 49 cm
Musée National d'Art Moderne,
Centre Georges Pompidou, Paris

137 ❖ *Jeux:* **Set design** 1913

Pencil, mixed media on paper laid on canvas,
73.7 × 104.1 cm
Robert L. B. Tobin,
courtesy of the McNay Art Museum,
San Antonio, Texas
Illustrated p.94

Cat. 136B

From designs by Léon **BAKST**

138 ❖ *Narcisse:*
Costume for Nymph 1911

Silk crêpe dress and silk wrap
Theatre Museum, London

139 ❖ *Le Dieu Bleu:*
Costumes 1912

A Temple Servant

Bodice and skirt
Theatre Museum, London

B Sacrificial Attendant

Bodice, skirt and trousers
Theatre Museum, London

C Costume for a Bayadère

Choli, collar, skirt and headdress
Theatre Museum, London

140 ❖ *Papillons:*
**Cloak for Morningson
as Konietzka** 1914

Silk satin
Theatre Museum, London

Alexandre **BENOIS**

A key member of the team which set up the Ballets
Russes, Benois's star began to set with the first
production of *Petrushka* in 1911. After this date,
with a few exceptions during 1914, Benois was
increasingly excluded from participation in
Diaghilev's enterprises.

141 ✣ *Petrushka:*
Costume designs 1911

A **Coachman**
Watercolour and gouache, 31 × 23.2 cm
State Museum of Theatre and Music,
St Petersburg

B **Police Sentry and Officer**
Watercolour and gouache, 31 × 23.2 cm
State Museum of Theatre and Music,
St Petersburg

C **Nursemaid** 1911
Pencil and watercolour heightened with white,
31 × 23.2 cm
State Museum of Theatre and Music,
St Petersburg

142 ✣ *Petrushka:* **Set designs**

A **The Fair** 1911
Watercolour and gouache heightened with white,
83.4 × 60 cm
Bolshoi Theatre Museum, Moscow
Illustrated p.63

B **Petrushka's Room** 1911 / 1921
Watercolour and gouache, 63 × 47.7 cm
Bolshoi Theatre Museum, Moscow
Illustrated p.83

C **The Moor's Room** 1911 / 1921
Watercolour and gouache, 64.6 × 48.7 cm
Bolshoi Theatre Museum, Moscow
Illustrated p.83

D **The Moor's Room** 1918
Watercolour, 83.5 × 35 cm
State Museum of Theatre and Music,
St Petersburg

143 ✣ *Le Rossignol:* **Costume designs**

A **The Emperor** 1914
Watercolour and body colour over black chalk,
47 × 33 cm
Ashmolean Museum, Oxford

Cat. 143A

B **Palace Marshal** 1914
Body colour and silver over red and purple chalks,
46.2 × 29.5 cm
Ashmolean Museum, Oxford
Illustrated p.74

C **Sword Dancer** 1914
Body colour and watercolour over black and green
chalks, 43.3 × 29.6 cm
Ashmolean Museum, Oxford
Illustrated p.109

D **Mademoiselle Briand** 1914
Watercolour, ink and highlight over pencil,
49.2 × 30.7 cm
Ashmolean Museum, Oxford
Illustrated p.74

From a design by Alexandre **BENOIS**

144 ❖ *Petrushka:* Costume for the Ballerina Doll 1920s

Silk, wool and linen
State Museum of Theatre and Music,
St Petersburg

Cat.144

Pierre **BONNARD**

1867 – 1947

Although Bonnard designed for the theatre, he was never directly associated with the Ballets Russes. However, he painted an important portrait of Misia Sert in 1909, the first year of the Ballet Seasons, which suggests that he was not unconnected with the milieu. It seems reasonable to suppose that his commission for the poster for *La Légende de Joseph* came through Misia, who in 1914 had already been living for six years with her future third husband, José-Maria Sert, the fashionable artist who designed the set. A sultry crimson portrait of Misia on a divan was executed by Bonnard the same year. He had already executed a poster incorporating a stylised portrait of Misia when, in 1894, he was asked to produce an advertisement for *La Revue Blanche*, with which he was associated and to whose editor Misia was then married.

145 ❖ La Légende de Joseph: Study for the poster *c.*1914

Pencil, 32 × 27 cm
Bibliothèque Nationale, Paris
Illustrated p.106

Bonnard has an important association with the history of the lithographic poster. In 1891, his *France-Champagne*, for which he had already completed the original design by 1889, appeared on the streets of Paris. It particularly impressed Toulouse-Lautrec, who was indebted to him when he came to design his posters for the Moulin Rouge later the same year.

Jean **COCTEAU**

1889 – 1963

A poet, writer, artist and film director, Cocteau was the author of scenarios for many ballets, starting with *Le Dieu Bleu* (1912) [see Production Notes]. He first entered Diaghilev's circle in the year 1909, and he has left brilliant descriptions of those years in his memoirs. He made innumerable sketches and caricatures of Diaghilev and his entourage. Cocteau particularly admired Stravinsky, with whom he tried to collaborate on several occasions, succeeding only once (*Oedipus Rex*, 1927).

146 ❖ Ballets Russes: Poster of Tamara Karsavina as the Young Girl in *Le Spectre de la Rose* 1911

Lithograph, 201 × 132 cm
State Museum of Theatre and Music,
St Petersburg
Illustrated p.64

147 ❖ Ballets Russes: Poster of Vaslav Nijinsky in the title role of *Le Spectre de la Rose* 1911

Lithograph, 201 × 132 cm
State Museum of Theatre and Music,
St Petersburg
Illustrated p.93

148 ❖ Caricature of Igor Stravinsky at the piano, playing *The Rite of Spring* 1913

Pen and ink, 29.2 × 31.8 cm
Theatre Museum, London
Illustrated p.82

Sergei **DIAGHILEV**

149 ❖ Ballets Russes: Theatre programmes

A **Théâtre de Monte-Carlo: Saison de Ballets Russes** 1911

31.5 × 18 cm
Mander and Mitchenson Theatre Collection,
Beckenham

B **Royal Opera Covent Garden: Coronation Gala** 1911

44 × 30 cm
Philip Dyer, Deal

C **Royal Opera Covent Garden: Season of Russian Ballet** 1911

24 × 18.5 cm
Mander and Mitchenson Theatre Collection,
Beckenham

D **Royal Opera Covent Garden broadsheet programme** 1911

38 × 25.5 cm
Mander and Mitchenson Theatre Collection,
Beckenham

E Royal Opera Covent Garden:
Russian Ballet 1912

25 × 19 cm
Mander and Mitchenson Theatre Collection,
Beckenham
Illustrated p.121

Mstislav **DOBUZHINSKY**

Although Dobuzhinsky had been associated with
Diaghilev during the World of Art period, he did not
follow him to Paris and did not belong to the Ballets
Russes circle. Instead, he became involved in
producing material for the propaganda and culture
of the new USSR. This included theatre, for which
he had designed since 1908. He travelled abroad,
however, and maintained his friendship with members of Diaghilev's circle, including Bakst, whom
he replaced as designer for *Midas* when Bakst was
ill. At the outbreak of the First World War,
Dobuzhinsky worked as a medical orderly.

150 ❖ Portrait of
Tamara Karsavina
in *Petrushka* 1914

Pencil, 18 × 17 cm
Valéric Dobužinskis, Paris

151 ❖ *Papillons:* Set design 1914

Watercolour and gouache on cardboard,
42 × 57 cm
Valéric Dobužinskis, Paris

152 ❖ *Midas:* Costume designs 1914

A Oréade

Watercolour, 30.4 × 20 cm
Valéric Dobužinskis, Paris

B Hamadriade

Watercolour, 30 × 23 cm
Valéric Dobužinskis, Paris

153 ❖ *Midas:* Set design 1914

Watercolour and gouache on cardboard,
30 × 50.5 cm
Valéric Dobužinskis, Paris

Michel **FOKINE**
1880 – 1942

Fokine left Diaghilev's Company voluntarily in
1912. He considered that disproportionate time
and effort had been expended on the two ballets
choreographed by Nijinsky [see Biographical
Notes], almost overlooking those by himself.
Persuaded by Diaghilev to return after Nijinsky's
marriage, Fokine was again ignored at the time of
his production in 1914 of Richard Strauss's ballet,
La Légende de Joseph [see cat.145 and Production
Notes]. Deeply resentful of Diaghilev's behaviour,
Fokine then left the Company for good. The
personal unhappiness and frustration which he
experienced for the rest of his life are described
in his memoirs [see Biographical Notes].

154 ❖ Michel Fokine's Travelling Trunk

101 × 52 × 53 cm
State Museum of Theatre and Music,
St Petersburg

Natalia **GONCHAROVA**

155 ❖ *Le Coq d'Or:*
Costume designs

A Russian Woman in
Yellow Flowered Skirt 1914

Watercolour and body colour, 38 × 26.5 cm
Victoria and Albert Museum, London
Illustrated p.65

B Russian Peasant in
Embroidered Shirt 1914

Watercolour and body colour, 38 × 27 cm
Victoria and Albert Museum, London

156 ❖ *Le Coq d'Or:*
Design for the backcloth
for Act I 1914

Watercolour, 53.4 × 73.6 cm
Victoria and Albert Museum, London

157 ❖ *Le Coq d'Or:*
Set design for
Finale (Act III) 1914

Pencil, watercolour, gouache and collage
on cardboard, 63.5 × 96.3 cm
A.A.Bakhrushin State Central Theatre Museum,
Moscow
Illustrated p.111

Konstantin **KOROVINE**

158 ❖ *Swan Lake:*
Backcloths for Acts I and IV,
Bolshoi Theatre Production 1901

Tempera on canvas, 10.7 × 16 m
Philip Dyer, Deal

Vaslav **NIJINSKY**

In Buenos Aires, during the Ballets Russes's American tour in 1913, Nijinsky married the Hungarian
Romola de Pulszky. Shortly afterwards, war broke
out and Nijinsky was interned in Budapest. During
this period, he worked at inventing a system of
choreographic notation. He started by retro-
spectively systematising his past ballet, *L'Après-
midi d'un faune* [see also Biographical Notes].

159 ❖ *L'Après-midi d'un faune:*
Choreographic notebook 1915

Notebook, bound volume,
open measurements 35.5 × 60 × 4 cm
British Library, London

In this ballet, which required, according to
Stravinsky, a hundred and twenty rehearsals,
Nijinsky was at pains to set up a system of written
choreographic notation. He subsequently filled
several manuscript and exercise books which
purported to achieve this objective.

Auguste **RODIN**
1840 – 1917

A stalwart supporter of Nijinsky's performance
in *L'Après-midi d'un faune*, Rodin had his name
ascribed to a long, supportive review, which
appeared in the French newspaper *Le Matin*
the day after the 'scandalous' first night. Rodin
subsequently saw every performance of the Ballets
Russes and became a particular admirer of Nijinsky,
whom he invited to his studio to sit for a portrait
which remained unfinished. It is possible that
the project was abandoned owing to Diaghilev's
unbridled and quite unjustified jealousy of the
sculptor.

160 ⁜ Vaslav Nijinsky:
   Study for a portrait 1912
   Bronze, height 17 cm
   Mr and Mrs S. Bawarshi,
   courtesy of Browse & Darby, London

It has been claimed by Serge Lifar that this unfinished work represents neither Nijinsky nor
the Faun. However, the intensely coiled figure
clearly represents a dancer of powerful physique
and vibrant energy; and the suggestion of high
cheek bones and slanted eyebrows in the face is
consistent with Nijinsky's own features and with
his appearance as the Faun [see also cat. 166].

Nikolai **ROERICH**

161 ⁜ *The Rite of Spring:*
   Costume designs

A   **Youth** 1913
   Pencil, gouache and watercolour on cardboard,
   25.2 × 16.8 cm
   A.A. Bakhrushin State Central Theatre Museum,
   Moscow
   Illustrated p.79

B   **Maiden** 1913
   Pencil, gouache and watercolour on cardboard,
   24.5 × 15.4 cm
   A.A. Bakhrushin State Central Theatre Museum,
   Moscow
   Illustrated p.79

C   **Maiden** 1913
   Pencil, pen and ink, watercolour and gouache,
   14 × 24 cm
   Bibliothèque Nationale, Paris
   Illustrated p.79

D   **Old Man** 1913
   Pencil, gouache, watercolour and silver paint
   on cardboard, 24.5 × 15.4 cm
   A.A. Bakhrushin State Central Theatre Museum,
   Moscow
   Illustrated p.79

Cat.164

162 ⁜ *The Rite of Spring:*
   Set designs

A   **Sketch** 1914
   Tempera on cardboard, 63.5 × 81 cm
   State Museum Reserve, Peterhof

B   **Sketch** 1914
   Tempera on cardboard, 57 × 83 cm
   State Museum Reserve, Peterhof

C   **Design with eight figures** 1913
   Charcoal, pastel and gouache, 29 × 60 cm
   Private collection, New York,
   courtesy of Julian Barran Ltd, London

From a design by Nikolai **ROERICH**

163 ⁜ *The Rite of Spring:*
   Costume for a Maiden in Scene I
   1913
   Robe with attached petticoat, cotton
   Theatre Museum, London

Sergei **SUDEIKIN**
   1882 – 1946
A stage designer from the year 1905, Sudeikin helped
Bakst to mount Diaghilev's Salon d'Automne exhi-
bition in 1906 and was involved with the designs for
Diaghilev's theatre productions from 1910. His wife,
the actress and artist Vera Sudeikina, married Igor
Stravinsky in 1939.

164 ⁜ *La Tragédie de Salomé:*
   Set design 1913
   Oil on canvas, 97 × 114 cm
   State Museum of Theatre and Music,
   St Petersburg

Valerian **SVETLOV**

1860-1934

A Russian ballet critic, writer and editor, Svetlov wrote innumerable articles on ballet both in Russian and French. His book *Le Ballet contemporain* was published simultaneously in Russian and French in St Petersburg in 1911. It contains superb colour reproductions of designs by Bakst and other illustrators. In 1917, Svetlov settled in Paris. He married the dancer Vera Trefilova and acted as mentor to the young balletomane Arnold Haskell.

165 ✣ *Sovremenny balet*
(*Le Ballet contemporain*) 1912

Designed by Léon Bakst
Published by Maurice de Brunoff
Book, 32 × 22 × 4 cm
David Elliott, Oxford

Una **TROUBRIDGE**

1887-1963

Born Margot Elena Gertrude Taylor, she married Sir Ernest Charles Troubridge, later Vice-Admiral. A sculptor, she made drawings of Nijinsky, without Diaghilev's knowledge, during Nijinsky's classes with Cecchetti [see Biographical Notes].

166 ✣ *L'Après-midi d'un faune:*
Vaslav Nijinsky as Faun 1912

Plaster, height 41 cm
Theatre Museum, London

This is the original plaster head, from which several bronzes have been made. Richard Buckle tells us that when it was discovered by Lydia Sokolova in a shop in Cecil Court in the early 1950s, it was marked 'from Temple of Mithras'.

With the outbreak of the First World War, Diaghilev and the members of his Company were cut off from their homeland and found themselves scattered throughout Europe and America. Also, by that time, principal associates such as Fokine, Nijinsky and Rubinstein had left Diaghilev's Company to set up enterprises of their own. From 1915, a caucus of Ballets Russes activists found themselves in Switzerland. In a villa at Ouchy, in Lausanne, Diaghilev, Massine, Stravinsky, Larionov [see pp.136 and 154] and Goncharova [see p.136] continued to discuss projects and create ideas until the end of the war.

However, during the course of the First World War, the Ballets Russes did not cease to operate. On 20 December 1915, Léonide Massine's *Soleil de Nuit*, to the music of Nikolai Rimsky-Korsakov and designs by Michel Larionov, was first performed at the Grand Théâtre in Geneva. *Las Meniñas*, again choreographed by Massine to music by Gabriel Fauré, with costumes by José-Maria Sert, was premièred on 25 August 1916 at the Teatro Eugenia-Victoria, San Sebastian, as was Massine's *Kikimora*, to the music of Anatoly Liadov, with sets and costumes by Mikhail Larionov. Nijinsky's *Till Eulenspiegel* was performed the same year at Manhattan Opera House and the year 1917 saw the premières of two major ballets, both choreographed by Massine: *Contes Russes* (music by Liadov, designs by Larionov, assisted by Goncharova) and *Parade*, with libretto by Cocteau, music by Erik Satie and designed, for the first time, by Pablo Picasso.

In 1917 the Revolution in Russia put a stop to tours, or even social visits there by members of the Company. The Diaghilev artists who returned to Russia made a commitment to the Bolshevik government. Diaghilev never saw his homeland again. Since fresh material was now hard to import from Russia, the composers and, especially, the artists associated with the post-war phase of the Ballets Russes were increasingly Western and mainly French or School of Paris.

It would be wrong, however, to describe the Ballets Russes as ceasing after the war to be Russian. The core of dancers remained so (supplemented by notable artists from Britain, including Alicia Markova, Lydia Sokolova and Anton Dolin), as did the main choreographers, Léonide Massine, Bronislava Nijinska and George Balanchine. Stravinsky continued to supply musical compo-

sitions and Prokofiev also contributed. Among visual artists, Goncharova and, especially, Larionov, enriched the ballets with designs. In his final immersion in the experimental avant-garde, even after meeting Picasso and his circle, Diaghilev did not overlook the importance of the Russian Constructivists. Ten years after the October Revolution, he made use of Naum Gabo and Anton Pevsner (*La Chatte*, 1927) and Georgi Yakulov (*Le Pas d'Acier*, 1927).

Diaghilev's Ballets Russes continued until his death, on 19 August 1929, after two highly charged decades, in which some seventy ballets and fifteen operas were performed.

[For the later careers of Fokine, Nijinsky, Rubinstein, Massine and Stravinsky, see Biographical Notes.]

Léon **BAKST**

From 1913 Bakst worked for various companies, and for individuals including Michel Fokine and Ida Rubinstein.

167 ✣ **Portrait of Ida Rubinstein** 1913

Charcoal and watercolour, 104.2 × 73.7 cm
Private collection
Illustrated p.101

Edited by Maurice **DE BRUNOFF**

Maurice and Jacques de Brunoff were the publishers of *Comoedia Illustré*, a weekly magazine of the performing arts. Cat. 169 was an edition containing a collection of magazines and souvenir programmes devoted to the *Saisons russes*. It included features on the Ballets Russes and on Ida Rubinstein.

168 ❖ *Comoedia Illustré*
(May 1914 issue)
Special Ballets Russes
Number 1914
Magazine, 32 × 25 × 1 cm
David Elliott, Oxford

169 ❖ *Collection des plus beaux numéros de Comoedia Illustré et des programmes consacrés aux Ballets et Galas Russes depuis le début à Paris*
1909-1921 *1922*
Bound copies of souvenir theatre magazines and programmes 1909-21, 34.5 × 26.5 × 3 cm
David Elliott, Oxford

Sergei **DIAGHILEV**

170 ❖ **Passport**
Issued in 1919 by the Russian Consulate in London
Bibliothèque Nationale, Paris

171 ❖ **Travel notebook**
Bibliothèque Nationale, Paris

Mikhail **LARIONOV**

Larionov was one of very few Russian artists who fought in the First World War. Invalided out in 1915, he was then invited by Diaghilev to join him in Lausanne, with his companion, Natalia Goncharova. They later emigrated to Paris. They had already worked with Diaghilev, participating in the Salon Exhibition in 1906 and *Le Coq d'Or* in 1914. Naturally gravitating to his circle, Larionov and Goncharova spent much time with him during the war, when they worked together on collaborative productions which were performed during and after the war.

172 ❖ **Sketchbook**
34 × 28.5 cm
Victoria and Albert Museum, London

173 ❖ **Group Portrait of Diaghilev, Goncharova, Massine and Beppo in a Café** 1917
Pencil on yellow paper, 21.8 × 27.5 cm
Victoria and Albert Museum, London

Vaslav **NIJINSKY**

After Nijinsky's marriage to Romola de Pulszky, Diaghilev dismissed him abruptly from his Company. After an abortive season at the Palace Theatre, London, in 1914, for which he had formed his own company, Nijinsky was interned at the outbreak of war in Hungary as an alien. Diaghilev pulled influential strings and secured Nijinsky's release to rejoin the Company in New York, in April 1916.

174 ❖ **Vaslav Nijinsky's wedding invitation and wedding photo** 1913
Private collection, courtesy of Julian Barran Ltd, London

Léon Bakst:
Narcisse:
**Costume design
for Bacchante** 1911
Cat.131G

Notes on Productions

OPERAS

BORIS GODUNOV

Opera-legend in seven scenes

Cat. **90, 91, 92, 93, 95 A-B**

Music: Modest Mussorgsky, revised and orchestrated by Rimsky-Korsakov in 1896 and, with Diaghilev, in 1908

Libretto: by the composer, after Pushkin's drama and Karamzin's *History of the Russian Empire*

Sets for Scenes 1, 3, 5, 6 and 7 by Alexandre Golovine and executed by Yuon, Anisfeld, Lanceray, Yaremich and Plekhanov

Set for Scene 4: Alexandre Benois

Costumes: Alexandre Benois, Ivan Bilibin, Alexandre Golovine and others

First performance: St Petersburg, 1874

Paris première: 19 May 1908, Théâtre National de l'Opéra

London première: 24 June 1913, Theatre Royal, Drury Lane

Director: Alexander Sanin

Conductors: Felix Blumenfeld (Paris), Thomas Beecham (London)

Soloists: Fyodor Chaliapin (Boris), Vladimir Kastorsky (Pimen), Natasha Ermolenko (Marina), Jean (Ivan) Altchevsky (Shuisky)

The libretto is taken from a history play in blank verse and with the same title by Alexander Pushkin, set in the reign of the elected successor to Tsar Ivan IV (the Terrible), his son-in-law Boris Godunov, who ruled Russia from 1598 to 1605. Godunov's death was followed by a period of utter devastation, traditionally referred to, with the understatement characteristic of Russian forbearance, as the Time of Troubles. A four-year interregnum ended with the election in 1613 of Tsar Mikhail, the first of the Romanov dynasty.

The opera dramatises the psychological anguish of Boris Godunov, who is torn between the desire to be a just and expedient ruler, and his personal guilt at having murdered Ivan's last surviving son, Dmitry, in order to remove the possibility of political unrest and to facilitate Boris's smooth transition from Regent to Tsar. (This theory has recently been disproved by historians, who believe that Dmitry accidentally stabbed himself during an epileptic fit.) Instead, Dmitry becomes a martyr, and a Pretender, apparently risen from his ashes, incites popular support. While an edict against the False Dmitry is being read, Boris suddenly dies.

In Mussorgsky's opera, intrigues at Court and in the Church are juxtaposed with powerful crowd scenes, making the Russian people the main protagonist in the action. Diaghilev brought the opera to Paris twice: in 1908, and again in 1913, after which it was performed in London.

THE MAID OF PSKOV

Opera in four acts

Cat. **94 A-E, 99**

Music: Nikolai Rimsky-Korsakov

Libretto: Rimsky-Korsakov, after Lev Mey

Sets: Alexandre Golovine, Nikolai Roerich

Costumes: Dmitry Stelletsky

First performance: Maryinsky Theatre, St Petersburg (as *Pskovitianka*), 1895

Paris première: 24 May 1909, Théâtre du Châtelet

Conductor: Nicholas Tcherepnine

Chorus-master: Ulric Avranek

Director: Alexander Sanin

London première: 8 July 1913, Theatre Royal, Drury Lane

Principal singers: Fyodor Chaliapin, Alexander Davydov, Vladimir Kastorsky, Lydia Lipkowska, Elizaveta Petrenko, Vasily Sharonov

In sixteenth-century Russia, the tyrannical Tsar Ivan IV inflicts terror on the independent city of Novgorod. A similar fate awaits the city of Pskov. Its subjects join to fight the Tsar and, in the surprise attack that follows, Princess Olga and her lover, Mikhail Toucha, both natives of Pskov, are killed. Olga is subsequently revealed as the secret daughter of the Tsar.

The opera is also known as *Pskovitianka* and *Ivan the Terrible*.

PRINCE IGOR

[For details of the ballet excerpt, *Polovtsian Dances*, see under 'Ballets'.]

The idea for a Russian national opera based on historical myth concerning medieval Russia was suggested to Borodin by the critic and champion of 'The Five', Vladimir Stasov, who had first launched the painter, Ilya Repin. Borodin devised his own libretto from the twelfth-century literary epic, *The Tale of Igor's Campaign* (*Slovo o polku Igoreve*). He worked on the music and its libretto for eighteen years and the work remained unfinished at his death. The opera was completed by Rimsky-Korsakov and Glazunov.

During the 1907 concert season, arias were performed from Act I of this opera, sung by Fyodor Chaliapin and Marianne Tcherkassky. On 18 May 1909, Act II was performed in Paris at the Châtelet Theatre. The principal male parts were taken by Dmitry Smirnov and Vasily Sharonov, and the part of Igor's wife Yaroslavna by Elizaveta Petrenko.

LE ROSSIGNOL

Opera in three acts

Cat. **143 A-D**

Music: Igor Stravinsky

Libretto: Stepan Mitusov and Igor Stravinsky; based on a story by Hans Christian Andersen

Choreography: Boris Romanov

Sets and costumes: Alexandre Benois

Director: Alexander Sanin, with Alexandre Benois

Chorus-master: Nicolas Palitzine

Conductor: Pierre Monteux

First performance: 26 May 1914, Théâtre National de l'Opéra, Paris

London première: 18 June 1914, Theatre Royal, Drury Lane

Principal singers: Pavel Andreyev, Alexander Belianin, Marie Brian, Aurelia Dobrovolska, Fyodor Ernst, Nicolas Goulaiev, Elisabeth Mamsina, Elisabeth Petrenko, Vasily Sharonov

Principal dancers: Max Frohmann, Nicolas Kremnev

The plot is set in legendary times, when a Chinese Emperor acquires a nightingale whose beautiful singing moves him to tears. When three ambassadors from Japan bring the Emperor a gift of a mechanical nightingale, the live one disappears. The Emperor, on his deathbed, is magically cured when the real nightingale returns to sing for him. The courtiers, expecting to find him dead, discover him in the best of health.

Stravinsky made three different uses of this story. The opera was the first version. He then converted the opera into a ballet, which was first produced by Ballets Russes on 2 February 1920 with Tamara Karsavina in the title role. It was revived in 1925 with Alicia Markova. Ultimately, Stravinsky developed the musical material of the first and second acts into a symphonic poem.

BALLETS

SADKO

Opera-legend in seven scenes

Cat. **89 A-D, 96**

Music: Nikolai Rimsky-Korsakov

Libretto: Rimsky-Korsakov and V.I. Belsky, after a Russian fairy tale, made famous by Pushkin

Choreography (for the ballet insert 'The Kingdom under the Sea': Scene 6 of the opera): Michel Fokine

Sets: Boris Anisfeld

Costumes: Boris Anisfeld, Léon Bakst

First Russian performance: 7 January 1898, Soldovnikov Theatre, Moscow

Paris première: (Scene 6 only) 6 June 1911, Théâtre du Châtelet

The wanderings of the minstrel Sadko bring him to Volkhova, Princess of the Sea, who promises that his net will be filled with golden fish. He wages his head against the wealth of the citizens of Novgorod that he can catch the golden fish. He succeeds and sets sail with some merchants to find his fortune, leaving behind his wife Lyubava.

Returning successfully twelve years later, they are becalmed, and throw gold overboard to pacify the King of the Sea; but his daughter Volkhova tells Sadko that one of the company must be sacrificed. Sadko is set adrift and sinks to the sea-bed, where his song wins Volkhova's hand.

At the wedding (Scene 6), Sadko's singing so arouses the sea that many ships are sunk. The chief knight of Novgorod orders Sadko back to the land. On the shore of Lake Ilmen, Sadko bids farewell to Volkhova, who is transformed into the river that bears her name. Lyubava, still watching, is reunited with Sadko, now the richest man in Novgorod.

L'APRÈS-MIDI D'UN FAUNE

Ballet in one act

Cat. **159, 160, 166**

Music: Claude Debussy

Libretto and choreography: Vaslav Nijinsky (after the poem by Stéphane Mallarmé)

Set and costumes: Léon Bakst

First performance: 29 May 1912, Théâtre du Châtelet, Paris

Principal performers: Vaslav Nijinsky (Faun), Bronislava Nijinska (Chief Nymph)

A faun reposes on a sunny hillside. He plays on a lute and enjoys a bunch of grapes. A group of nymphs come into view at the base of the hill, on their way to bathe at a pool near by. Curious, the faun descends the hillside and approaches them. At first they, too, are curious; then, nervously, they take flight. Presently they return and the faun seeks to woo them. Again they run away. But one, bolder than the rest, returns. They link arms, but the nymph, suddenly afraid, escapes, leaving behind her scarf. Disconsolate at the loss of his playmate, the faun is sad. Then, seeing the scarf, he takes it up in his arms and bears it to his retreat, where he consoles himself by fondling it.

The ballet was originally called *Prélude à l'après-midi d'un faune*, the title given by Debussy to his symphonic suite, to which the ballet was composed. The theme of the ballet was ascribed to Nijinsky, but on this point the evidence of contemporaries is contradictory. Stravinsky declares that Diaghilev suggested the theme: a tableau in which an amorous faun would pursue a group of nymphs. Stravinsky further claims that the idea was changed by Bakst, who advised Diaghilev to mount a ballet in the form of an animated bas-relief, with figures in profile. Stravinsky also states that Bakst inspired the actual choreography down to the last detail.

Madame Romola Nijinsky, in her biography of Nijinsky, claims that the theme of *Faune* was first conceived by Nijinsky when staying with Diaghilev at Carlsbad in 1911. It is the story of a youth's awakening to adolescence. But Nijinsky, realising the difficulties of presenting the theme on stage, transferred the action to Ancient Greece.

According to Stravinsky, this ballet required 120 rehearsals. The poses were an attempt to adapt the two-dimensional figures on Greek vases to the service of ballet. The result corresponded to a frieze of living figures – the bodies facing the audience,

heads and limbs in profile in an attempt to sustain the impression of a two-dimensional surface. Arms and hands, with palms parallel to the spectators, were used with especial effect. Feet were bare.

CARNAVAL

Cat. **118 A-C, 120**

Music: Robert Schumann, orchestrated by Anton Arensky, Alexander Glazunov, Anatol Liadov, Nikolai Rimsky-Korsakov, Nicholas Tcherepnine

Libretto: Léon Bakst, Michel Fokine

Choreography: Michel Fokine

Sets and costumes: Léon Bakst (adapted from *Le Bal Poudre [The Fairy Doll]*)

First performance: 20 February 1910, Pavlov Hall, St Petersburg (at a charity masquerade ball sponsored by *Satyricon* magazine)

Berlin première: 20 May 1910, Theater des Westens

Paris première: 4 June 1910, Théatre National de l'Opéra

Principal dancers: Tamara Karsavina (Columbine), Vera Fokina (Chiarina), Ludmilla Schollar (Estrella), Bronislava Nijinska (Papillon), Vaslav Nijinsky (Harlequin), Adolph Bolm (Pierrot), Enrico Cecchetti (Pantalon), Michel Fokine (Florestan), Joseph Kchessinsky (Eusebius), Vsevolod Meyerhold (Pierrot)

A plotless divertissement, with *commedia dell'arte* character roles, set in the ante-chamber of a ballroom, its deep blue curtain with black and gold frieze; two striped settees.

Carnaval:
Vera Fokina as Chiarina
and Michel Fokine as Florestan, 1911
A.A.Bakhrushin State Central Theatre Museum, Moscow

Léon Bakst:
Le Dieu Bleu:
**Costume design
for the Young Rajah** 1911–12
Cat.132A

Léon Bakst:
Le Dieu Bleu:
**Costume design for
the Pilgrim** 1911–12
Cat.132C

CLÉOPÂTRE

Ballet in one act

Cat. **103 A-B, 104, 116**

Music: Anton Arensky. Additional music by Alexander Glazunov, Mikhail Glinka, Modest Mussorgsky, Nikolai Rimsky-Korsakov, Sergei Taneev, Nicholas Tcherepnine.

Libretto: Léon Bakst

Choreography: Michel Fokine

Set and costumes: Léon Bakst

First performance: 8 March 1908, Maryinsky Theatre as *Une Nuit d'Egypte*

Paris première: 2 June 1909, Théâtre du Châtelet

Principal dancers: Anna Pavlova (Ta-Hor), Ida Rubinstein (Cleopatra), Michel Fokine (Amoun), Tamara Karsavina and Vaslav Nijinsky (Favourite Slaves of Cleopatra)

Amoun, an amorous Egyptian youth, has seen the Queen of the Sapphire Nile. Renouncing his humble mistress Ta-Hor, and defying Cleopatra's courtiers, he offers his life for a sign of Cleopatra's favour. The Queen languorously accepts his devotion. While her slaves dance a celebratory bacchanal, Cleopatra, on her gilded couch, succumbs to her new lover's passion. But his triumph is short lived. Amoun meets a swift death by a rare poison, prepared by the High Priest and administered by the Queen. As the royal retinue leaves the Temple, the faithful Ta-Hor falls lifeless on the body of her faithless lover.

The arrival and ceremonial disrobing of Ida Rubinstein as Cleopatra was an unforgettable experience to many who saw it and is described in the memoirs of Alexandre Benois, Valentin Serov and Jean Cocteau.

Cléopâtre:
Tamara Karsavina as Cleopatra's Favourite Slave, 1909
Bibliothèque Nationale, Paris

LE COQ D'OR

Opera-ballet in three acts, burlesque style

Cat. **155 A-B, 156, 157**

Music: Nikolai Rimsky-Korsakov

Libretto: Vladimir Belsky, after Alexander Pushkin, revised by Alexandre Benois

Sets and costumes: Natalia Goncharova

Choreography and stage direction: Michel Fokine

Chorus master: Nicholas Palitzine

First performance: 7 October 1909, Soldovnikov Theatre, Moscow

Paris première: 24 May 1914, Théâtre National de l'Opéra

Conductor: Pierre Monteux

London première: 15 June 1914, Theatre Royal, Drury Lane

Principal singers: Jean (Ivan) Altchesky, Alexandre Belianin

Principal dancers: Enrico Cecchetti (Astrologer), Tamara Karsavina (Queen of Shemakha), Alexei Bulgakov (King Dodon)

The golden cockerel has a gift for prophecy. It is brought to King Dodon by an astrologer to protect him from danger. In return, the King offers the astrologer whatever he should request. Feeling secure, the King falls asleep, but is awakened by the cockerel's crowing, warning him of imminent danger. The King dispatches his army to ward off the enemy, but the next time the cock crows, the King himself goes off to head his forces. In the field of battle, he finds that his sons have been killed. But he also meets the Queen of Shemakha, with whom he falls in love and whom he brings back to his kingdom. When the astrologer demands the Queen as the price for his cockerel, the King murders him. The cock in turn avenges the astrologer's death by killing the King and then flies off.

The Fokine production of this opera was unique. The cast was divided in two parts, one operatic, the other balletic, and each character was played by two artists, one singing, the other dancing. Its undercurrent of pointed political satire prevented the work being performed in Rimsky-Korsakov's lifetime.

DAPHNIS AND CHLOË

Ballet in three scenes

Cat. **135 A-C, 136 A-B**

Music: Maurice Ravel

Libretto: Michel Fokine, after Longus

Choreography: Michel Fokine

Sets and costumes: Léon Bakst

First performance: 8 June 1912, Théâtre du Châtelet, Paris

Principal dancers: Tamara Karsavina (Chloë), Vaslav Nijinsky (Daphnis), Adolph Bolm (Darkon)

Scene 1 is set in a grove sacred to Pan and his nymphs. A religious ceremony is being held at the altar of nymphs. Young girls bearing garlands prostrate themselves. Daphnis and Chloë join in. The company proposes a contest between Daphnis and the clownish herdsman, Darkon. A kiss from Chloë is proposed to reward the victor. Darkon dances a grotesque figure. Daphnis follows with lithe step. Daphnis and Chloë fall into a mutual embrace while the crowd admires their beauty. Chloë runs away. Daphnis lapses into dreaming languor.

There is a sudden commotion. A group of women is being pursued by a band of brigands. Realising that Chloë is in danger, Daphnis hastens to help her; but, in the meantime, Chloë, who has taken refuge near the altar of nymphs, is seized by the brigands. Daphnis returns, finds an abandoned female sandal, and fears the worst. He curses the gods and falls down in despair. At this moment, in the temple, the statues of the nymphs are one by one endowed with life. They leave their pedestals to console Daphnis, and invoke the god Pan, who emerges from a rock.

In Scene 2, in the camp of brigands, the imprisoned Chloë performs a dance of supplication. Briaxis, the pirate chief, woos her. Suddenly, Pan appears in a cloud and enfolds Chloë. When Daphnis beholds his beloved, he knows that Pan has intervened.

In a coda, Lammon, the old countryman, informs all that Pan has graciously acted in memory of his ancient love for the nymph Syrinx: whereupon, the assembled company join in a dance to celebrate the old love-tale.

Michel Fokine devised the original theme for this ballet in 1904. At the same time, he formulated a system for reforming contemporary ballet. This work was therefore much cherished by Fokine. When, despite the importance of Ravel's score, the first production of this ballet proved somewhat unsuccessful, Fokine resigned from Diaghilev's Company.

His decision was accepted by Diaghilev, who, at this time, was still absorbed in building the choreographic reputation of Nijinsky. However, at the end of the summer, Nijinsky married during the Company's South American tour, and was dismissed by Diaghilev. This event necessitated the return of Fokine to the Ballets Russes.

LE DIEU BLEU
Ballet in one act on a Hindu theme
Cat. **132 A-C, 133, 139 A-C**

Music: Reynaldo Hahn

Libretto: Jean Cocteau, Frédéric de Madrazo

Choreography: Michel Fokine

Sets and costumes: Léon Bakst

First performance: 13 May 1912, Théâtre du Châtelet, Paris

Principal dancers: Vaslav Nijinsky (Blue God), Tamara Karsavina (Young Girl)

A young hero is invested with the robes of priesthood. After his investiture, the young man's fiancée enters and appeals to him to renounce his religious vows. The elders, enraged, thrust her into a dungeon to be devoured by strange monsters. Overcome with terror, she prays to the Blue God, who suddenly appears and delivers the helpless girl into the hands of the stupefied priests. She is quickly restored to her lover, and the Blue God of love and happiness disappears in radiant glory.

This ballet was performed for one season only, its strongest element being its designs by Léon Bakst. In contributing the libretto, the twenty-three-year-old Jean Cocteau fulfilled his intense and long-held desire to collaborate with Diaghilev and his Company.

LE FESTIN
Suite of dances
Cat. **102**

Music: Alexander Glazunov, Mikhail Glinka, Modest Mussorgsky, Nikolai Rimsky-Korsakov, Pyotr Tchaikovsky

Choreography: Michel Fokine, Marius Petipa, Alexander Gorsky, Nikolai Goltz, Felix Kchessinsky

Sets and costumes: Léon Bakst, Alexandre Benois, Ivan Bilibin, Konstantin Korovine

First performance: 18 May 1909, Théâtre du Châtelet, Paris

Principal dancers: Vera Fokina, Tamara Karsavina, Vaslav Nijinsky, Mikhail Mordkin, Georgy Rosai, Vera Karalli

THE FIREBIRD
Ballet in one act and two scenes
Cat. **124, 125 A-C, 126**

Music: Igor Stravinsky

Libretto: Michel Fokine

Sets: Alexandre Golovine

Costumes: Alexandre Golovine, Léon Bakst

First performance: 25 June 1910, Théâtre National de l'Opéra, Paris

Principal dancers: Tamara Karsavina (the Firebird), Michel Fokine (Ivan Tsarevich), Alexei Bulgakov (Koshchei, the Immortal), Vera Fokina (the Tsarevna)

The ballet is based on a selection of traditional Russian fairy stories and a prose poem by Alexander Pushkin.

The Tsarevich has captured a bird with flaming golden plumage while out hunting. But he cannot resist its mute appeal and lets his precious captive escape, accepting one of its magical feathers as a token of gratitude. Hardly has the Firebird flown away when he is warned by a group of exquisite maidens that the forest is enchanted and that its ruler, the green-eyed monster Koshchei, will petrify him if he remains. However, he is captivated by the grace and beauty of one maiden-princess and refuses to flee. The weird retinue of the ogre rushes upon him, but, with the aid of the feather, the Tsarevich calls the Firebird to his aid. The power of the wicked ogre Koshchei is broken by the bird, which forces his evil followers to dance madly until they fall asleep, overcome by exhaustion. Meanwhile, Ivan finds and destroys the huge egg which contains the ogre's soul. The monster is killed, the Tsarevich and his love live happily ever after.

Although Stravinsky was later to see his score for this ballet as derivative, the first performance made the twenty-eight-year-old composer an international success overnight.

GISELLE
Fantastic ballet in two acts
Cat. **122**

Music: Adolphe Adam

Libretto: Vernoy de Saint-Georges, Théophile Gautier and Jean Coralli; inspired by Heine's *Zur Geschichte der neueren schönen Literatur in Deutschland* [Original Production]

Choreography: Jean Coralli, Jules Perrot, Marius Petipa

Sets: Pierre Ciceri

Costumes: Paul Lormier

First performance: 28 June 1841, Théâtre National de l'Opéra, Paris

Principal dancers: Carlotta Grisi (Giselle), Lucien Petipa (Albrecht), Adèle Dumilâtre (Myrtha, Queen of the Wilis)

Saisons russes première: 18 June 1910, Théâtre de l'Opéra, Paris

Sets and costumes: Alexandre Benois

Choreography: Jean Coralli, Marius Petipa, adapted by Michel Fokine

Principal dancers: Tamara Karsavina (Giselle), Vaslav Nijinsky (Albrecht)

The ballet is set in the Rhine Valley. Giselle, a peasant girl, loves Albrecht, unaware that he is a count engaged to Bathilde, daughter of the Duke of Courland. Albrecht loves Giselle in return, which arouses the jealousy of the gamekeeper Hilarion, whose love for Giselle is unrequited. At a hunting picnic for the Duke, his daughter and his entourage, Hilarion reveals Albrecht's identity, whereupon Giselle goes mad and dies.

In Act II, both Hilarion and Albrecht come to worship at the tomb of Giselle. At the stroke of midnight, the Wilis appear, led by their Queen Myrtha. They are the embodiment of spirits of dance-loving fiancées, who died before their wedding day.

They perform their ghostly rites, discover Hilarion and drive him into the lake. Albrecht, too, almost meets his death, but Giselle intervenes by dancing with him until dawn breaks, when the Wilis must return to their graves, and Albrecht is saved.

The ballet still retains the reputation acquired at its first production; it is considered to be the very essence of the Romantic movement. Before long, it was being performed all over the world. It was first produced in London, St Petersburg and Vienna in 1842, in Berlin and Milan in 1843 and Boston in 1846. The work became a display piece *par excellence* for ballerinas of all future generations. The Paris production was last performed in 1868. Modern versions are based traditionally on Marius Petipa's last production in St Petersburg in 1884.

Most of the later productions make some reference to Diaghilev's which, while not a failure, was not enthusiastically received in Paris, though the London reception was warmer and tribute was paid to the partnership of Karsavina and Nijinsky.

JEUX
Ballet in one act
Cat. **137**

Music: Claude Debussy

Libretto and choreography: Vaslav Nijinsky

Set and costumes: Léon Bakst (supplemented by Paquin)

First performance: 15 May 1913, Théâtre des Champs-Elysées, Paris

Principal dancers: Vaslav Nijinsky, Tamara Karsavina, Ludmilla Schollar

The first contemporary subject in the repertoire of Diaghilev's Company: three tennis-players, a boy and two girls, meet by chance in a garden. The boy flirts with both the girls, but cannot make up his mind which one to choose. They depart in different directions.

This ballet was dismissed by critics as obscure. The costumes and gestures are consciously anti-balletic, the dancers being clothed in sportsgear. Unhappy with Bakst's costume designs, Diaghilev insisted that the girls visit the dress designer, Paquin. Nijinsky performed in his rehearsal clothes.

Jeux:
Tamara Karsavina, Ludmilla Schollar and Vaslav Nijinsky, 1913
Bibliothèque Nationale, Paris

Details of Nijinsky's original inspiration can be gleaned from his biographies and diaries. Lady Ottoline Morrell declares that it came from a game of tennis seen at a party in Bedford Square in London. The movements are based on gymnastic gestures loosely associated with a ball game, and

the whole is intended to suggest a futuristic plot. The ball was the size of a football.

Nijinsky's own diaries reveal an overtly sexual subtext to his libretto:

Diaghilev wanted to love two boys at the same time, and he wanted them to love him. The two boys are the two young girls, and Diaghilev is the young man. I have disguised the characters, because I wanted people to feel disgust. I was disgusted, so I couldn't finish this ballet. Diaghilev didn't like the idea either, but they had given him ten thousand francs for this ballet, so he had to finish it . . .

LA LÉGENDE DE JOSEPH
Ballet in one act
Cat. **145**

Music: Richard Strauss

Libretto: Count Harry Kessler, Hugo von Hofmannsthal

Choreography: Michel Fokine

Set: José-Maria Sert

Costumes: Léon Bakst

First performance: 4 May 1914, Théâtre National de l'Opéra, Paris

Principal dancers: Maria Kuznetsova (Potiphar's wife), Vera Fokina (the Shulamite Woman), Alexis Bulgakov (Potiphar), Léonide Massine (Joseph)

The authors set the Biblical story of the shepherd Joseph and his rejection of the wife of Potiphar in the Venice of Paolo Veronese, c.1530, stressing the contrast of oriental riches and corrupt voluptuousness with boyish rectitude and chastity. At the end, Joseph is led towards apotheosis, while Potiphar's wife strangles herself with a rope of pearls. This marked Massine's début with Diaghilev's Company.

Cyril Beaumont explains that the work was 'not so much a ballet as a wordless play' with the dance inserts 'more in the manner of embroidery than a necessary adjunct to the plot'.

MIDAS
Ballet in one act
Cat. **152A-B, 153**

Music: Maximilian Steinberg

Libretto: Léon Bakst, after Ovid

Choreography: Michel Fokine

Set and costumes: Mstislav Dobuzhinsky

First performance: 2 June 1914, Théâtre National de l'Opéra, Paris

Principal dancers: Tamara Karsavina, Adolph Bolm, Max Frohman, Ludmilla Schollar, Sophie Pflanz, Lubov Tchernicheva

Midas, a king famous for his stupidity, attends a musical contest between Apollo and Pan, who has dared challenge the God of Music. At the end of the contest, Apollo is declared the victor. Midas protests against this verdict and Apollo, to punish him, gives him donkey's ears.

NARCISSE
Ballet in one act
Cat. **131A-J, 138**

Music: Nicholas Tcherepnine

Libretto: Léon Bakst, after Ovid, Pausanias

Choreography: Michel Fokine

Set and costumes: Léon Bakst

First performance: 26 April 1911, Théâtre de Monte-Carlo, Monaco

Paris première: 6 June 1911, Théâtre du Châtelet

Principal dancers: Vaslav Nijinsky (Narcisse), Tamara Karsavina (Echo), Bronislava Nijinska (Bacchante), Vera Fokina (Young Boeotian girl)

Narcisse:
Vera Fokina as Young Boeotian Girl, 1911
Victoria and Albert Museum, London

The shy, graceful Echo is in love with the vain youth Narcissus who proudly rejects her. He is punished by the gods, who make him the victim of a love which cannot be returned.

At the start of the ballet, Narcissus has been sporting with a bevy of nymphs, all of whom are enamoured of him. He stoops to drink from a crystal pool which mirrors his beauty. In vain he attempts to make his reflection share his passion for himself. As he falls exhausted by the cool waters, he is transformed into the golden flower which still bears his name.

PAPILLONS
Ballet in one act
Cat. **140, 151**

Music: Robert Schumann; arr/orch. Nicholas Tcherepnine

Libretto and choreography: Michel Fokine

Set: Mstislav Dobuzhinsky

Costumes: Léon Bakst

First performance: March 1912, Maryinsky Theatre, St Petersburg (Literary Fund Benefit)

Western première: 16 April 1914, Théâtre de Monte-Carlo, Monaco

Principal dancers: Tamara Karsavina, Ludmilla Schollar, Michel Fokine

The scene is Carnival night in 1830. A melancholy Pierrot wanders in the park when a group of girls, with little wings attached to their shoulders, enter and dance round him. Pierrot, believing them to be butterflies, tries to attract them with a candle flame. He succeeds in capturing one but is so rough with her that her wings break and she falls down dead. Her companions return and the distraught Pierrot appeals to them for help. They succeed in re-attaching her wings and she comes back to life. Pierrot is happy again and they all dance joyously.

Suddenly a clock strikes to denote the end of the Carnival. All the girls, including Pierrot's captive, disappear to return accompanied by their chaperones. The last to leave is a young masked girl escorted by a gentleman. Pierrot looks at her, and as she passes him she half raises her mask and smiles. Pierrot, realising that that he has been tricked, stares after her, overcome with bitterness. Finally he turns and falls to the ground, stricken with grief.

LE PAVILLON D'ARMIDE
Ballet in one act and three scenes
Cat. **106A-F, 107A-E, 108A-E**

Music: Nicholas Tcherepnine

Choreography: Michel Fokine

Libretto: Alexandre Benois from Théophile Gautier's story *Omphale*

Designs: Alexandre Benois

First performance: 28 April (annual pupils' graduation performance) and 25 November 1907, Maryinsky Theatre, St Petersburg

Paris première: 19 May 1909, Théâtre du Châtelet

Principal dancers 1907: Anna Pavlova (Armida), Pavel Gerdt (Marquis), Vaslav Nijinsky (Armida's Slave), Michel Fokine (Vicomte)

Principal dancers 1909: Vera Karalli (Armida), Tamara Karsavina (Armida's confidante), Vaslav Nijinsky (Armida's slave), Michel Fokine (Vicomte)

The ballet is set in the period of Louis XIV. A young Vicomte stays the night in a pavilion decorated with exquisite tapestries. These come to life during the night. In his dream, the young man becomes infatuated with the embroidered Armida. His happiness is crowned by the consent of King Hydrao (whom he recognises as his host – a notorious magician) to their nuptials. When the Vicomte awakens, he finds, to his amazement, Armida's scarf at his side. Realising he is the victim of enchantment, he dies of fear and horror before the gloating eyes of his villainous host.

Le Pavillon d'Armide:
Vaslav Nijinsky as Armida's Slave, 1909
Bibliothèque Nationale, Paris

The designs, by Benois, were conceived, according to his memoirs, as 'the quintessence of baroque architecture and decoration'.

PETRUSHKA
Ballet in one act and four scenes
Cat. **141A-C, 142A-D, 144, 150**

Music: Igor Stravinsky

Libretto: Igor Stravinsky, Alexandre Benois

Sets and costumes: Alexandre Benois

Choreography: Michel Fokine

First performance: 13 June 1911, Théâtre du Châtelet, Paris

Principal dancers: Vaslav Nijinsky (Petrushka), Tamara Karsavina (the Ballerina Doll), Alexander Orlov (the Moor), Enrico Cecchetti (the Showman)

The ballet takes place at the Shrovetide Fair in 1830. In St Petersburg's Admiralty Square, crowds come and go. To the background leitmotif of the organ-grinder, we see a kaleidoscope of dances by groups of gypsies, street dancers, nurses, coachmen, grooms, organ-grinders, vendors, officers, soldiers, gentlemen, ladies, children, policemen and a bear-leader.

At a showman's booth, a second, inner curtain goes up. The old necromancer, manager of a puppet show, displays his grand, life-size marionettes; a dancing girl and her two admirers, Petrushka, ugly and romantic, the Moor, wicked but fascinating. Their creator has endowed these images with human emotions. The hero bitterly resents his unattractiveness as contrasted with the Moor's gorgeous appearance, which enslaves the dancing girl. Petrushka is mad with jealousy. When festivities are at their height, Petrushka is suddenly killed by his rival. Consternation seizes the crowd. But the old showman assures them that Petrushka is only a thing of sawdust and plaster – his own creature. However, when the people disperse, the showman is horrified to see the tragic ghost of the marionette menacing him from the quiet shadow of the booth.

In this ballet, where character is as important as dancing, Nijinsky won many hearts as the tragic figure of the mawkish clown whom nobody takes seriously.

POLOVTSIAN DANCES

Ballet in one act, from the opera *Prince Igor*
[For the background of the opera, see p. 156]
Cat. 109, 111-12, 113A-C

Music: Alexander Borodin (see above), partly
orchestrated by Nikolai Rimsky-Korsakov

Scenario: Vladimir Stasov

Libretto: Alexander Borodin

Set and costumes: Nikolai Roerich

Choreography: Michel Fokine

First performance: 19 May 1909, Théâtre
du Châtelet, Paris

Principal dancers: Sophie Fedorova (Young
Polovtsian Girl), Helen Smirnova (Polovtsian
Woman), Adolph Bolm (Polovtsian Chief)

The scene is a Polovtsian camp at dawn.
Prince Igor of Novgorod and Seversk and his son
Vladimir have been captured by the Polovtsy, a tribe
of marauding Tatars. The main action of the opera
takes place in the camp of Khan Kontchak, where
they have been taken prisoner along with their men.
The Khan is impressed by his captive's high principles, and, assuring Igor that he is a guest and not
a slave, offers him inducements to make peace with
the Tatars and join his empire and forces with
Kontchak's. Igor refuses all his offers, including
those that would make his captivity more luxurious.
It is at this point that the Khan brings on his dancing
Polovtsian slaves to lighten the tedium of Igor's life
without liberty.

As an independent entity, the *Polovtsian
Dances* have been performed many more times
than the opera *Prince Igor*, particularly in the West,
where, for every person who knows of the opera, one
thousand are familiar with its ballet insert. After its
Paris première, during the first Season in 1909, this
wild, ferocious number received six curtain calls.

THE RITE OF SPRING

A picture of Ancient Russia in two acts
Cat. 148, 161A-D, 162A-C, 163

Music: Igor Stravinsky

Libretto: Igor Stravinsky and Nikolai Roerich

Choreography: Vaslav Nijinsky

Sets and costumes: Nikolai Roerich

First performance: 29 May 1913, Théâtre des
Champs-Elysées, Paris

Principal dancers: Maria Piltz (the Chosen
Maiden), Mme Goulik (an Old Woman 300 Years
Old), M. Woronzov (a Wise Man)

Act I is devoted to ritual movements in
which the members of the tribe, at the direction
of the aged seer, dance in adoration of the earth.
Act II turns on the selection of the Spring Victim,
the initial rites before the sacrifice, and ends with
the extremely long and energetic dance by the
Chosen Maiden, which culminates in her death.

The second episode provides the peak of
the ballet. The movements made by the Chosen
Maiden work up to a repetitive, forceful rhythm
which borders on delirium. It was at the time
the most exhausting dance, both physically and
mentally, in the history of the choreographic art.

This ballet created an atmosphere of savagery, mingled with profound ritualism. Coming
after the romantic beauty of Fokine's choreography,
it was a tremendous shock to an audience nurtured
on the traditional conception of ballet. Nijinsky here
choreographed movements which were ugly and
uncouth. Stravinsky's music, with its insistent,
throbbing rhythm emphasised by dancers' feet
pounding on stage, becomes irresistible and
dominating. The music and choreography were
united not by steps danced to notes but by rhythmic
responses and counterpoint achieved through mass
movement. This ballet, which required endless rehearsals, was given five times in Paris and three in
London.

SCHÉHÉRAZADE

Ballet taken from the Prologue
of *One Thousand and One Nights*
Cat. 119A-D, 121, 129

Music: Nikolai Rimsky-Korsakov (Overture, Parts
II and IV of the Symphonic Suite of the same name)

Libretto: Alexandre Benois (also Bakst, Fokine)

Choreography: Michel Fokine

Sets and costumes: Léon Bakst

First performance: 4 June 1910, Théâtre National
de l'Opéra, Paris

Principal dancers: Ida Rubinstein (Zobéide), Vaslav
Nijinsky (Zobéide's Favourite Slave 'Golden
Negro'), Alexis Bulgakov (Shahryar, Sultan of
India and China), Basil Kissilev (Shah Zeman, his
brother), Enrico Cecchetti (Chief Eunuch), Sophie
Fedorova (Odalisque)

The scene is Shahryar's harem. The Shah
Zeman is incredulous when his brother Sultan
Shahryar sings the praises of his favourite wife
Zobéide. He persuades the Sultan to test her fidelity
by pretending to go on a hunting expedition for
several days.

Hardly have the lords departed when the
harem is in uproar. The fat eunuch is soon wheedled
into opening the bronze and silver doors which lead
into the apartment of the sleek negro slaves. Finally,
he opens the door behind which Zobéide's favourite
slave and lover, the 'Golden Negro', is waiting.

He bounds into Zobéide's embrace, and the
two start a mass orgy which reaches its maddest
height when the Sultan returns unexpectedly. His
vengeance is swift. All are massacred. Zobéide, after
vainly imploring pardon of her royal spouse, stabs
herself at his feet, to avoid the fate of the other
inmates of the harem.

This is the most voluptuous of Diaghilev's
ballets and, as such, was a triumphant sensation
wherever it was performed. Bakst's designs were
immortalised and much copied at this period. The
ballet received some adverse criticism in musical
circles, especially from the family of the late Rimsky-
Korsakov, who objected to the truncation of the
work, and to its use as incidental music to the violent
climax of an erotic ballet. The composer's original
intention was that his symphonic poem should
illustrate the adventures of Sinbad the Sailor, also
from *One Thousand and One Nights*, but giving a
quite different interpretation of these tales.

THE SLEEPING BEAUTY
Ballet in two acts
Cat. **58**

Music: Pyotr Tchaikovsky

Libretto and choreography: Marius Petipa

Sets and costumes: Ivan Vsevolozhsky

First performance: 15 January 1890, Maryinsky Theatre, St Petersburg

London première: 2 November 1921, Alhambra Theatre (Ballets Russes production) as *The Sleeping Princess*

Principal dancers, 1890: Carlotta Brianza (Aurora), Pavel Gerdt (Prince Charming), Marie Petipa (Lilac Fairy), Enrico Cecchetti (Carabosse)

Act I, Scene I shows the Palace of King Florestan XXIV in the seventeenth century, where guests assemble for the christening of Princess Aurora. These include a swarm of fairies, each of whom approaches the cradle to breathe upon the baby Princess a magic spell, endowing her with desirable qualities. A sudden clap of thunder announces the arrival of the wicked Fairy Carabosse. Displeased at not having been invited to the christening, she berates the palace officials, and instead of a magic spell, she bestows a curse on the baby Aurora: the Princess will grow in beauty and accomplishments until the day she shall prick her finger and die. The Lilac Fairy commutes this sentence to deep slumber until the Princess shall be awakened by a kiss from the son of a King.

Act I, Scene 2 takes place in the garden of King Florestan's Palace, sixteen years later. A coming-of-age party is being held for the Princess Aurora, who has become renowned for her beauty and accomplishments. Four Princes have arrived to seek her hand. The local villagers are also making merry. When the celebrations are in full swing, a furtive newcomer glides in. It is the Fairy Carabosse, with a spindle under her cloak. Without difficulty, she entices the Princess to touch this curious object. The Princess pricks her finger and loses consciousness. The Lilac Fairy arranges for her to be carried indoors. Foliage begins to grow around the palace.

Act II, Scene I is set in a forest glade, one hundred years later. Prince Charming is hunting with his entourage. He becomes bored and detaches himself from the company. The Lilac Fairy appears and offers him a meeting with the sleeping Princess. Entranced by an enchanted vision of Aurora, the Prince is drawn to the castle where the Princess awaits the kiss of a King's son.

Scene 2 is the dusty hall of King Florestan's Palace. Prince Charming enters the palace, where a grey stone tomb supports the body of the sleeping Aurora. He approaches the Princess and embraces her. She awakes and, with her, the palace comes to life. A joyous party begins, in which fairy-tale characters, exotic nobles and fabled animal heroes join in celebration.

Tchaikovsky began working on this ballet in December 1888. The first Gala Rehearsal was on 1 January 1890. The Imperial Court accorded it a cool reception, but the intelligentsia, including members of Alexandre Benois's circle, gave it a much warmer reception. Léon Bakst reported: 'I lived in a magic dream for three hours intoxicated with fairies and princesses, splendid palaces flowing with gold, in the enchantment of the old tale.'

In the year 1921, Carlotta Brianza, who had played the part of Aurora in 1890, appeared as Carabosse. On 5 January 1922, Enrico Cecchetti, who had created the role of Carabosse, danced it again in London, to celebrate fifty years of his career.

LE SPECTRE DE LA ROSE
Ballet in one scene
Cat. **130, 146, 147**

Music: Carl Maria von Weber, orchestrated by Hector Berlioz

Libretto: Jean-Louis Vaudoyer, after a poem by Théophile Gautier

Choreography: Michel Fokine

Set and costumes: Léon Bakst

First performance: 19 April 1911, Théâtre de Monte-Carlo, Monaco

Principal dancers: Vaslav Nijinsky (The Spectre), Tamara Karsavina (Young Girl)

The scene is a young girl's bedroom with tall French windows thrown open to reveal rose bushes. The girl falls asleep after her return from a ball, with a full-blown rose in her hand. The delicate flower is the symbol of her romance. As she dreams, she clasps it to her breast. It comes to life in the shape of a phantom, with whom she dances. She awakens to find only a few fragrant petals scattered about her feet where, an instant before, her dream lover had been kneeling.

This was one of the early ballets which forged in the public memory the historic partnership of Nijinsky and Karsavina. It was the Western production in which Nijinsky's renowned ethereal leap was recalled in the memoirs of many contemporaries, including Fokine and Cocteau. It received rapturous applause at every performance.

SWAN LAKE (*Le Lac des Cygnes*)
Ballet in four acts
Cat. **158**

Music: Pyotr Tchaikovsky

Libretto: Vladimir Begichev, Vasily Geltzer

Choreography: Marius Petipa and Lev Ivanov, revised by Michel Fokine

First performance: 15 January 1895, Maryinsky Theatre, St Petersburg

London première: 2-act version, 30 November 1911, Royal Opera House, Covent Garden

Sets: Konstantin Korovine, Alexandre Golovine, 1901 (purchased by Diaghilev from the Bolshoi Theatre, Moscow)

Principal dancers: Mathilde Kshessinska (Odette-Odile)

Act I is set in a magnificent garden, a castle in the background. It is Prince Siegfried's coming-of-age and his party is attended by bucolic guests. His mother rebukes him and his tutor taunts him for having no associates of rank and no suitable fiancée. A flock of swans passes overhead.

In Act II it is midnight by a lakeside, with a ruined chapel in the distance. A group of swans, one wearing a crown, glides to the shore. As they approach land, the swans turn into young girls. Disguised as an owl, the wicked enchanter Rotbart watches over them from the shadow of the chapel. Siegfried and his male companions enter with crossbows. The swan-girls explain that they are humans under a spell and beg the young men not to shoot them. Siegfried falls for their Princess, Odette, but Rotbart comes between them. The Prince invites Odette to the ball where he must choose his bride. She warns him that the spell of Rotbart is not yet broken and begs Siegfried to be true to her meanwhile. Dawn breaks and the girls turn back into swans.

The setting for Act III is a splendid ballroom. Siegfried, his mother, noble guests and dancers in national costumes are gathered for the selection of Siegfried's bride. Fanfares announce new arrivals. Enter Rotbart and his daughter Odile, attired as a black swan. Siegfried, thinking she is Odette, pays court to her. Odette knocks on the window, trying vainly to warn him of the danger. Siegfried announces to Rotbart that he will marry Odile. Delighted that Siegfried's vow is broken, the magician and his daughter vanish. Realising his error, Siegfried goes out to find Odette.

Act IV is again set by the lake. Odette enters and tells the swan-girls of Siegfried's betrayal of his troth. Siegfried enters. At first Odette hides, but when he explains how the enchanter duped him, she forgives him. They dance. A storm blows up. Siegfried carries Odette to a hilltop. He announces his readiness to die with her, thus breaking Rotbart's spell. The lake is restored to its former calm and the girls regain their human state.

LES SYLPHIDES

Ballet in one act

Cat. **105, 115**

Music: Frédéric Chopin, orchestrated by Alexander Glazunov, Igor Stravinsky, Alexander Taneev

Choreography: Michel Fokine

Set and costumes: Alexandre Benois

First performance: 1907, Maryinsky Theatre, St Petersburg

Paris première: 2 June 1909, Théâtre du Châtelet

Soloists: Anna Pavlova, Tamara Karsavina (Sylphides), Vaslav Nijinsky (Poet)

Les Sylphides:
Anna Pavlova, 1909
Bibliothèque Nationale, Paris

This ballet, first known as *Chopiniana,* is set in a sylvan glade. In its day, the ballet was unusual in having no story line, no conventional characters and a male dancer as the main soloist. The whole is conceived as a kaleidoscopic spectacle in white, closely allied to the music of Chopin. Performed as a poetic ensemble by the *corps de ballet,* the work culminated in the appearance of the male soloist. The dances consisted of four variations and a *pas de deux* framed in two ensembles: an overture and a conclusion. The female costumes were of the romantic, Taglioni type.

THAMAR

Ballet in one scene

Cat. **134**

Music: Mili Balakirev

Choreography: Michel Fokine

Libretto: Léon Bakst, after a poem by Mikhail Lermontov

Set and costumes: Léon Bakst

First performance: 20 May 1912, Théâtre du Châtelet, Paris

Principal dancers: Tamara Karsavina (Queen of Georgia), Adolph Bolm (Wandering Prince)

The curtain rises on the interior of a castle, disclosing the fantastic court of the seductive Caucasian Queen, Thamar. Her castle is surrounded by the turbulent waters of the river Terek, where so many of her unfortunate lovers have met their fate. Her strange companions dance grotesques, trying to free Thamar of her ennui. She ignores them but, surveying the wild Dariol mountain pass, she sees a stranger approach. She commands that he be brought in and disrobed in her baleful presence. He proves handsome, and is led away to her chamber. For a brief hour, he enjoys the feverish pleasures of Thamar's favour, while her barbaric entourage perform wild elemental dances. But even as the court collapses exhausted, the Prince, also quite spent, is dragged into the hall by the glaring vampire Queen, who stabs him dead, flinging him through a hatch to his doom in the cruel depths of the dark river. Thamar's hungry eyes are soon seeking the next victim . . .

The impact of this ballet can be imagined through its magnificent Caucasian costumes and its music, a symphonic poem in the oriental style characteristic of Balakirev. As a production, it was remarkable for the power of its acting, especially of Karsavina as the cruel Queen. Its theme, the smouldering of insatiable lust, is effectively harnessed through the dramatic device of suspense. The Prince's pleasure is at first repeatedly postponed by the Queen, who has devised a ritual, which leads to consummation offstage, echoed by the antics of the waiting court.

LA TRAGÉDIE DE SALOMÉ

Ballet in one act

Cat. **164**

Music: Florent Schmitt

Libretto: After a poem by Robert d'Humières

Choreography: Boris Romanov

Set, front cloth and costumes: Sergei Sudeikin

First performance: 12 June 1913, Théâtre des Champs-Elysées, Paris

Conductor: Pierre Monteux

Principal dancer: Tamara Karsavina (Salomé)

The ballet uses the New Testament story of the stepdaughter of King Herod, who asks to be rewarded for her dance with the head of John the Baptist (Mark 6, 17–29). The plot, which includes political intrigue, finishes with the visionary sequence of Salomé and John, liberated from his chains, in a landscape of love. Earlier dance treatments of the story were mostly based on Oscar Wilde's homonymous tragedy. The costume designs owe something to Beardsley.

La Tragédie de Salomé:
Tamara Karsavina as Salomé, 1913
Hulton Deutsch Collection Limited, London

Biographical Notes

Adolph **BOLM** / 1884 – 1951
Cat. **109, 124**

Graduating in 1903 from the Imperial School in St Petersburg, Bolm became a soloist at the Maryinsky Theatre in 1910. He organised and danced in Pavlova's first tours abroad but joined Diaghilev's troupe in 1909. He created the roles of Chief Warrior in the *Polovtsian Dances* of *Prince Igor* in 1909, the first year of the *Saisons russes*; and of Pierrot in *Carnaval* in 1911, the year he resigned from the Maryinsky Theatre to join Diaghilev's Company.

Bolm danced for Diaghilev until the second USA tour of Ballets Russes in 1916, when he decided to settle in the USA. There he founded his Ballet In Time, with which he was later to do pioneer work in films. He worked with Chicago Grand Opera / Ballet, where he staged seventy modern ballet productions. In later life, he worked in Hollywood, where he died.

Thamar:
Adolph Bolm as the Wandering Prince
and Tamara Karsavina
as the Queen of Georgia, 1912

Enrico **CECCHETTI** / 1850 – 1928
Cat. **119B, 127, 128**

One of the greatest teachers in ballet history, Enrico Cecchetti was born in Rome (appropriately, in a theatre), the son of two Italian dancers. He made his first stage appearance in Genoa at the age of five. He studied with Lepri in Florence, made his début at the Milan School, in 1870, then toured Europe as *premier danseur*.

Cecchetti made his St Petersburg début in 1887. His brilliant technique amazed the Russians and occasioned his appointment, in 1890, as second ballet master to the Imperial Theatres, and in 1892, as instructor at the Imperial School.

He created the roles of both the Bluebird and Carabosse (*Sleeping Beauty*), a testimony to his virtuosity and mimetic gifts. While at the Maryinsky Theatre, he created some choreography, notably refurbishing *Coppélia* in 1894, but his chief claim to fame lies in his extraordinary gifts as a teacher. His pupils included Anna Pavlova, Tamara Karsavina and Vaslav Nijinsky.

Cecchetti became ballet master of the Imperial School, Warsaw, in 1902. In 1905, he returned to Italy, then to Russia, opening a private school in St Petersburg and devoting much time to private work with Pavlova. In 1909 he became the official teacher for Diaghilev's Ballets Russes and created roles with that company, notably the Chief Eunuch in *Schéhérazade*, the Charlatan in *Petrushka* and the Astrologer in *Le Coq d'Or*. In 1918, he and his wife Giuseppina opened a school in London, where his pupils included nearly every famous dancer of the time.

In London, Cyril Beaumont initiated the formation of the still flourishing Cecchetti Society in 1922 to perpetuate his teaching methods. At Beaumont's instigation, the Manual of the Méthode Cecchetti was first published the same year.

Fyodor **CHALIAPIN** / 1873 – 1938
Cat. **97, 100, 101**

Widely considered the greatest singing talent of his day and largely self-taught, Chaliapin was born in Kazan, the son of very poor peasants: an attribute which was to stand him in good stead when, in the Soviet period, he was to become 'People's Artist of the USSR'.

His first experience of music was as a choirboy, which he became on impulse and to the displeasure of his father, who beat him. After running away from home to work on the Volga ferries, the young Fyodor began to dabble in theatre first as an actor and later as a singer. From the age of seventeen, he sang, first in the chorus, later in progressively more important roles in small provincial opera and operetta troupes, before he had received any formal training. After studying in Tblisi with Dmitry Usatov, a former Bolshoi soloist, Chaliapin successfully sang a wide variety of French and Italian roles in Tblisi and St Petersburg.

From 1894 to 1896, he belonged to St Petersburg's Imperial Opera, which offered him no roles. In the meantime, he became interested in Russian opera and was easily induced by Savva Mamontov to leave the Imperial Theatres and join his Private Opera Company, which boasted the best theatre designers and the best musical exponents of Russian opera.

With Mamontov, Chaliapin further developed his musical and artistic powers and became renowned for carefully thought-out performances of such roles as Boris and Varlaam (*Boris Godunov*), Dosifei (*Khovanshchina*, also by Mussorgsky), Ivan the Terrible (*The Maid of Pskov*), the Viking Guest (*Sadko*), the Miller (Dargomizhsky's *Rusalka*) and Holofernes (Alexander Serov's *Judith*).

In 1900, he left Mamontov's company to join the Bolshoi Opera, making frequent guest appearances at the Maryinsky and at provincial opera houses. In 1901, Chaliapin's international career began at La Scala, Milan, where he returned in 1904 and from 1907 to 1908, and at the Metropolitan Opera House, New York.

Diaghilev first discovered Chaliapin when he was performing for Mamontov's Private Opera. In 1907, Diaghilev invited him to perform as soloist in his first Paris Season. Thereafter, Chaliapin was associated with Diaghilev's enterprises until the outbreak of the First World War. He performed in the Paris *Saisons russes* of 1908, 1910 and 1913 and in London in 1913 and 1914. In 1918, Chaliapin rejoined the Maryinsky Theatre as soloist and art director, before leaving Russia in 1921.

With the celebrated Russian theatre director Stanislavsky, who gave him lessons in acting, Chaliapin was one of the first Russians to become interested in the totality of a theatrical production. His career was marked by his historic creation and transformation of operatic roles, which he achieved by entering wholly into the personality of the character he played.

A high bass baritone, Chaliapin's voice was sufficiently flexible to allow him to sing a wide range of bass and baritone roles. In *Prince Igor* he sang the parts of Galitzky, Kontchak and Igor.

Accounts of his character by people who knew him on and offstage reveal a superhuman personality, set off by unusual physical height, which gave him stature in and out of roles. Although he had received only four years of formal education, Chaliapin was intelligent as well as energetic, warm and responsive. Remarkably versatile, his talents extended beyond music to painting and sculpture. Generous in all personal dealings, he was grasping in financial transactions and commanded the highest salary of his day. Chaliapin died in Paris, where his funeral was attended by thousands of mourners. He was recently reburied in Moscow's Novodevichy Cemetery.

Isadora **DUNCAN** / 1877-1927
Cat. **53**

Born in San Francisco, Isadora Duncan was the pioneer of 'free' dance. Inspired by the natural movements of waves and trees, she rebelled against stereotyped conventions of ballet with what she considered its contortions of the body and restrictive costume. She danced in filmy shifts, barelegged and barefoot, which added a sensational element to her reputation.

Since her performances were largely improvisations based on personal response, and containing a high degree of personal charisma, Duncan had no direct followers, although she has ever since had an enormous influence on choreographers.

In 1899, the twenty-two-year-old Isadora Duncan left America with her family on what became a long European tour. They first visited London, where she was acclaimed in artistic circles. The discovery of Greek sculptures and vase paintings in the British Museum gave her a new ideal for achieving beauty and emotional expression.

Still imitating the flowing rhythms of nature, she began to dance to the music of the great composers, particularly Beethoven, Chopin and Schubert. Between 1900 and 1902, she made triumphant European débuts in Paris, Budapest, Vienna, Munich and Berlin.

Duncan would often deliver discourses from the stage on her art, which was based on theories about the workings of the human body and the forces of gravity.

In December 1904, during her Russian début at the Hall of Nobles, St Petersburg, she was an immediate sensation, winning the admiration of major Russian exponents of all the arts. She won particular praise from Diaghilev, the young Michel Fokine (later to become his choreographer) and the theatre director Konstantin Stanislavsky, all of whom were already battling against convention in the performing arts.

Duncan's connection with Russia continued into the Bolshevik period, when her personal life became tinged with dramatic notoriety. In 1921, she was invited to open a dance school in Moscow and

in 1922 she married the poet Sergei Esenin, who committed suicide in 1925. She composed two dances for Lenin's funeral and made a tour of the Ukraine, distributing her earnings to the poor. In 1924, she left Russia and settled in France. She was accidentally killed in Nice when her scarf caught in the wheel of her open car.

Michel **FOKINE** / 1880-1942
Cat. **110, 113A, 118C, 120, 154**

Mikhail (later Michel) Fokine graduated from the Imperial Theatre School, where he had already made an impression with his versatility, talent and application in 1898. He joined the Maryinsky Ballet Company with the immediate rank of soloist. He began to teach in the Imperial School in 1902.

His first choreography was for *Acis and Galatea*, staged for a pupils' performance in 1905. In 1907, he choreographed *Le Cygne* for Anna Pavlova. The same year, Fokine choreographed to music by Tcherepnine a student production based on the libretto by Alexandre Benois for *Le Pavillon d'Armide*. Later the same year, he worked with Benois on a full production for the Imperial Theatres. This was the beginning of Fokine's collaboration with Diaghilev's circle.

In 1908, Fokine was invited by Diaghilev to produce ballets for his 1909 Paris Season. He worked with Diaghilev until 1913, creating works that included *Les Sylphides*, *Carnaval*, *Le Spectre de la Rose*, *Prince Igor*, *The Firebird*, *Petrushka* and *Daphnis and Chloë*. The variety of styles represented in these and later ballets which he composed is unprecedented in the work of a single choreographer. He also danced the leading roles in his own and other ballets with the greatest ballerinas, starting with Pavlova.

Fokine's influence on the course of ballet in this century and its consequent transformation from a pretty entertainment to a potent art force is summarised in his own writings. His theory was formed in 1904, when he created the scenario for his later ballet *Daphnis and Chloë*. He submitted both the scenario and his opinions to the Director of the Imperial Theatres, but his reforms were only implemented when Fokine joined the Ballets Russes. An awkward character, given to explosions of rage, his refusal to compromise made him difficult to work with.

At the start of the First World War, Fokine returned to Russia, where he choreographed six works for the Maryinsky Theatre. He left Russia for Sweden in 1918, eventually settling in New York in the early 1920s. He travelled widely, staging his

famous ballets and producing new ones. Towards the end of his life he worked for the De Basil Ballet Russe de Monte-Carlo. His last two important works were the comedy ballet *Bluebeard* (1941) and *The Russian Soldier* (1942).

Pavel **GERDT** / 1844-1917
Cat. **106A-B**

Graduating in 1864 from St Petersburg Theatre School, where he had studied in the classes of Marius Petipa and Johansson, Gerdt started dancing at the Maryinsky Theatre at the age of sixteen. He created the roles of Siegfried, Prince Charming and Abdérâme, and danced all the other classical roles. He taught at the St Petersburg School from 1880 to 1904, forming Anna Pavlova, Tamara Karsavina, Michel Fokine and others.

Tamara **KARSAVINA** / 1885-1978
Cat. **118A, 124, 146, 150**

The daughter of the dancer Platon Karsavin, she studied at the St Petersburg Imperial School and later worked with the Italian Caterina Beretta to strengthen her technique. She graduated in 1902 as soloist and by 1909 was dancing ballerina roles. She maintained her connection with the Maryinsky until the Russian Revolution.

Karsavina's artistic education was furthered by Fokine. She took part in all the early Diaghilev seasons, created immortal roles and formed memorable partnerships with Nijinsky, in *Les Sylphides*, *Carnaval*, *Petrushka*, *Le Spectre de la Rose*, *Thamar* and *The Firebird*.

La Tragédie de Salomé:
Tamara Karsavina as Salomé, 1913
Bibliothèque Nationale, Paris

Her intelligence and the deeply expressive nature of her dancing endeared her to Diaghilev, who invested in her a deep friendship based on a mutual respect rare in his relationships with the dancers of his troupe. In the post-war period, Karsavina returned to dance for Diaghilev in 1919, creating the role of the Miller's Wife in *Le Tricorne* and dancing Bronislava Nijinska's *Romeo and Juliet* with Lifar.

Tamara Karsavina's second husband was the British diplomat Henry James Bruce, with whom she escaped from Russia during the Revolution. Eventually, she made her home in London, became a Vice-President of the Royal Academy of Dance at its inception in 1920 and later devised important teaching syllabuses.

Savva **MAMONTOV** / 1841–1918
Cat. **23**

Mamontov was an industrialist and arts patron of fabulous wealth. He was also a considerable artist and musician in his own right.

In 1870, he bought the Abramtsevo estate, near Moscow, where he ran an arts colony. Initially, his protégés were chiefly traditionalists of national bent such as Repin and Viktor Vasnetsov. Later, he commissioned work from the more avant garde members of the younger generation, including Konstantin Korovine [see p. 133] and Mikhail Vrubel [see p. 131].

In the early 1900s, Mamontov founded both a successful ceramics workshop and a Private Opera Company in Moscow, which ran at a loss but produced Russian operas to a standard unequalled by the Imperial Theatres. Indeed Mamontov's artists and performers were lured with huge cash incentives to the Imperial Theatres by their director, Vladimir Teliakovsky. The most famous of them was Fyodor Chaliapin. In 1899, Mamontov was accused of fraud and imprisoned for some months. When subsequently he was cleared of the charge, he had been reduced to bankruptcy. Despite being the patron of a wide circle of artists, not one of his protégés supported him at the time of his disgrace. He died a sculptor.

Mamontov joined forces with Princess Tenisheva in 1898 to support *World of Art* magazine, on the understanding that it would perform the function of a platform for the applied and industrial arts in Russia. When, after the first issue, the magazine failed to do this, both parties withdrew.

MARYINSKY BALLET COMPANY

Selected graduates of the Imperial Theatre Schools were allowed to enter the Imperial Companies on graduation. Diaghilev's first dancers, Bolm, Fokine, Gerdt, Karsavina, Nijinsky, Pavlova and Rubinstein all shared this background. For the most outstanding dancers, an eventual rise to the status of principal dancer was assured.

More average débutants would have been promoted through gradual stages. At the Maryinsky Theatre in St Petersburg, in 1902, the Ballet Company (of 180) consisted of the following hierarchy: *corps de ballet*, *coryphée*, first and second soloists, ballerina or *premier danseur*.

Léonide **MASSINE** / 1895–1979

Léonide Fyodorovich Miasin (*sic*) studied at Moscow's Bolshoi Theatre School, graduating in 1912 to join the Bolshoi Theatre. He was toying with the idea of becoming a dramatic actor when, in 1914, he found himself enrolled into Diaghilev's Ballets Russes. Miasin at first studied intensively under Cecchetti, with Diaghilev his watchful mentor. Selected by Diaghilev for his suitable appearance, Massine (as he came to be called) successfully created the title role in Fokine's *La Légende de Joseph* [see cat. 145], essentially a mimetic role.

Massine was installed in the Company, following the departure both of Nijinsky and Fokine, as a potential choreographer and he was groomed by Diaghilev as Nijinsky's replacement in every respect. After a tentative beginning, Massine did not disappoint. He became an excellent dancer and a choreographer of vision and inventiveness.

The first ballet choreographed by Massine, *Le Soleil de Nuit*, was performed in 1915; two others, *Les Femmes de bonne humeur* (1917) and *Parade* (1917), were staged towards the end of the First World War. After the war there appeared:

Igor Stravinsky and Léonide Massine
in Lausanne, 1915
Bibliothèque Nationale, Paris

La Boutique Fantasque (1919), *Le Tricorne* (1920), *Le Chant du Rossignol* (1920), *Pulcinella* (1920), *Astuzie Femminili* (1920) and a new version of *The Rite of Spring* in 1920.

In 1921, Massine left Diaghilev to tour with some colleagues and, during the next three years, he choreographed several ballets independently of the Ballets Russes. In 1925, he joined Diaghilev again for three years, creating the ballets *Les Matelots* (1924), *Zéphyre et Flore* (1925), *Le Pas d'acier* (1927) and *Ode* (1928). In 1938 he became artistic director of René Blum's rival Ballet Russe de Monte Carlo. He was married three times: to the dancers Vera Savina, Evgenia Delarova and Tatiana Orlova.

Vaslav **NIJINSKY** / 1888–1950
Cat. **102, 106C-E, 111, 114, 119A, 122, 147, 159, 160, 166, 174**

The most brilliant graduate of the Imperial Theatre School, a legendary performer in the history of dance and a revolutionary choreographer, Vaslav Fomich Nijinsky was born in Kiev, the son of the Polish dancers Thomas Nijinsky and Eleonora Bereda, and the brother of Bronislava Nijinska.

Vaslav Nijinsky (second from left) and graduates
from the Imperial School of Dancing, St Petersburg, 1907
State Museum of Theatere and Music,
St Petersburg

From 1898 to 1907, as a student at the Imperial School, Nijinsky's powerful musculature and extraordinary elevation soon attracted notice, both in his interpretation of works in the old repertoire and in the early ballets of Fokine. In 1908, he met Diaghilev, who became his mentor, replacing Prince Lvov, previously his patron and close companion from the time of his graduation.

On 19 May 1909, the first night of Diaghilev's first Paris Season, Nijinsky became a legend.

In 1911, in a much-publicised scandal over the inadequacy of his costume in *Giselle*, Nijinsky was dismissed from the Imperial Company, left Russia for good and became *premier danseur* of Diaghilev's now independent Ballets Russes, as well as Diaghilev's constant companion. Most of Nijinsky's famous roles (almost all of which were created specially for him) were in the new Fokine works: *Le Pavillon d'Armide*, *Cléopâtre* and *Les Sylphides* (1909); *Schéhérazade* (1910); *Le Spectre de la Rose*, *Carnaval*, *Petrushka* and *Narcisse* (1911); *Le Dieu Bleu* and *Daphnis and Chloë* (1912). His partner was nearly always Karsavina [see p.168].

Nijinsky's prodigious technique was surpassed by his interpretative genius, the ability to transform himself completely in each of his roles. His choreography, in *L'Après-midi d'un faune*, *Jeux* and *The Rite of Spring*, was uniquely innovative, at once building on the traditions of classical ballet, and laying enduring foundations for dance as a significant branch of modern art.

Vaslav Nijinsky in New York, 1916
Bibliothèque Nationale, Paris

Diaghilev seems to have had faith in Nijinsky as a choreographer. He planned with him a Bach ballet and Richard Strauss's *La Légende de Joseph*, and had in mind also Stravinsky's *Noces*, which was eventually produced by his sister Bronislava Nijinska.

Following Nijinsky's marriage during the Ballets Russes's first South American tour, his relationship with Diaghilev was strained, and Nijinsky left the Company in 1913 [see cat. 174]. Nevertheless, Nijinsky rejoined the Company's second US tour (winter 1916-17): he took over as artistic director and Diaghilev returned to Europe. The staging of Nijinsky's last ballet, *Till Eulenspiegel*, which he had conceived while a prisoner in Hungary [see cat. 174], was vitiated by his now marked mental

illness, his increasingly unpredictable behaviour and dissension within the Company. None the less, it was a popular success and had twenty-two performances. After a dispiriting tour, Nijinsky rejoined Diaghilev in Spain, and was obliged to dance in the second South American season. There his persecution mania gained ground, and he gave his last performance with the Diaghilev Ballet on 26 September 1917 in Buenos Aires.

The Nijinskys retired to Switzerland, where, after a frightening dance recital on the theme of war at St Moritz early in 1919, Vaslav Fomich was pronounced insane. His famous notebooks and drawings date from this period. Nijinsky spent most of the next twenty years in sanatoria, but was again interned in Budapest during the Second World War. The Nijinskys escaped to Austria in 1945 and moved to England in 1947. Nijinsky died in London three years later, leaving his widow and two daughters. In 1953 he was reburied in Paris, near the grave of Auguste Vestris (1760-1842), the previous bearer of the legendary title, 'Le Dieu de la danse'.

Anna **PAVLOVA** / 1881 – 1931
Cat. **115, 117**

After seeing a performance of *The Sleeping Beauty* at the Maryinsky Theatre in 1890, Anna Pavlova resolved to become a dancer and appear as Aurora. In 1891 she won a place at the St Petersburg Theatre School, where she was taught by Pavel Gerdt, Johansson and later Cecchetti. She graduated on 11 April 1899 and immediately attracted the attention of critics. She first danced her incomparable Giselle in 1903 and received ballerina status in 1906, achieving in 1908 her role of Aurora in *The Sleeping Beauty*.

Anna Pavlova, 1909
Bibliothèque Nationale, Paris

Although sympathetic to the ideas of Fokine, Pavlova danced only in the first Diaghilev Season, opting thereafter to star in her own company and tour worldwide. Moreover, she was antipathetic to modern music, preferring to concentrate on perfecting the art of classical ballet. More than any other dancer, Pavlova epitomises the public image of a ballerina.

Pavlova danced no fewer than eighteen leading parts on the Maryinsky stage. She was Fokine's first Armida in *Le Pavillon d'Armide* (1907) and, in the same year, he created for her *Le Cygne* (*The Dying Swan*) which became her most famous solo. Her partners included the powerful Mikhail Mordkin (originally of the Moscow Ballet), who was to partner her on tours abroad, Anatoly Obukhov (with whom she created the *pas de deux* to the C-sharp-minor Waltz in *Chopiniana*) and Nijinsky, with whom she performed the same number in *Les Sylphides*. She last appeared in Russia in a full-length work on 25 February 1913, in *La Bayadère*.

Pavlova began to tour abroad in 1908, visiting Stockholm, Copenhagen and Berlin. From 1912 she lived in Golders Green, London. She died of pneumonia in The Hague at the age of fifty.

Ida **RUBINSTEIN** / 1885 – 1960
Cat. **116**

A performer of breathtaking androgynous beauty, Ida Rubinstein, who came from a wealthy Jewish family, was not a dancer by training, having studied acting at the St Petersburg Theatre School and ballet privately with Michel Fokine. She made her début in 1909 in a private performance of *Salomé* which Fokine choreographed for her. The same year, she played the title role in *Cléopâtre* in Diaghilev's first Paris Season and, in 1910, the part of Zobéide in *Schéhérazade*. In both roles she created a sensation with her arresting, statuesque appearance and her understated mime technique, suggesting depths of eroticism.

After her triumph with the Ballets Russes as Zobéide in *Schéhérazade*, Rubinstein left Diaghilev's Company to start up a theatrical enterprise of her own. The same year, she commissioned *Le Martyre de St Sébastien* from Debussy, to a text by Gabriele d'Annunzio, and played the title role in a lavish production of her own at the Châtelet Theatre on 22 May 1911. In 1928, her company presented ballets devised, composed and designed by some of the greatest artists of her time: the choreographers Bronislava Nijinska, Léonide Massine, Michel Fokine and Kurt Jooss; the composers Ravel, Stravinsky, Sauguet, Honegger and others; the writers Paul Valéry and André Gide; and the artists Bakst and Benois. The company disbanded in 1935.

Igor **STRAVINSKY** / 1882–1971
Cat. **123, 148**

At the age of twenty-eight, Igor Fyodorovich Stravinsky became a celebrity inextricably linked with the Ballets Russes. With the first performance of *The Firebird*, he began a meteoric career, which he shared with the Ballet Company. The years 1910 to 1914 saw the premières of *The Firebird*, *Petrushka*, *The Rite of Spring* and *Le Rossignol*.

This period coincided with the first part of his exile from Russia, most of which he spent in France and Switzerland, becoming finally cut off from his homeland by the First World War.

The son of a fine bass singer, who performed first with Kiev Opera, then with the Maryinsky Company, Igor was the third of four sons. The family lived on the Kryukov Canal in St Petersburg and they spent their summers in the country at various estates, including Ustilug, the summer residence of the Nossenko family. Igor was to marry his first cousin, Ekaterina Nossenko, in 1906, and continued to do important work at Ustilug until he left Russia.

Like other outstanding individuals in this catalogue, Stravinsky's career at school and in the Law Faculty of St Petersburg University was undistinguished. However, from childhood, he took lessons in piano and, later, in harmony and counterpoint. He composed naturally by improvising at the piano. As a student, in summer 1902, he met Vladimir Rimsky-Korsakov, the youngest son of the composer, and his association with the family began that summer. From winter 1902, when Igor's father died, Nikolai Rimsky-Korsakov became a kind of father-figure to the twenty-year-old Stravinsky, who was now too old to start studying at the conservatoire where Rimsky-Korsakov was professor. The latter therefore began to tutor Stravinsky privately. An early work that Stravinsky showed to his mentor was his original draft for *Le Rossignol* (*Solovei*).

In spring 1908, Stravinsky wrote *Feu d'artifice* to celebrate the forthcoming wedding of Rimsky-Korsakov's daughter. But by the time it was written, the older composer was dead. The same year, the work was played, along with Stravinsky's *Scherzo fantastique*, at a concert in St Petersburg. It was well received and made an especially deep impression on Sergei Diaghilev, who immediately saw Stravinsky as necessary to his enterprise.

For the 1909 Paris Season, Stravinsky was commissioned to orchestrate Grieg's *Kobold* (as part of the ballet divertissement *Le Festin*) and two piano pieces by Chopin (for *Les Sylphides*). *The Firebird*, which Diaghilev invited him to write for the 1910 Season, was Stravinsky's first large-scale commission. It took nine months to compose and was first performed on 25 June 1910 at the Paris Opéra.

Although derivative (above all, it showed the influence of Rimsky-Korsakov's own symphonic opera *Koshchei the Immortal*), it was the first of Stravinsky's works to win and hold a place in the repertoire. It presented Stravinsky with a series of challenges: the transformation into musical terms of the elements of drama, characterisation, physical gestures and movements, narrative and colour. Stravinsky's forte, as shown in this piece for the first time, was in orchestral innovation, which made good harmonic use of a distinctive melodic vocabulary. The success of *The Firebird* altered the course of Stravinsky's life. From 1910 to 1914, Paris and the Ballets Russes were to form its central point.

The first performance of *Petrushka*, on 13 June 1911 at the Théâtre du Châtelet, proved just as successful with the public and critics as *The Firebird*. Undoubtedly a more original work, it had an authentic voice. Stravinsky was able to compose this work with authority, as he had played a leading part in the creation of the scenario. *The Cry of Petrushka* was an independent inspiration, which he was able to harness to a childhood memory that he shared with Alexandre Benois of the annual Butter Week Fair held in St Petersburg's Admiralty Square.

After the 1911 Season, Stravinsky retired to Ustilug, where he worked on *The Rite of Spring* until the autumn, when he and his family moved to Clarens in Switzerland. The first half of this work, projected for the 1912 Season, was ready by New Year 1912, but, when Nijinsky's *Faune* proved to be requiring too many rehearsals, the production of *The Rite of Spring* was postponed until the Season of 1913, and Stravinsky was able to work more

slowly on it. During this period, he travelled around Europe, visiting the composers of his day. In winter 1912–13 he collaborated with Ravel on an adaptation of Mussorgsky's opera *Khovanshchina* for the Ballets Russes production in Paris and London that summer.

The scandal surrounding the first night, on 29 May 1913, of *The Rite of Spring* was a trauma for its participants. Stravinsky fell ill a few days later with typhoid fever. The composition itself had achieved Stravinsky's aim to produce, through convulsive asymmetry, a new rhythmical and harmonic system expressed through a distinctive voice.

However, Stravinsky was still aware of the need to find an enduring individual vocabulary. His work on *Le Rossignol*, following *The Rite of Spring*, represented an aspect of this quest. Following the 1913 Season, he worked on this new opera, for which he had received a commission from the newly founded Private Theatre of Moscow for 1914. In the event, the Moscow theatre project collapsed. Diaghilev offered to assume responsibility for a production of *Le Rossignol* during the Seasons in Paris and London that summer. It was duly performed as an opera with ballet inserts.

Between 1914 and 1920, Stravinsky lived permanently in Switzerland. His life was generally dislocated and, with a growing young family, he was in considerable financial straits. His German publishers had been cut off in enemy territory; and his income from his Russian estate had become unreliable. He was able to bring his mother to London from St Petersburg through the good offices of Sir Thomas Beecham.

In October 1917 he completed *Les Noces*, a work dedicated to Diaghilev, who had wept on hearing the first sketches. But, for six years, he could find no instrumental formula for accompaniment to the vocal line of the score and the opera-ballet was not performed until 1923. Stravinsky died at the age of eighty-nine. He is buried near Diaghilev on the island of San Michele in Venice.

Diaghilev (centre), Igor Stravinsky,
Mme Kovchinsky and Léon Bakst
Lausanne, 1915
Bibliothèque Nationale, Paris

SELECT BIBLIOGRAPHY

Bartlett, Rosamund, *Wagner in Russia*, Cambridge University Press, 1994

Beaumont, Cyril, *The Complete Book of Ballets*, Putnam, London, 1937 (revised 1949, 1951)

Beaumont, Cyril William, *Michel Fokine and His Ballets*, London, 1945

Benois, Alexandre, *The Russian School of Painting* (trans. Abraham Yarmolinsky), T. Warner Laurie, London, 1916

Benois, Alexandre, *Reminiscences of the Russian Ballet*, Putnam, London, 1941

Benois, Alexandre, *Memoirs* (trans. Moura Boudberg), 2 vols, Chatto and Windus, London, 1960-4

Blanche, Jacques-Emile, *Portraits of a Lifetime*, London, 1937

Borovsky, Viktor, *Chaliapin: A Critical Biography*, Hamish Hamilton, London, 1988

Brunoff, M. de (ed.), *Collection des plus beaux numéros des programmes consacrés aux Ballets et Galas Russes 1909-1921*, Paris, 1922

Buckle, Richard, *In Search of Diaghilev*, London, 1955

Buckle, Richard, *Nijinsky*, Weidenfeld and Nicolson, London, 1971

Buckle, Richard, *Diaghilev*, Weidenfeld and Nicolson, London, 1979

Cocteau, Jean, *The Journals of Jean Cocteau*, Museum Press, London, 1957

Debussy, Claude, *Letters* (ed. François Lesure and Roger Nichols), London, 1987

Diaghilev, Sergei Pavlovich, *Mir Iskusstva/Le Monde de l'art*, St Petersburg, 1898-1904

Diaghilev, Sergei Pavlovich, *Ezhegodnik imperatorskikh teatrov*, direktsiia imperatorskikh teatrov/Ministerstvo imperatorskogo Dvora, St Petersburg, 1898-9 (1 vol.), 1899/1900 (2 vols)

Diaghilev, Sergei Pavlovich, *Russkaia zhivopis' v VIII Veke (Levitskii)*, St Petersburg, 1902

Diaghilev, Sergei Pavlovich, *Istoriko-khudozhestvennaia vystavka russkikh portretov*, exhibition catalogue, St Petersburg, 1905

Diaghilev, Sergei Pavlovich, *Salon d'Automne: Exposition de l'Art Russe à Paris*, exhibition catalogue, Paris, 1906

Dobujinsky, M.V., *Memoirs* (Vospominaniia), vol. 1, New York, 1976

Duncan, Isadora, *My Life*, Gollancz, London, 1928; Sphere, London, 1968

Fokine, Michel: *Memoirs of a Ballet Master* (trans. Vitale Fokine, ed. Anatole Chujoy), Little Brown, Boston, 1961; Constable, London 1961

Garafola, Lynn, *Diaghilev's Ballets Russes*, Oxford University Press, 1989

Gold, Arthur and Fitzdale, Robert, *Misia: The Life of Misia Sert*, Macmillan, London, 1980

Grigoriev, S.L., *The Diaghilev Ballet 1909-29*, Constable, London, 1953; Penguin, London, 1960

Haskell, A.L. (in collaboration with Walter Nouvel), *Diaghileff. His Artistic and Private Life*, Gollancz, London, 1935

Kamensky, Alexander (ed.), *The World of Art Movement in Early 20th-Century Russia*, Aurora Art Publishers, Leningrad, 1991

Karsavina, Tamara, *Theatre Street*, Heinemann, London, 1930 (revised edition, Constable, London, 1948, Columbus, London, 1988)

Kchessinskaya, M.F., *Dancing in St Petersburg*, Gollancz, London, 1960

Kennedy, Janet, *The Mir iskusstva group and Russian Art 1898-1912* (published dissertation), Gartland, New York, London, 1977

Kochno, Boris, *Diaghilev and the Ballets Russes* (trans. Adrienne Foulke), Harper and Row, New York, 1970; Allen Lane/Penguin Press, London, 1971

Lieven, Prince Peter, *The Birth of Ballets-Russes* (trans. L. Zarine), Allen and Unwin, London, 1936

Lifar, Serge, *Diaghilev. His Life. His Work. His Legend. An Intimate Biography*, Putnam, London, 1940

Macdonald, Nesta, *Diaghilev Observed by Critics in England and the United States 1911-1929*, Dance Horizons, New York, 1975

Massine, Léonide, *My Life in Ballet* (ed. Phyllis Hartnoll and Robert Rubens), Macmillan, London, 1968

Nijinska, Bronislava, *Early Memoirs*, Duke University Press, Durham and London, 1992

Nijinsky, Romola, *Nijinsky* and *The Last Years of Nijinsky*, Gollancz, London, 1980

Nijinsky, Vaslav, *Cahiers* (unexpurgated version: trans. Christian Dumais-Lvowsk and Galina Pogojeva), Actes Sud, Paris, 1995

Percival, John, *The World of Diaghilev*, Studio Vista, London, 1971; revised edition Herbert Press, London, 1979

Pospelov, Gleb Gennadievich, *Bubnovyi valet, primitiv i gorodskoi fol'klor v moskovskoi zhivopisi 1910-kh godov*, Moscow, 1990

Pozharskaia, Militsa and Volodina, Tatiana, *The Art of the Ballets Russes, The Russian Seasons in Paris, 1908-1929*, Aurum Press, London, 1990

Propert, W.A., *The Russian Ballet in Western Europe, 1909-1920*, Bodley Head, London, 1921

Rimsky-Korsakov, N.A., *My Musical Life* (trans. J.A. Joffe, ed. Carl van Vechten), Secker, London, 1924; Eulenberg Books, London, 1974

Sarabianov, D.V., *Russian Art: From Neoclassicism to the Avant-Garde*, Thames and Hudson, London, 1990

Schouvaloff, Alexander, *Léon Bakst, The Theatre Art*, Sotheby's Publications, London, 1991

Schouvaloff, Alexander and Borovsky, Viktor, *Stravinsky and the Stage*, Stainer and Bell, London, 1982

Sitwell, Osbert, *Great Morning*, Macmillan, London, 1948

Sokolova, Lydia, *Dancing for Diaghilev* (ed. Richard Buckle), Murray, London, 1960

Spencer, Charles, *The World of Serge Diaghilev*, Paul Elek, London, 1974

Stravinsky, Igor, *Chronicles of My Life*, Gollancz, London, 1936

Stravinsky, Igor (with Robert Craft), *Memories and Commentaries*, Faber and Faber, London, 1960

Svetlov, Valerien, *Le Ballet Contemporain* (with designs by Léon Bakst; trans. M.D. Calvocoressi), de Brunoff, Paris, 1922

Valois, Ninette de, *Invitation to the Ballet*, Bodley Head, London, 1937

Vershinina, Irina Yakovlevna, *Rannye balety Stravisnkogo. Zharptitsa, Petrushka, Vesna sviashchennaia*, Moscow, 1967

Wolkonsky, Prince Sergei, *My Reminiscences*, 2 vols (trans. A.E.I. Charnot), Hutchinson, London, 1925

Zilberstein, I.S. and Samkov, V.A., *Sergei Diagilev i russkoe iskusstvo*, 2 vols, Moscow, 1982

INDEX OF ARTISTS

This index covers the artists and designers
in the exhibition.
Works are referenced by catalogue numbers.

Anisfeld, Boris | 89A–D
Bakst, Léon | 3, 4A–B, 5A–B, 6, 53, 90, 91, 102,
        103A–B, 104, 118A–C, 119A–D, 120, 121,
        130, 131A–J, 132A–C, 133, 134, 135A–C,
        136A–B, 137, 138, 139A–C, 140, 165, 167
Benois, Alexandre | 7, 8, 50A–E, 54, 61, 62, 63, 64,
        65, 66, 67, 92, 105, 106A–F, 107A–E, 108A–E,
        122, 141A–C, 142A–D, 143A–D, 144
Bilibin, Ivan | 9A–B, 10, 93
Blanche, Jacques-Emile | 123
Bonnard, Pierre | 145
Chekhonin, Sergei | 11
Cocteau, Jean | 146, 147, 148
Dobuzhinsky, Mstislav | 13A–D, 50F–H, 68, 69, 150,
        151, 152A–B, 153
Frodman-Kluzel, Boris | 109, 110
Gaudier-Brzeska, Henri | 124
Golovine, Alexandre | 56, 94A–E, 95A–B, 125A–C, 126
Golubkina, Anna | 70
Goncharova, Natalia | 71, 155A–B, 156, 157
Knight, Laura | 127
Korovine, Konstantin | 57, 96, 158
Kruglikova, Elizaveta | 14A–B
Kuznetsov, Pavel | 97
Lanceray, Evgeny | 15, 16A–C, 17A–C, 50I
Larionov, Mikhail | 72, 73, 172, 173
Levitan, Isaak | 18, 19, 74, 75
Maliavine, Filipp | 20
Milioti, Nikolai | 76
Nijinsky, Vaslav | 111, 159
Ostroumova-Lebedeva, Anna | 21A–D, 50J–L
Pasternak, Leonid | 98
Polenova, Elena | 22A–B
Repin, Ilya | 1, 2, 23, 77
Rodin, Auguste | 160
Roerich, Nikolai | 99, 112, 113A–C, 161A–D, 162A–C, 163
Ryabushkin, Andrei | 24
Schwabe, Randolph | 128
Serov, Valentin | 25, 26, 100, 114, 115, 116, 129
Shcherbov, Pavel | 27
Somov, Konstantin | 28, 29, 30, 31, 32, 33, 34, 35,
        36, 37, 38, 39, 40A–G, 41, 42, 79, 80, 81, 82, 83
Sudeikin, Sergei | 164
Troubridge, Una | 166
Trubetskoi, Pavel (Paolo) | 43, 44, 101, 117
Vrubel, Mikhail | 45, 46, 47, 48, 49, 84, 85, 86, 87
Vsevolozhsky, Ivan | 58
Yakunchikova-Weber, Mariya | 51, 52
Yuon, Konstantin | 88

PHOTOGRAPHIC ACKNOWLEDGEMENTS

The publishers and the organisers of the exhibition would like to thank all those lenders who have kindly supplied photographic material for the catalogue and the exhibition display.
We extend particular thanks to the following:

Ashmolean Museum, Oxford
A. A. Bakhrushin State Central Theatre Museum, Moscow
Julian Barran Ltd, London
Bibliothèque Nationale de France, Paris
British Library, London
Central State Archive of Cinema and Photo Documents, St Petersburg
Asya Chorley
Diaghilev Foundation, Perm
Hulton Deutsch Collection Limited, London
Victor Kennett
Mander and Mitchenson Theatre Collection, Beckenham
Fraser Marr
Jonathan Morris-Ebbs
Musée des Arts Décoratifs, Paris
Villi Onikul
Roger-Viollet Documentation Photographique, Paris
State Museum of Theatre and Music, St Petersburg
State Russian Museum, St Petersburg
State Tretyakov Gallery, Moscow
L. Sully-Jaulmes
Thames and Hudson Limited, London
Theatre Museum, London
Victoria and Albert Museum, London

ACKNOWLEDGEMENTS

Barbican Art Gallery
would like to thank its
Corporate Members:

Barclays Bank of Ghana Ltd, Zambia Limited
      and Zimbabwe Limited
The Bethlem Maudsley NHS Trust
British Petroleum Company plc
British Telecommunications plc
Chemical Bank
Robert Fleming & Co. Limited
Save & Prosper plc
Sun Alliance Group
TSB Group plc
Unilever plc

Barbican Art Gallery
also would like to thank

for their support for
Diaghilev: Creator of the Ballets Russes